The British Toy Business

The British
Toy Business

A History since 1700

Kenneth D. Brown

THE HAMBLEDON PRESS

LONDON AND RIO GRANDE

Published by The Hambledon Press, 1996

102 Gloucester Avenue, London NW1 8HX (UK)
PO Box 162, Rio Grande, Ohio 45674 (USA)

ISBN 1 85285 136 8

A description of this book is available from
the British Library and from the Library of Congress

Typeset by Carnegie Publishing, 18 Maynard St, Preston

Printed on acid-free paper and bound in
Great Britain by Cambridge University Press

Contents

Illustrations

Preface

Children's toys have an appeal that transcends all differences of age, class, gender and nationality. Much has been written about them but the history of the indigenous British toymaking industry has never before been comprehensively investigated.

Acknowledgements

In writing this book I have incurred many debts, not least to the army of toy enthusiasts whose works populate the footnotes and bibliography. I must also thank the numerous people who responded to my requests for information about Meccano, especially Bev Stokes, George Perry and J. G. Thomas, who all gave me first hand information based on their experiences of the company. Richard and Graeme Lines did the same for Lines Brothers Ltd, and while they will not find my account of their family firm uncritical, they will, I trust, find it to be fair.

The staff of the British Library, British Library of Political and Economic Science, Hackney Archives Department, Lloyd's Bank Archives, the Museum of London, the Public Record Office, the Rylands Library and Sheffield City Archives were uniformly helpful. I am especially grateful to Dr S. Lawrence and her colleagues at the Bethnal Green Museum of Childhood, all of whom shared with me their profound knowledge of the industry and its history. I was courteously received by the British Toy and Hobby Association and given free access to their invaluable records. The Director General, David Hawtin, subsequently read the manuscript and eliminated a number of errors. Mr David Le Mare, curator of the Merseyside Maritime Museum, guided me through the Meccano archives, and provided an hospitable welcome in more ways than one. Particular thanks are due to the staff of the interlibrary loan department of my own university. In the face of repeated requests from a senior professor for books on model railways, Dinky cars, tinplate toys, dolls, teddy bears and toy soldiers, their collective eyebrows never flickered.

The research on which this work rests was funded in the main by a grant from the Economic and Social Research Council, whose support for historical projects is always welcome. I am thankful, too, that the authorities at Queen's still believe that new life can be breathed into expired deans through the granting of sabbatical leave.

Finally, my thanks are due to my colleague, Alun Davies who gave to my draft manuscript the same care and attention he always gives to his students. I can think of no higher compliment.

The Queen's University of Belfast
January 1995

To my children, Stephen (1971), Rachel (1972), Beth (1975),
Judith (1977), Kirsty (1980), Andrew (1987) and Michael (1989),
who between them have allowed me to prolong my practical
interest in toys for more than a quarter of a century

Chapter 1

Conception

On a summer's day shortly before the outbreak of the First World War
C. F. G. Masterman, a junior Minister in Herbert Asquith's Liberal
Government, called to see his friend, H. G. Wells. He found the famous
writer deeply absorbed in a game of toy soldiers which he was playing
with another Cabinet member, Sidney Buxton. The President of the
Board of Trade was 'sprawled full length on the floor and with unerring
accuracy picking off the flower of Wells' Imperial Guard, which he
thought he had concealed and protected in a thick pine forest'.[1] Masterman was not in the least surprised by this somewhat unlikely scene.
On previous occasions he had himself participated in similar games.
The most memorable had lasted all day and ended only when Buxton's
'magnificent shot from the other end of the nursery' had 'destroyed a
missionary fleeing .on a dromedary – the last representative of the
nation which had marched so gaily into battle so many hours before'.[2]

It is tempting to speculate on the deeper significance of such martial
preoccupations on the part of Britain's political leaders in the days
immediately before 1914, but such war games were nothing new.[3] As
early as 1760 Laurence Sterne had portrayed Tristram Shandy's Uncle
Toby ploughing up the family bowling green in order to play out a
miniaturised version of Marlborough's campaigns against Louis XIV.
Sadly, his fortifications proved vulnerable, though not to the cannons
which he made by melting down the lead weights from the sash windows.
Rather, they were mortally damaged by nocturnal activities, first of a
marauding cow and then of some amorous interplay between Corporal
Trim and a servant girl. These resulted in the complete destruction of
a drawbridge, 'somehow or other crushed all to pieces'.[4] Apart from
the obvious gap between fiction and fact, there was one other essential
difference between the games played by Shandy's uncle on the one
hand and those of Wells on the other. Whereas the former had to make
for himself all the necessary equipment, Wells was able to buy everything

he required from ordinary retail outlets. In the intervening 200 years a new industry, the commercial manufacture of playthings for children and hobbyists, had grown up in Britain.

During the twentieth century toy and game making has assumed many of the characteristics of modern big business – national and international trade associations, government regulations on standards and safety, multinational corporations, annual production and trade running into millions of pounds, and a domestic market worth about a billion pounds a year.[5] Yet the emergence and development of British toy manufacturing have not attracted much attention from professional historians: 'The rise of toy making as an industry', observes one popular history of toys, 'is a mysterious process. Its history has seldom been charted.'[6] Children's toys, it seems, have become so much a part of modern life that their existence and the processes by which they have been provided are taken largely for granted. As G. C. Bartley complained in 1876, contemporaries were

> so accustomed to fix . . . attention on those articles, whose use is prin-
> cipally confined to persons of adult age . . . that we are apt to lose
> sight of the fact that children too have their wants, which are to be
> supplied by those little trifles that we call toys, and to ignore the extent
> to which their manufacture in England is carried on.[7]

A century later this remains substantially true for, as J. H. Plumb suggested in his pioneering study of eighteenth-century childhood, 'we have too long neglected some of the most vital fields of human experience as if unworthy of a professional historian's attention'.[8] It is true of course that there exists a considerable literature on the toy as artifact or antique.[9] There are also a number of studies concerned with the history of particular products and firms. By definition these tend to be narrowly focused and, as Linda Hannas suggests of her own study of jigsaw puzzles, are 'motivated by the verve and enthusiasm of an amateur, rather than the opus magnum of a professional historian'.[10] There is nothing pejorative about her use of the word amateur; the very best of these works contain much that is relevant to the wider issues with which the economic and social historian is concerned. Nevertheless, the industry as a whole still remains unexplored. References to toy making are non-existent in virtually every account of Britain's industrial history, save that of the magisterial J. H. Clapham.[11]

One possible reason for this neglect of the industry may lie in the fact that, historically, most items with which children played were not commercial products at all, but homemade, utilising whatever materials came freely to hand. Thus when a distressed Joseph Tysoe discovered that his hand-made clay figures broke up when put in the oven, his mother 'ran into the garden and pulled lead from an old, small, leaded window frame . . . After softening it in the fire she made fantastic little men with it.'[12] This sort of activity continued even into the twentieth century. Robert Roberts found plenty of inspiration in the contents of his family grocer's shop, creating for himself a whole world of cottages made from gas-mantle boxes. They were set among cliffs made of soda, sandy beaches composed of flour and sugar and 'peopled. . . with figures carved from pop bottle corks'.[13] His contemporary, Laura, the heroine of Flora Thompson's *Lark Rise to Candleford*, was similarly self-reliant, able only to '*read* about children whose lives were very different' from her own because they possessed 'nurseries with rocking-horses'.[14] Ernest Shepard was one about whom she might have read, since he was given a factory-made rocking-horse for his seventh birthday in 1887. 'He arrived, carefully packed, on the tenth of December . . . he stood, with eyes dilated and distended nostrils, pawing the air with his two forelegs, as though yearning to discard his three wooden wheels.'[15] If homemade toys remained important even into the present century, their gradual ousting at all social levels by commercial products constitutes an important historical development, revealing much about attitudes to children and shifting patterns of prosperity, as well as the growth of consumerism.

Interest in the British toy industry may also have been deterred by the commonly held assumption that the domestic market has been dominated by foreign toys. This has certainly been the case since the collapse of the industry in the late 1970s.[16] It is perhaps less true of the nineteenth century than has sometimes been asserted by manufac-turers, importers and wholesalers, often, it seems, in the hope of securing short-term political or economic advantages.[17] The frequently-made claim that before 1914 'most toys were made in Germany . . . or France' is at the very least questionable.[18] Contemporary official statistics do show significant growth in imports before 1914, but the failure to collect comparable data for domestic production renders direct comparison impossible, while the estimates included in the 1907 Census of Production are highly questionable.[19] Even if indigenous firms did dominate the domestic market only for a short period in the middle six decades of the twentieth century, the study of their success and subsequent failure does have an important contribution to make to the long-standing debate about the quality of British industrial management.

It is only natural that this debate, as with discussions of the economy in general, should usually be couched in terms of industries such as coal, steel, cotton, shipbuilding and engineering, statistically the most important contributors to the Gross National Product, to exports and to employment. Yet, by themselves, such quantitative measures are not always an appropriate or an accurate guide to the importance of an individual sector, although an undue emphasis on quantification may well help to explain why small industries have been relatively neglected by historians.[20] Prince Kropotkin could claim in 1900 that such minor enterprises 'were hardly taken into account', even though almost a half of the country's manufacturing labour force still worked in small work-shops and factories rather than in the larger units associated with the major businesses.[21] An industry such as toy making, where the typical unit had fewer than ten employees, was therefore more characteristic of nineteenth-century manufacturing than raw employment figures might suggest. This has remained the case in the twentieth century. In the early 1970s about a quarter of the employed population still worked for small firms – defined now as those employing less than 200 people – and all but a few toy manufacturers fell comfortably within this categorisation.[22] To examine the toy industry, therefore, is to study a representative of an important part of Britain's industrial fabric.

Furthermore, it should not be assumed that the predominance of the small-scale producer precluded the emergence of a few giants. By the 1960s the Triang empire, built up by the Lines Brothers, claimed to be the largest toy making concern in the world. Other British firms had capitalisations comparable with those of major engineering con-cerns. Toy companies were among the most profitable of all British manufacturing enterprises in the late 1960s and were frequent winners of export awards.[23] Recorded retail sales of toys in Britain reached £920,000,000 by 1987, a substantial figure and certainly one worthy of more detailed exploration and explanation.[24]

In any case, it is misleading to assess the significance of a consumer industry solely in terms of its scale or output, although a cost-conscious and present-minded age might be tempted so to do. To a utilitarian, the study of the British toy industry might at first glance appear to be yet another example of that dilettantism to which the sometimes esoteric interests of social and economic historians can give rise. But toy manu-facture, which is after all nothing less than a specialised branch of engineering, has been and remains more significant than mere figures and superficial consideration might suggest. Its development provides important insights into relatively unexplored aspects of the country's economic and social past.[25] This was something Bartley pointed out in his 1876 survey of the industry. 'Objects which we all require to use during a greater part of our early life', he wrote, 'and which have such an immense influence on us cannot in any way be considered as unimportant.'[26]

It is of course a commonplace that the culture of any society can be better understood through the study of its artifacts, but most attention has been lavished on the products of high culture, such as architecture, art and sculpture. However, anthropologists have suggested that toys reveal more about the society that produces them than most of its other products, because they represent the dreams and aspirations of adult rather than childish imagination.[27] For example, a recent American study examined the production of indigenous dolls in order to explore notions of gender and sexual stereotyping. The dolls made by women, it contends, were very different from the 'idealised feminine domesticity' characteristic of those manufactured by men.[28] The physical appearance of toys can also sometimes provide important historical information. Costumed dolls, for instance, have provided some tangible evidence of changing fashions. Likewise, much has been learned about the costume, architecture and personnel of the nineteenth-century theatre from items originally made for the popular juvenile drama.[29] As Cyril Connolly once observed, it is often the case that 'we can penetrate into the past more easily through the small things which people loved than through the great'.[30]

More important perhaps, the development of commercial toy manufacturing mirrors society's changing perceptions of childhood. Toys have accordingly figured in some of the controversial debates about European attitudes towards children.[31] Equally, their educational function has been much discussed, for, as a modern sociologist has pointed out, 'civilisation reflects the manner in which man's play focuses his conceptions of reality'.[32] In this context toys are deployed 'as socialising mechanisms, as educational devices, and as scaled down versions of the realities of the larger adult-dominated world'.[33] Such claims have a very long pedigree, reflecting the growth of interest in children's education. Historically, they did not always go unchallenged, although by the twentieth century it was possible for toy makers such as the Abbatts to have built successful businesses on the appeal of educational toys, while the instructional value of toys and play have been increasingly stressed in advertising and by the burgeoning toy library movement.

Finally, study of the industry's history has been retarded by a relative

lack of source materials. This is a function first of its product and
second of its scale. For the most part toys, as a French scholar has
observed, 'sont absents du commerce, absents des testaments, absents
des recits, des souvenirs'.[34] This has been compounded by the fact that
in the past little information was gathered on small firms, partly because
they were difficult to study and partly there was not much public interest
in them.[35] Toy makers did not generate many statistics of their own
until the market researchers got busy in the 1970s. As recently as 1984
the chairman of the British Toy and Hobby Association (hereafter
BTHA) was asking members to cooperate in providing quantitative
information because the association was 'unhappy at the dearth of
statistics within the toy trade . . .'[36] The high failure rate typical of small
firms has also deprived the historian of much archive material.

As might be expected, the sources are more abundant for the twentieth than for earlier centuries. Government interest in wages and safety
matters generated some useful official documentation. Although the
collapse of 1979–84 left behind virtually nothing of major firms like
Airfix and Lesney, some records survive, albeit of variable quality and
utility, from Cascelloid, Meccano, Mettoy, Lines and the Abbatts.[37]
These can be supplemented by information drawn from market reports,
although like the remaining archives, these are useful in the main for
the period since 1945. So, too, are oral reminiscences, which in any
case have to be interpreted with all the caveats usually attached to this
type of evidence. Two important toy makers of the same era produced
autobiographies, although both are of limited use. Peggy Nisbet eschewed a straightforward history of her soft toy company in favour of
writing 'about my family, my staff, customers, suppliers and colleagues'.[38] The recollections of Walter Lines, founder of the Lines group
of companies, were written at the height of his success and tend to
verge on the heroic.[39] So, too, does the earlier biography of Frank
Hornby, developer of Meccano. It reflects all too obviously the author's
conviction that 'we like books that are exciting to read and rouse our
ambitions and make us long to be like the people we read about'.[40]
These sources can be most usefully supplemented by reference to the
toy trade press, which first appeared towards the end of Queen Victoria's
reign.

For most of the nineteenth century, however, the evidence is much
skimpier. No business archives are extant and the two known autobiographies of toy makers are extremely thin. Hamlet Nicholson's patented
composition cricket ball won a prize at the Paris Exhibition in 1878
but, in his autobiography, his business interests are totally overshadowed

by religious and political matters.[41] Equally slight are the memoirs of an earlier, part-time toyman.[42] Apart from what can be gleaned by combing through a variety of fictional, biographical, journalistic and official sources, most of what can be learned of the nineteenth-century industry comes from the work of Henry Mayhew, G. C. Bartley, Charles Booth and E. E. Williams. Published in 1850, Mayhew's three articles in the *Morning Chronicle* can serve as a very rough map to the shape of the industry in the first half of the nineteenth century.

The historian of the early industry, however, lacks even this modest guidebook, for childhood, it has been remarked in a recent survey of the eighteenth century middle classes, 'is one of the few subjects covered . . . on which it has been difficult to find good sources'.[43] It is thus possible to do little more than grope short-sightedly at the past, relying on constructive and deductive detective work to give shape to such isolated landmarks of evidence as are encountered. Yet the landmarks can be treacherous and misleading, for they are further blurred by the fog of semantics.

The word 'toy' originally referred to trifles or small objects. Its first known literary deployment as a child's plaything occurred in the late sixteenth century. In the course of the next 200 years it came also to be applied to a wide range of items such as buckles, buttons, hat pins, brooches, small utensils and ornaments, usually intended for adult use. These were the staple output of the toy trade whose growth in eighteenth-century Birmingham earned that town the sobriquet of 'the toy shop of Europe'.[44] Another, though less common, application was to small pieces of haberdashery, ribbons, patchwork prints and the like.[45] China figurines were also included in the term. Charles Shaw, who worked at a pottery in the 1840s, later recalled that 'the figure of Napoleon Buonaparte was the leading article of our industry at this *toy* factory'.[46] Anthony Trollope was still using it in this sense in 1874, describing a drawing-room in one of his novels as being full of 'precious toys lying here and there about the room – toys very precious but placed there not because of their price but because of their beauty'.[47] The Victorian poet, Coventry Patmore, confuses matters still further, listing his son's toys as

> A box of counters and a red-vein'd stone
> A piece of glass abraded by the beach,
> Six or seven shells,
> A bottle with bluebells
> And two French copper coins.[48]

The word's catholic and evolving meaning was well caught in an encyclopaedia definition of 1845 which encapsulated both the older and
the newer usages: 'any showy trinket, a plaything, a play or sport,
anything trifling or fanciful'.[49]

Early references to toys, toy makers and toyshops, therefore, all have
to be carefully interpreted. The toys mentioned in early port books
and other accounts of trade were often, though not exclusively, of the
trinket type. Those featuring in Samuel Pepys' diary were small gifts
and did not necessarily have anything to do with children.[50] Similarly,
the £500,000 worth of toys claimed to have been exported from the
midlands in the middle of the eighteenth century probably consisted
in the main of metal items associated with the adult fashion trade.[51]
These were also what Daniel Defoe had in mind when he wrote of
forged iron, wrought brass and copper being made into 'cutlery ware
and . . . toys innumerable'.[52] Other industries turned out similar toys,
using different base materials including wood, ivory, bone, and clay.
The 'porcelain toys' advertised in one newspaper in 1754, for instance,
consisted of snuff boxes, smelling bottles and trinkets for watches, suitable for jewellers, goldsmiths, cutlers, china sellers and toyshops.[53] Such
goods formed the main stock in trade of the early eighteenth-century
London establishments designated as toyshops.[54] When Horace Walpole
decided to have a watch made for a friend, he ordered it from John
Deard because he was widely regarded as 'one of the first jewellers and
toymen here'.[55] Walpole actually purchased his house from another
well-known contemporary toy dealer, Paul Chevenix, whose shop near
Charing Cross had a magnetic attraction for at least one royal European
adult.[56]

Even so, some of these trinkets, though not perhaps playthings in
the modern sense, were intended for children. Josiah Wedgwood turned
out miniature figurines especially for children.[57] Two centuries earlier,
the goods imported into London in 1565 included children's rings
worth £60.[58] But the customs clerks were not at all consistent in their
use of the term 'toy'. In some entries it appears by itself with no further
qualification. In others, the phrase 'children's toys' is found. Sometimes,
the entries are sub-divided into categories, not all of which are relevant
to children. 'Babies', 'puppets', 'marbles' and 'whistlecocks' were quite
clearly intended for children; 'nest boxes', 'pill boxes' and mechanical
'singing birds' less obviously so. In some years, children's playthings
are not entered under the generic heading at all but appear in their
own rights as 'marbles', 'joynted babies' and so on.

Quite evidently the numerous objects which the word 'toy' commonly defined were not always very age specific in their use. This was probably most true of the equipment produced for games such as chess or battledore and shuttlecock. It is hardly surprising that children should have taken to playing with the small-scale models sometimes produced by furniture makers, even those of the standing of Sheraton and Chippendale, in order to give potential adult customers an idea of what they were ordering for their dining rooms and parlours. A similar fate sometimes befell the costume dolls, originally used by fashionable European couturiers as a way of advertising their styles. Other miniatures were less functional, serving purely decorative purposes, but they were also readily adaptable to childish ends. Collecting miniatures was a well-established aristocratic fashion in England by the early seventeenth century. Silver ones were imported from Europe and they were frequently imitated in baser metals for a less exclusive clientele. Although inventories rarely, if ever, referred to toys as such, it seems highly likely that some of the goods hidden under the generic name of 'pewter', especially when combined with the adjective 'littell', consisted of ornaments and miniatures, which would have appealed to children.[59] So, too, did playing cards. Their use for the construction of model houses was, in the words of one contemporary observer, 'a very common amusement with children'.[60] In so far as adult possessions were colonised by children in this way they became de facto toys.[61]

The converse of this also occurred. Items which to a modern eye would appear to have been intended for juveniles were often utilised by adults. It was not children, for example, who used 'all kinds of dolls and scarecrows with leeks on their heads' to taunt Welshmen on St David's Day in 1662.[62] Dolls' or baby houses were something of a fad among the adult aristocracy of Hanoverian England and Horace Walpole wrote disparagingly on one occasion of a prince of George II's family being busy 'building baby houses at Kew'.[63] In another letter he commented on the habit of 'women of the first quality' going to Chevenix's shop and returning home 'laden with dolls and babies not for their children, but for their housekeepers'.[64] Indeed, some of the miniatures being manufactured in the eighteenth century were specifically designed for use in such dolls' houses. Swift referred in *Gulliver's Travels* to 'sets of silver dishes and plates and other necessaries' made for his use at the Court of Brobdingnag, 'not much bigger than what I have seen of the same kind in a London Toy-shop for the Furniture of a Baby house'.[65]

This is exactly what is to be expected of a world in which, it has been argued, children tended to be regarded as little adults.[66] Although the experience of childhood naturally varied according to social hierarchy, it was still generally the case in the seventeenth and eighteenth centuries that the roles of children and adults were not yet as distinctively separate as they were subsequently to become. Their worlds intermeshed both at work and in leisure. This provides yet a further complexity for the historian intent upon tracing the early development of children's toy making in Britain.

Chapter 2

Birth and Childhood, 1700–1850

Guided only by inadequate sources and with vision partially obscured by semantic mists, the historian can do little more than sketch in the very barest outlines of toy manufacturing as it existed in England prior to the middle of the eighteenth century. The landscape was still dominated by what Paul Abbatt was later to denominate as secondary and tertiary types of toys. By these terms he meant respectively items turned to childish entertainments from other purposes, and those artifacts, such as sticks and stones, which occurred naturally.[1] Yet commercially made primary toys (i.e. items conceived as children's playthings) were becoming increasingly common. It is quite possible that the dressed wooden doll bequeathed in an English will of 1548 to a granddaughter was home-made.[2] On the other hand, there is no doubting the commercial provenance of the Noah's Arks which appeared in growing quantities from the beginning of the seventeenth century. At about the same time John Earle described English children playing with whipping tops, kites, drums, rattles and hobby horses.[3] Virtually identical items appeared a century later in Dodsley's rather heavy-handed satirical play, *The Toy-Shop*. A wife, suggested one character, was a toy for life:

> a Rattle in a Man's Ears which he cannot throw aside: a Drum that is perpetually beating him to the point of war: a Top which he ought to whip for his Exercise, for like that she is best when lashed to sleep: a hobby Horse for the Booby to ride on when the Maggott takes him.[4]

A similar range of children's goods, as usual mixed with adult trinkets, was stocked by Chevenix, Deard and the other London toyshops. Mid century advertisements for Coles Child's establishment on London Bridge referred to steel and metal toys, pill boxes, nest boxes, babies, marbles, alleys, children's trumpets, balls and counters.[5] It was from such a store that in 1701 Dr Claver Morris purchased for his daughter a quite sophisticated product, 'a Wax Baby with an invention to make it cry and turn its eyes'.[6]

Writing later of the mid eighteenth century, one contributor to a survey of British industry claimed baldly that 'toys were at that time all of foreign make'.[7] The Southampton Port Books certainly show that children's musical instruments were being imported in the early sixteenth century.[8] So, too, were German dolls, probably from Nuremberg, where dollmakers are known to have been established as early as 1413. When Thomas South railed against the import of frivolities in 1549 he specifically listed balls and 'puppets'.[9] As the seventeenth century drew to a close the import ledgers for England and Wales recorded imports of babies, joynted babies, puppets, marbles, daggers, fiddles, pipes, rattles and balls, all specifically described as being for children, worth £1457. If to this are added the other toys listed (but not those described as alabaster, wrought iron and glass because they were most likely ornaments intended for adults), the figure rises to £2761 (Table 1).

Table 1
Foreign Trade in Toys: England and Wales[10]

Year	Imports £	Re-exports £	Exports £
1699	2,761	113	284
1710	912	126	212
1720	883		110
1730	869	42	8,410
1740	735	77	7,831

To nearest pound

This is not a huge sum but, since toys were cheap, the quantities could be quite considerable. Although the fiddles imported from Germany were valued at just over £261, for example, there were almost 4000 of them. Similarly, there were 15,000 balls in a 1699 consignment valued at £38. The importance of these foreign supplies is illustrated by the fact that Henry Crouch's survey of import duties distinguished between three categories of toys 'for children'. From 1660 unrated toys were taxed at about 24 per cent of their sworn value. 'Babies or puppets for children' paid sixteen pence in the pound, as did 'all other toys for children'. Fiddles and rattles 'for children' were also separately enumerated.[11] When in 1678 the English Parliament, concerned at the adverse balance of trade between France and England, imposed a three-year ban on French imports, it specifically referred to 'an innumerable variety of Frippery, Millinery and Haberdashery Wares, Toys etc'.[12]

The French were in fact best known for the manufacture of very complex mechanical toys, in most cases intended for adult entertainment.[13] Most foreign toys were indeed generally acknowledged in England as being of high artistic and mechanical quality, as a 1747 description of occupations made clear. Toymen, it commented, were dealers in toys, 'of all Sorts for the diversion of Children, which are pretty numerous, made Abroad, as most of the nicer Sorts are, *as well as at Home*'.[14] The final phrase is of great significance, however, for, contrary to later assertions, it clearly implies the existence of indigenous British toy makers by the middle of the eighteenth century. Although the broad parameters of Britain's occupational structure at this time can be drawn, very little in detail is known about it before the nineteenth century.[15] It is hardly surprising that minor activities like toy making for children, catering only for a market restricted in both size and nature, should remain largely anonymous in the historical record. It is likely that a whole range of artisans in metal, wood, canework and pottery produced miniature items specifically for children on an irregular or seasonal basis, particularly when demand for the adult version of their product was low. Hoops, for example, were easily turned out by coopers and wheelwrights. Whips and tops were readily produced by anyone with a sharp knife and access to timber, as were wooden dolls. Some of the 20,000 or so employed in the Birmingham toy trades by 1759 appear to have been catering for children. Charles Shipman, for example, newly arrived in New York in 1767 after serving an apprenticeship in Birmingham as a wood and ivory turner, announced in the press his intention of carrying on the same business in America, making billiard balls, cups and balls, drumsticks, backgammon and chessmen, along with ivory counters engraved with alphabet and figures – all 'very popular with children'.[16] A few years earlier, the *Boston Newsletter* was advertising 'English and Dutch Toys for children', while Walter Shee was advising readers of another colonial paper, the *Pennsylvania Gazette*, that he had for sale 'Dutch and Manchester Pretties'.[17]

That commercial English toy makers were active even before the middle of the eighteenth century is apparent from other isolated pieces of evidence. There is, for example, Crouch's reference to the ban on the import of painted toys which might be taken to indicate that there existed indigenous makers who required some protection. Crouch also mentioned a duty of sixteen pence in the pound on 'earthen heads for babies'.[18] Unless these were being re-exported, which seems highly improbable, the implication must be that they were for the use of English producers. This is perhaps confirmed by some American evidence. In 1695 the Reverend John Higginson wrote to his brother, an English merchant, to say that small quantities of toys might sell well in New England. Dolls were among the first such imports and 'Bartholomew Babies', associated with Bartholomew Fair, were mentioned in *Poor Robin's Almanac* in the same year.[19] Finally, there is the tangible evidence in the form of more than two dozen English-made wooden dolls dating from the seventeenth century.[20]

Well before the middle of the eighteenth century, then, there were Englishmen, and probably women too, who gained their livelihood by making toys for children. A few, almost certainly resident in London, may have been full-time but the majority probably drifted in and out of the trade, since demand could not yet have been sufficiently widespread or stable to sustain production on a permanent basis. The uncertainties of the toy market, broadly defined, have been well illustrated in a recent survey of eighteenth-century business bankrupts, which includes some Birmingham toy makers.[21] That the domestic demand for what were essentially luxury items, despite their often rather commonplace nature, was quite restricted, is further suggested by the low volumes of imports recorded. The official value of toy imports from France in 1785, for example, was put at £66.00.[22] High levels of infant mortality, low incomes and a requirement that children become earners as soon as possible, all signified that for the majority of English children playthings still consisted in the main of what was provided by nature or could be adapted from the adult world. It was all very well for the philosopher John Locke to urge that children should have various types of toys, but he was writing as the son of a landed gentleman, albeit of modest standing.[23] Only the relatively wealthy had the disposable income necessary to indulge their children with playthings in any quantity. The late seventeenth-century privy purse accounts of the fifth Earl of Bedford, for example, show that he always purchased toys for his grandchildren when visiting them.[24] They could be quite expensive, too. One of his descendants paid 9s. 6d. for battledores and shuttlecocks, 5s. 2d. for cups and balls in the 1750s.[25] Inevitably, the spatial and social distribution of wealth in England before the onset of the industrial revolution also meant that demand was heavily concentrated in London. For most of the eighteenth century the capital was unique among British towns in possessing toy shops, and the fortunes of the Birmingham trades certainly varied in accord with the state of the London market.[26]

In 1856 a writer in *Chamber's Journal* commented that there was now such an abundance of toys available that 'grandmothers may feel that they lived a century too early'.[27] This may have been an over-generous estimate of grandmotherly longevity but there is no doubt that sometime in the middle of the eighteenth century the tempo of toy manufacture picked up. Further acceleration after 1780 later prompted J. H. Plumb to claim that by 1820 'the trade in toys had become very large indeed'.[28] Like other contemporary consumer industries both the production and distribution of toys were beginning to cast off some of their pre-industrial characteristics, although the process was hardly completed even by the start of the twentieth century.

The most obvious manifestation of change was a growing range of primary toys. Increasingly the whips, tops, drums, dolls and marbles most frequently mentioned in the sources of the preceding centuries were being supplemented and overshadowed by newer products. Although expressing a preference in 1812 for the older, long-standing favourites like tops, hoops and balls, because they 'afford trials of dexterity and activity', the Edgeworths also commented favourably on the availability of little sets of carpenter's tools, garden implements, cheap microscopes and plaster bricks for model making, as well as listing a considerable number of items which they found objectionable – 'disjointed dolls, maimed horses, coaches and one horse chairs without wheels . . . a nameless wreck of gilded lumber . . . a working cart . . . a fully furnished baby house, automata'.[29] The reference to automata is revealing because there is some indication that the diversification of English toy manufacture included the production of mechanical toys. Christopher Pinchbeck had advertised his musical automata quite early in the century, although they were probably meant for adults rather than children.[30] Such lines had previously been associated mainly with French watch and clock makers. At least one of the new London manufacturers catering for children was a Frenchman. Monsieur Crouchet, who settled in the capital in 1815 after his release as a prisoner of war, made cheap, simple automata, including a model guillotine. It was an Englishman, however, who told Henry Mayhew that he had been at work since 1815 as a fancy toy maker, producing mechanical and moving novelties which went to warehouses before being sold to a mainly middle-class market.[31] By the 1820s a Manchester merchant, James Nicholson, was selling more complex varieties of automata, *'la plupart anglaise*, d'une belle construction.'[32]

There appears also to have been some expansion in the scale of doll production. Thomas Osler, a glass trinket maker from Birmingham, told the Select Committee on Artisans in 1824 that when in London in 1806 he had been offered a contract worth £500 for the supply of glass eyes for dolls. Although unable to accept the work, he had subsequently calculated that the potential business in glass eyes alone could have produced 'a circulation of a great many thousand pounds'.[33] New types of doll were also appearing. Although little is known about them, it is generally accepted that the common features of the Queen Anne Dolls – turned bodies and heads with features carved on afterwards – suggest that they were the work of a particular individual or group of workers with woodworking and carving experience.[34] It was also in these years that there appeared the pedlar dolls, which were unique to Britain, although it is likely that initially at least they were homemade rather than commercially manufactured.

The lead in expanding toy output, however, was taken by a group of well-known printers and publishers. When they first appeared in the 1740s Thomas Boreman's *Gigantick Histories* were among the first books produced directly for children. In the same decade John Newbery advertised a book for children costing 6d. but which, for an extra 2d., was supplied along with a ball and a pincushion. By 1800, twenty-three years after Newbery's death, the firm he founded had about 400 children's titles on its list.[35] Newbery was also responsible for the first juvenile periodical, the *Lilliputian Magazine*, which was published in 1751. Eleven others followed between 1752 and 1800, all designed to instruct and improve their young readers.[36] In cooperation with another printer, John Wallis, Newbery also published 'The New Game of Human Life' in 1790. This was one of a new genre of pastimes, the board game, produced in the wake of the first commercial success, 'A Journey Through Europe', published in 1759.[37] Along with William Darton, from whom he pirated ideas, Wallis and later his son, Edward, were also prominent publishers of jigsaw puzzles. These had evolved quite quickly from dissected maps, made and sold by John Spilsbury from 1762 onwards.

Printers and publishers were also prominently involved in turning out some of the other novel categories of playthings. Paper toys had been associated primarily with German makers, but English-made paper dolls were being advertised in the German press by 1791. From about 1810 the Fullers published toy books in which the characters could be redressed with changeable paper costumes. Others were turning out prints of furniture and figures capable of being stuck on to wood.[38] While the origin of paper sheets illustrating various aspects of the contemporary theatre is uncertain, the fact that at least five London publishers were producing such material by 1811 suggests both some prior development and the existence of a healthy demand. From these prints the juvenile drama developed and by 1822 Hodgson and Company were turning out such materials for seventy different plays, complete with props, characters and words.[39] According to Mayhew, the model theatres in which these dramas could be appropriately presented were first made in London in 1813. They subsequently became one of the most popular toys in the first half of the nineteenth century, as numerous memoirs confirm.[40] Robert Louis Stevenson later described the shop where as a boy he had purchased his sheets as 'a loadstone [sic] rock for all that bore the name of boy. They could not pass it by, nor, having entered, leave it. It was a place besieged.'[41]

Such was the growing range of British toy production that by 1800 one shop in Margate, hardly a major town, could carry a stock of more than 200 different lines. In turn this points up another feature of the industry's emergence in the years around the turn of the century – changes in the nature of retail operations. Here, too, the old and the new continued to coexist. The selling of toys by pedlars and street-traders remained a common feature of distribution for many years. Thus the five-year old George Sims, taken to watch Wellington's funeral procession in 1852, had his tears of tiredness somewhat assuaged when his mother bought him a penny coloured picture book from one of the numerous vendors working in Fleet Street.[42] Printed items like books were usually obtained from one of the London warehouses, but the street-sellers of cheap mechanical and wooden toys more usually made their own. Alternatively they worked directly for a small maker. One such arrangement came to grief when the female hawker employed by a Scottish toyman proved to be so chronically and heavily inebriated that she was unable to keep accurate accounts of her sales. It says much about the transitory nature of toy making that the frustrated manufacturer, who had already tried his hand at tailoring, teaching and preaching, promptly abandoned toys and apprenticed himself to a china mender.[43] Another early nineteenth-century hawker was William Green, who later recalled meeting a colleague in the 1830s: 'When I first met him he was at low ebb, and with his wife . . . was assisting another party stuffing dolls ready for Birmingham June fair.'[44]

Although by this time fairs were losing something of their traditional importance in the nation's distributive chain, they still retained a vestigial role. A contributor to *Chamber's Journal* in the 1850s recalled that his first acquaintance with toys had been made at a country fair. 'What toys we bought! – jacks-in-the-box, watchmen's rattles . . . tin

Wellingtons, Cossacks and Bluchers, spinning jennies and industrious cobblers.'[45] It is known that toys were being sold at Bartholomew Fair in the sixteenth century and they were still much in evidence at the same venue in the 1830s. 'The variety and abundance are so great', wrote one visitor, 'that you are quite confounded with the scene.'[46] A similar profusion was evident at Greenwich Fair, where 'richly furnished booths [were] groaning with toys and gingerbread'.[47] Even in the 1850s several of the manufacturers interviewed by Mayhew relied mainly on the fairs in order to sell their goods. A toy basket maker, for example, stressed that his goods were 'chiefly for fairs', even though they were now 'few and far between'.[48]

If such long-established retail mechanisms proved resilient in the face of change, the new were developing apace. In a way the establishment in 1760 of what, as Hamleys, was to become the world's most famous toyshop, symbolised the new world that opened up for British toy makers from the middle of the eighteenth century. It was only one of a number of new toy outlets established in London in the years after 1750. By 1822 the capital possessed no fewer than seventy-one retail toy shops and thirteen wholesalers.[49] Such was the proliferation by 1800 that some degree of specialisation emerged, with at least two concentrating solely on rocking-horses. By 1784 Green's in Crooked Lane had virtually abandoned the trinket types of toy in favour of playthings intended only for children. These included model cattle, boxes of soldiers (imported from Germany), and Bristol toys (heavy and light wooden toys named after the location of their manufacture). London was also acquiring a growing number of bazaars which, like the one opened in Soho in 1815, contained a number of toy stalls. Successive attempts to sustain a toy shop in Exeter Arcade near the Elephant and Castle may have failed but by mid century the Burlington Arcade was acknowledged as a major toy centre. Best known of all, however, was Lowther Arcade, running into the Strand from St Martin's churchyard. 'Enormous, preposterous, marvellous is Lowther in respect of toys', was George Sala's opinion.[50] *Punch* agreed, though in a rather roundabout fashion, warning potential visitors to Lowther against the dangers of putting their feet through drums or of falling over trays full of children's tea things. 'The toy makers', it suggested, 'should be told to take their shops indoors.'[51]

Distribution was also undergoing change outside London although, not surprisingly, provincial developments lagged behind those in the capital. The reliability of eighteenth-century trade directories is notoriously suspect but they can generally be relied upon to indicate general trends and orders of magnitude.[52] The provincial distribution network developed most rapidly after the end of the Napoleonic War, encompassing most of the major population centres by the middle of the nineteenth century. Norwich, Manchester and York all had toy dealers by the 1820s where none had existed in the 1780s.[53] Elsewhere in the north Liverpool had ten toy dealers by 1822.[54] Outside London there were probably no shops dealing exclusively with children's playthings, since demand was still too volatile and restricted to sustain them on a permanent basis. The evidence suggests, however, that all manner of outlets were beginning to stock them. In Leeds, for example, Pellegrino Vassalli, described as an optician, also sold Sheffield, Birmingham, London, French and German goods.[55] Even the inhabitants of relatively small rural communities had access to toys, although the village toyshop, as Thomas Hood pointed out in 1839, was

> Not a whole one, for a village can't
> Compare with the London shops;
> One window sells drums, dolls, kites, carts, bats, Clout's balls,
> And the other sells malt and hops.[56]

Rather earlier, the metropolitan villages around the city of London had been similarly provided for. Such a store, it was accurately observed, could not

> keep its head above water unless it monopolises the commerce of the whole neighbourhood. It is grocer and tea-dealer, and stationer and bookseller, and draper and haberdasher, and chemist and druggist, and jeweller and ironmonger, and seedsman and toyman . . .[57]

The scope of the distribution system that had developed by the middle of the nineteenth century can be seen from Table 2.

Table 2

Toy Dealers in Selected British Towns[58]

Town	Date	Numbers of Toy Dealers etc.	
Birmingham	1847	Toy Warehouse	24
		Toy Dealer	13
Bristol	1848	Toy Dealer	21
Cardiff	1848	Fancy Goods Repository	2
Darlington	1847	Toy Dealer	5
Dublin	1849	Toy/Fancy Good Wholesaler	1
		Toy/Fancy Good Importer	4
		Rocking-Horse Maker	1
		Perfumer and Toy Dealer	2

Town	Date	Numbers of Toy Dealers etc.	
Durham	1847	Toy Dealer	5
Edinburgh	1850	Toy/Fancy Warehouse	6
Leeds	1853	Toy Dealer	9
		Toy Maker	4
Liverpool	1849	Fancy Repository	28
		Toy Dealer	30
London	1846	Doll Maker	12
		Fancy Repository	56
		Foreign/Fancy Good Importer	72
		Rocking-Horse Maker	5
		Toy Dealer	252
		Toy Importer	17
		Toy Maker	47
Manchester	1850	Fancy Repository	6
		Toy Dealer	30
Newcastle	1847	Fancy Repository	3
		Toy Dealer	6
Swansea	1848	Toy Dealer	5
Sunderland	1847	Toy Dealer	2

The list is derived from contemporary directories and, as far as possible, the figures have been adjusted in order to eliminate the double counting of those businesses appearing under more than one classification. Conversely, those described in vague terms, such as importers of French and German goods or as owners of fancy repositories, have been included since it is apparent from cross-referencing and advertisements that some of them did deal in children's toys, even if their activities concerned the much wider range of consumer items known generically as fancy goods. Although Birmingham had a highly developed system of factoring by the 1830s, it was more generally the case that individuals operated across the range of distributive functions, since wholesale, import, retail and even manufacture were not yet totally separated.[59] Three of the twenty-one toy dealers in Bristol, for example, were also manufacturers. Seven of the toy makers listed in the Post Office directory of London for 1846 also appeared in the list of importers.

The distributors were also now deploying some quite sophisticated selling methods. They were not slow to spot the commercial potential of Christmas, the celebration of which began to assume some of its modern characteristics from the late 1830s onwards, particularly among the middle classes.[60] Since much of the inspiration behind the new customs was German (the Christmas tree, for example) it was not surprising that a trade in which Germans were so prominent, both as makers and distributors, should be quick to encourage the role of the toy in the growing habit of present-giving.[61] It is true that this was generally regarded by most contemporaries as being of minor importance until well into the second half of the century, but the main exception was for children. By 1856 Nathaniel Hawthorne could write that 'especially the toy shops' prospered at Christmas time.[62] "Christmas presents", wrote another observer in 1852, 'form a master line in the posters on the walls and in the shop windows.'[63] Even more remarkable, perhaps, was the use of an early form of character merchandising which became such a prominent feature of toy marketing in the twentieth century. Even in the 1850s toys were presented in association with the names of well-known characters, both actual and fictional, in order to increase their appeal to children. 'They were enticed', wrote George Sala, 'to purchase Uncle Buncle's Noah's Ark, Peter Parley's balls, or Jenny Lind's doll's mansion.'[64]

It is significant that several of those listed in Table 2 were described in the directories as importers, either of toys or of French and German goods, for imports, too, showed a sustained rise after the middle of the eighteenth century, notwithstanding the disruptions arising from the Seven Years War (Table 3).

Table 3
Foreign Trade in Toys: England and Wales[65]

Year	Imports £	Re-exports £	Exports £
1750	1,152	34	19,780
1760	727		7,075
1766	1,347	72	3,275
1770	1,427		3,163
1779	1,805	1	715
1812	31*		
1814	1,022*		

To nearest pound
* imports from Belgium, France, Germany and Holland only

Table 4
British Toy Imports, 1820–55[66]

Year	Value £	Year	Value £
1820	5,748	1839	18,432
1821	5,638	1841	22,736
1822	7,138	1842	21,503
1823	8,722	1843	26,578
1824	9,488	1844	31,728
1825	8,760*	1845	39,691
1826	9,733	1846	40,455
1827	11,572	1847	35,114
1828	15,062	1848	31,432
1829	15,755	1849	35,826
1830	18,026	1850	46,310
1831	19,050	1852	39,617
1832	17,345	1855	49,789

* official value: otherwise declared value in pounds

The official published statistics show an even more rapid growth occurring from the mid 1820s (Table 4). Yet the accuracy of the evaluations made in these years, whether official or declared, is questionable. For example, official figures suggest (Table 5) that the level of imports from France remained fairly static in the 1820s and then grew marginally in the following decades. French sources, however, convey a rather different impression. In 1825 the French valued their exports of toys to Britain at almost £27,000 while British customs men gave these a lower official value of £8685.

Table 5
French Toy Imports to Britain, 1825–47[67]

Year	British Official Values £	French Values £
1825	8,685	26,965
1826	3,140	5,209
1827	2,187	22,226
1828	3,791	2,197
1829	2,603	4,050
1830	1,946	2,968
1831	2,052	5,332

Year	British Official Values £	French Values £
1845	3,821	
1846	3,801	
1847	3,001	

It is difficult, too, to know what to make of the figures for 1827 when French exports to Britain were apparently ten times larger than their declared customs value, and appear to have been virtually twice as large as the entire official value of Britain's total toy imports. Such discrepancies and inconsistencies are not altogether rare in nineteenth-century trade statistics and official values are in any case misleading. Oddly, there was some illicit trade in toys; or at least a collection of dolls exhibited at Kidderminster in 1932 was said to include one item bought a century earlier from French smugglers at Rye.[68] Such transactions could not have been of any significance, given the low value of toys, but it was this same low value that caused customs officials to be indifferent to the accuracy of the information they recorded. A more useful measure, therefore, is perhaps provided by weight. French figures indicate that almost ten tons of toys dispatched to Britain in 1830 had become more than 113 tons by 1850.[69]

Such an increase is not incompatible with the broad impression given by official figures that the proportion of British imports provided by the French diminished as the century approached its midpoint. J. R. McCulloch commented in 1835 that 'considerable quantities' of cheap toys, particularly wooden ones made in Germany, were now being shipped to Britain through Dutch ports.[70] Fifteen years further on, and the official figures contained in Table 6 indicate that almost three-quarters of Britain's toy imports arrived from what were still classified as the Hanseatic towns, the old confederation of German traders which had long-established links with Britain.

Table 6
Origins of British Toy Imports, 1850[71]

	£		£
Belgium	1,056	Holland	6,201
France	4,209	Hanse	33,828
Others	513	Denmark	323

The major impetus behind the growth of imports was the progressive lowering of the duties on toys, culminating in their final abolition in

1853. The effects of the reductions from 50 to 20 per cent in 1842 are clearly evident from the subsequent surges apparent in Table 4. Reduced tariffs had a downward effect on toy prices and many of the small-scale makers interviewed by Mayhew found it increasingly difficult to compete. One fancy toy maker told him that demand for his goods had fallen by about half in the face of stronger French competition since 1842.[72] The same reduction, a whitewood toy maker said, 'affected me a wonderful sight'.[73]

He went on to suggest that the foreign toy makers had some wage advantages:

> This lamb can't be made in London for a penny, but it is brought from Germany and sold here retail at a penny. If people, even girls and boys, are paid anything abroad for making such toys, it must be next to nothing. How they who depend upon such work live at all, is a puzzle to me.[74]

In fact, the wage evidence is ambiguous and difficult to interpret, not least because the level of payments could fluctuate so much from one year to the next. A married couple who sewed cotton dresses for the London doll trade, and who at one time had earned up to 30s. a week, were down to a paltry 6s. when Mayhew met them in 1850.[75] T. C. Barfield, who published quite extensively on the German economy in the 1840s, reckoned that the general level of urban industrial wages was about half that prevailing in major British cities like Birmingham, Glasgow and Leeds.[76] This may have reduced production costs in towns such as Nuremberg but it was probably not relevant in the case of rurally-based wooden toy makers, most of whom were part-timers anyway: as J. H. Clapham put it, Germany's wooden toys were the 'products of a hard living peasantry's winter evenings'.[77] It would in any case be unwise to make too much of these apparent wage advantages since it is not at all clear that like can be compared with like.

A far more significant advantage of the German makers of wooden toys was the abundant supply of cheap timber in a country still much more heavily forested than Britain. Although population pressure was gradually pushing up its price, soft wood from fir trees grown in Baden was still only 12.5 kreutzers – slightly over four imperial pence – per cubic foot in 1843. Even imported timber was available more cheaply to German toymen because the duty on it was only 1s. 6d. per fifty cubic feet. This compared with the British duty on imported pine which had been kept at the high level of 55s. per fifty cubic feet in order to protect the few importers of north American timber.[78]

In metal toys the German advantage lay in higher levels of technical prowess. The skills of the Nuremberg metal workers were enshrined in and protected by the masters' and journeymen's guilds. They were further enhanced from the 1820s by the progressive adoption of a French technique which used modified lathes to hollow out and shape sheet metal. All their goods were collected, packaged and shipped by well-connected merchants, who in some cases had been issuing trade catalogues since the eighteenth century.[79] These entrepreneurs had a similar role in the wooden toy trade, again gathering products at Nuremberg for further distribution.

Some French toy makers also enjoyed a high reputation for technical skill, which gave them, too, an edge in the British market. No one, Mayhew was told by a major London toy dealer

> can be compared to the French in the ingenuity of their toys; they surpass the skills of the English workmen. . . the English toy maker can hardly so much as repair a broken French toy. Few watch-makers here can repair a broken clock-work mouse; they will generally charge 2s. 6d. for repairing a mechanical mouse which I sell new for 3s. 6d. Such a mouse could not be made here, if it could be made at all, for less than 15s.

Skilled workers in the French industry were capable of earning up to 4s. 10d. a day, although the average daily wage of a male toy worker in Paris was 2s. 8d.[80] By contrast, Mayhew reckoned on a weekly London wage of 12s. 6d., rather lower than the French figure, but he arrived at this by including both the earnings of employees and the profits of one-man businesses. Since the latter were usually quite small, they gave a downward bias to his estimate. On Mayhew's own evidence, employees of whitewood and Bristol wood toy makers could make between 3s. and 3s. 6d. a day, rocking-horse makers about 18s. a week, although these still fell short of the skilled Parisians. However, as with the German case, the basis of the comparison between London and Paris is uncertain. At most the figures may imply that any advantages enjoyed by the French in the British market had more to do with innate quality rather than the cost of labour. It is possible, too, that any such advantage was further enhanced by the economies of scale arising from relatively large units of production. Birmingham certainly had some toy factories but Mayhew's researches indicate that the structure of the London industry was not at all comparable with Paris, where about a sixth of the masters employed more than ten workers in 1847.[81]

Comparative advantages such as these enabled some French and

German makers to penetrate the British market despite the burden of the import duties (until 1853) and transport costs. But their success, as illustrated in Tables 4, 5 and 6, must be kept in perspective. It patently was not by Mr McGregor, a Joint Secretary at the Board of Trade. He informed the Select Committee on Import Duties in 1840 that 'almost all the toys used in this country are imported'.[82] He later contradicted himself by adding that 'the toys they manufacture in this country are of a different description' from those made abroad.[83] This was not strictly accurate either. Indeed, commenting in 1835 on the import of cheap wooden toys from Germany, McCulloch noted that 'in late years these have been made in greater abundance in England than formerly'.[84]

If Mayhew's later work did reveal that domestic makers in some sectors were increasingly troubled by the growth of imports, it was also true that the British industry, just like the French and German, had its own areas of specialisation based on comparative advantages in skill or novelty. Prominent among these were board games and also the outdoor games produced from 1810 by F. H. Ayres. Equally important were paper toys, certain types of doll and rocking-horses. There was no serious foreign competition, either, in other heavy wooden goods. 'It's heavy work, sir', one maker told Mayhew, 'and foreigners like light work best.' As a result, he went on, his own tops and skipping ropes were shipped to America 'in immense numbers'.[85] English-made dolls' eyes were also much sought after both in America and France, and it was claimed than ten pairs were exported for every one finding its way into the home trade.[86] Cheap tin toys should probably be added to this list as well. Nuremberg's preeminence in this field did not really emerge until the 1860s, its contribution prior to that being largely confined to items such as trumpets and rattles. Only recently has it been appreciated that some tin playthings, formerly believed to be of continental origin, were in fact made at Wolverhampton, confirming Charles Dickens's accuracy in referring to 'rosy cheeked dolls . . . tables, chairs, bed-steads . . . and various other articles of domestic furniture (wonderfully made in tin, at Wolverhampton) . . .'[87]

Doubtless such toys found their way also into the expanding British export trade, which in itself was further evidence of the industry's development. Systematic export figures were not published on a regular basis until 1853 but the total for that year, £46,825, is indicative of an earlier growth suggested in Tables 2 and 3. However, the figures before 1853 are patchy and of dubious accuracy. The continued ambiguity in the use of the word 'toy' in trade statistics still precludes the drawing of any too precisely enumerated conclusions, although the general expansionary tendency is supported by other evidence. Even in the eighteenth century the pattern of toy exports was quite clear, with the bulk of English manufactures going to western Europe, the West Indies and the American colonies. English paper dolls were selling in Germany from the 1790s, while English-made toy books and the Fullers' paper costumes were being imported by American merchants in the first decade of the nineteenth century. Russia, too, imported some English toys. (Germany made the largest contribution to the 83,144 roubles worth of foreign toys imported into Russia's Baltic ports in 1802.) But according to a contemporary publication the British also had a stake in the market and the phrasing suggests that the author was making a distinction between adult and children's toys. 'It is easy for Russia to say, England must have our tallow, hemp, flax, iron, timber etc., but we can do without their cloth, cutlery, toys, trinkets, or articles of luxury and taste.'[88] To this can be added some expansion of exports to France. Given the almost permanent state of hostility between Britain and its nearest overseas neighbour it was hardly surprising that trade between the two was irregular and small. The official value of English toy exports to France in 1789 was formally recorded at a mere £30.[89] With the ending of the Napoleonic Wars, cross-Channel trade picked up and by 1825 the official worth of British toy exports to France had risen to £2680, with a declared value of £5524.[90] Although the actual figures cannot be taken at face value, they can perhaps serve as an indication of trends and orders of magnitude.

It is impossible to know with any certainty what these growing exports represented in terms of total British toy production at mid-century, since no formal attempt was made to measure the latter until 1907. Seventy years earlier, however, an anonymous contributor to a volume edited, among others, by Nathaniel Whittock, used contemporary price information to calculate that the annual value of toy whips sold in Britain was £2340. Multiplying this up to embrace all other types of toy, which he assumed to be 250, he arrived at a total output with a sales value of £583,000 a year.[91] Henry Mayhew attempted a similar exercise for the year 1841, concluding that the total cost of toys produced in Great Britain was almost £134,000, to which he added the value of imports and arrived at total sales worth £155,997, about a quarter of the sum suggested by Whittock's book.[92] In the absence of any alternative contemporary estimates these two figures may perhaps be taken as the likely parameters of British production, although neither should be taken too literally. The application by Whittock's contributor of an arbitrary multiplier to the price of a single toy hardly inspires much confidence, and faith in his accuracy is further undermined by his claim that there were fifteen whipmakers in London, when the Post Office Directory for 1846 shows three times that number. Allowing for average weekly earnings of about a pound, his suggestion that labour's share of the industry's income was about £308,600 implies a workforce of about 6000, or more than 9500 if Mayhew's average wage estimate of 12s. 6d. is accepted. Even allowing for the gross undercounting evident in the 1831 occupational census, and the fact that the Whittock calculation took into account not just children's toys but 'toy-books, twopenny trash, valentine letters, and pretty pictures' as well, this still seems somewhat on the high side.[93]

In its defence, however, it can be said that the final result was not inherently implausible. It represented only about a third of 1 per cent of the combined contribution made by the mining, building and manufacturing sector to the gross national product in 1841.[94] If production had remained at that level in 1853 then exports would have comprised about 12 per cent of total output, a rather more realistic figure than the 35 per cent implied by Mayhew's lower production estimate. It must also be allowed that the method used in Whittock's book did mean that retail and wholesale mark ups were included. It is by no means clear that Mayhew allowed for these in his estimates, although they may have been covered by what he termed 'interest for capital'. He certainly did not take into account sellers' margins on foreign toys, using only their official valuations in his calculations. Apart from the fact that official valuations bore little relation to actual value, it seems likely that mark ups on foreign toys could be very high. One story that Mayhew himself recorded involved a speculator who 'when the duty was highest . . . now and then would venture £1000 in buying foreign toys. It was, he said, a speculation, but he generally got £2000 for his £1000.'[95]

In some respects, it is true, Mayhew's approach, assessing the total costs of production by adding up the value of labour and raw material inputs, was the more rational, but there is a disquieting orderliness in his surmise that these costs and indeed the 'interest for Capital' were all equal at slightly over £44,622. His wage data were drawn from 1850, even though his calculations related to the year 1841, and from his own reports it is evident that returns to labour varied enormously from one year to the next. His average wage estimate of a weekly 12s. 6d. was derived by adding the incomes of highly-skilled journeymen to the profits made by one-man businesses. No allowance was made for the

relative numbers of these categories. As with Whittock's contributor, it
was also taken for granted that London rates applied in the provinces,
even though Mayhew himself acknowledged the importance of the
midland trade and was told by at least one of his informants that, unlike
London, it was more factory-based. Such considerations almost certainly
built into Mayhew's sums an excessive downward bias. So, too, did his
most erroneous assumption of all – that the count of toy makers
reported in the 1841 census was accurate. It was not. If the statistics
of output are uncertain, those of employment are almost equally so.

Table 7
The Toy Making Population of Britain, 1831–51[96]

Occupation	1831	1841	1851
Toy Maker	1,139	1,866	2,539
Ball/Bat Maker	25	97	294
Doll Maker	1		
Figure/Image Maker		287	378
Fishing Rod Maker	36	229	376
Mask Maker		10	
Modeller	1	381	583
Pewterer	98	321	
Tinplate Worker	27		
Wax Modeller		34	56
Total	1,327	3,225	4,226

The problems of early census interpretation are particularly intract-
able in the case of the toy industry, not least because it was possible to
move in and out of it relatively easily.[97] At one time, for example, the
manufacture of magic lanterns was dominated by opticians who 'had
the trade to themselves'.[98] A fancy toy maker to whom Mayhew talked
had once been a tailor, while the inventor of the juvenile drama began
life in the haberdashery and circulating library business.[99] A toy basket
maker followed the trade 'only in the summer'.[100] The census returns
of 1831 listed about 1100 toy makers, but this figure referred only to
males over the age of twenty (Table 7).

The next census did attempt an individual enumeration but it is
apparent that many women and children were missed. The sexes were
distinguished in 1851 and it showed that over a third of those designated
as toy makers were adult females. Children were also widely employed
and Dickens got it right on two counts, therefore, when he gave his
fictional toy maker, Caleb Plummer, a daughter to assist him in his

business.[101] Mayhew came across several instances of toy makers whose only other labour input came from their families or other juveniles. This was particularly so in the case of those working at the cheap end of the trade, where narrow profit margins made low wages imperative. A manufacturer of Bristol toys reported employing 'two boys . . . one was an apprentice, a well grown lad; the other was a little fellow, who had run away from a City institution'.[102] Further inaccuracies occurred because the enumerators described as unoccupied those who were currently unemployed. Unemployment was particularly likely in a trade with a demand as elastic and as seasonal as that for children's toys. Small toys and fancies sold well in summertime at fairs for example. Once again, Mayhew's researches provide an invaluable insight into the fragile nature of the market and its vulnerability to the weather and the seasons, and to the whims of impulse and fashion. 'When the labouring people are out of employ', one individual told him, 'I feel it in my business.'[103] Another pointed out that there was 'little chance of selling basket-toys in the streets in bad weather. But in summer the children are walking out with their mothers, and the children are our best friends, for they tempt the mothers to buy of us.'[104]

Nor were all of those described as toy dealers and makers actually engaged in making for children, as the word still retained its connotations of trinkets. Conversely, it was still the case that many who made toys for children appeared in the occupational census under different guises, including some of those whose occupations have been included in Table 7. It is significant in this context that although a survey of contemporary English trades, published in 1821, did not mention toy manufacturers as such it did remark that pewterers made 'a variety of articles' and that manufacturers of small-scale tin-ware could be found 'in every part of the metropolis'.[105] Even more specific was the reference in another early nineteenth-century description of trades. The account of each type of employment was prefaced with a short poem. Under the heading of 'turner' was the following verse.

> In ivory white and box so bright
> My cup and ball most rare is
> And tops and toys for girls and boys
> And wooden bowls for dairies.[106]

The involvement of the various types of woodworker in both the adult and juvenile markets is particularly relevant to calculations of employment in the toy trade because the manufacture of heavy wooden toys was one of the major areas of British specialisation at mid-century.

It was not without reason that a rocking-horse was used to symbolise centres of toy production on the map of industrial locations published along with the 1851 census.

Table 8
Location of Toy Dealers and Makers: England and Wales[107]

Place	Males	Females	Male (under 20 yrs)	Female (under 20 yrs)	Total
London	846	273	174	64	1,357
Warwickshire	541	105	220	69	935
Lancashire	150	39	38	5	232
Staffordshire	59	24	19	18	120
Yorkshire	67	20	15		102
Kent	59	14	12		85
Sussex	32	19	12	2	65
Wales	41	13	6		60
Worcestershire	27	1	12		40
Others	329	130	71	22	552
Total	2,151	638	579	180	3,548

As might be expected of an industry still not emerged from its pre-industrial chrysalis, toy makers were to be found in most counties. There was already, however, a degree of specialisation, as Table 8 indicates. Just under a third of those described in the 1841 census as toy makers were located in the midland counties of Warwickshire, Worcestershire and Staffordshire. These were the regions associated with the adult trinket industry centred on Birmingham and the Black Country. On the other hand, the trinket trade was in decline and some of those listed, therefore, were almost certainly engaged on making children's playthings in small toy making factories. Items such as model horses and carts were mass-produced by machines in such premises, though they were dismissed by a London artisan as nothing more than slop toys.[108] In Wolverhampton the Evans and Cartwright factory was also turning out large quantities of tin toys, while another Black Country firm, T. and C. Clark, had a sufficiently thriving business to seek to protect it by means of a registered trade mark.[109] Lancashire's importance rested mainly on the role assumed by Manchester as a distribution centre. The city itself had thirty-eight toy repositories and warehouses by 1853, while its satellite towns of Bury and Oldham boasted fourteen and five respectively.[110]

The other main centre of the industry for both production and distribution was in London, particularly in the parishes stretching away to the east from the city. Here were congregated not only the main wholesale warehouses but also clusters of jewellers, watch-makers, workers of various woods and metals, and a host of small handicraft tradesmen, most of whom eked out a precarious living in the interstices of the industrial revolution. St Georges in the East was fairly typical, a survey of 1848 identifying seventy-six carpenters, ten tin men, two brass workers, and ten cabinet makers, as well as turners, japanners, carvers and pewterers, some of whom probably drifted in and out of toy making, although only two were officially classified as such.[111] The majority of the commonest type of toy maker was to be found here, the self-employed, one-man or family business, whose goods were seldom manufactured to order but rather

> when they have produced a small number, [they] hawk them about the streets. Without capital, and compelled to work almost literally from hand to mouth, they continue to exist only, without any material advance . . . making much the same kinds . . . one year after another.[112]

Typically supplying the poorest end of the market, such individuals were operative, manufacturer, merchant and labourer all rolled into one or, as George Sala accurately described them, 'street mechanics, manufacturers of the articles they sell'.[113] Their enterprises required almost no capital and, it was said, produced profits that 'must fall short of those of an average workman'.[114] Mayhew certainly found plenty to fit this description – a tin toy maker who made about twelve shillings a week, and a whitewood toy maker and a pewterer who both paid out half of their weekly earnings on raw materials, leaving them respectively with ten and nine shillings. Wooden doll makers were equally vulnerable. The trade was so easy to enter and competition so fierce that the quality was continually deteriorating, sometimes to the extent that the dolls possessed legs 'innocent of calves, insteps and ankles', with bodies turned on lathes and 'confounding all distinction of front and back, left and right'.[115] The problem, as a High Holborn shop owner told Mayhew, was that in goods like these competition was unrestricted, with the result that the makers 'cut one another's throats for want of combination. I know the workmen do, I tell them so. They starve in trying to outdo one another in cheapness, which injures them and is no benefit to the tradesman.'[116]

Equally poor were some of those engaged in the putting out processes which were most commonly found in dollmaking. Mayhew was told that the relatively wealthy customers who bought sewn dolls rarely bothered to think about the circumstances under which they were made.[117] Typically, the stuffing and sewing of bodies and limbs was put out to women who by 1850 were earning perhaps 2s. 6d. a gross. Composition heads were manufactured from papier maché before going off to be finished in wax, and have eyes and hair inserted. To Mayhew the whole appearance of one head maker 'showed grinding poverty. His cheeks were sunk . . . and altogether he seemed, from grief and care, like a man half dead.' His weekly income, he claimed, did not exceed twelve shillings. A married couple who provided dresses for these dolls told him that their income was currently six shillings a week.[118]

A second group comprised those who, like the garret masters, worked at home but generally produced to order for an individual wholesaler or retailer. This was why some of Mayhew's interviews were delayed by the periodic arrival of dealers' delivery men.

> My informant, while giving his statement, was interrupted now and then by the delivery of orders . . . sounding very grandiloquent – 'a dozen large steamers', 'two dozen waggons' and then a customer had room left in his sack for 'half a dozen omnibuses with two horses'.[119]

This same individual had toys piled all over his workshop rather in the manner of Dickens' Caleb Plummer, whose output for the merchants Gruff and Tackleton, included

> dolls, Noah's arks, melancholy little carts . . . small fiddles, drums, no end of cannons, shields, swords, little tumblers in red breeches, boats of all sorts, dozens upon dozens of grotesque figures.[120]

Not all such makers were beholden to particular customers, producing instead on their own account and then seeking to sell directly to a range of wholesalers and retailers. If they were not successful they had other ways of offloading surplus stock, arranging their own auctions and getting accomplices to bid up the prices. 'Up goes a wooden rocking-horse which has been in Higgins' garret for the last three years; and after galloping up from ten shillings to three pounds ten, is knocked down . . .'[121] 'If you buy anything at one of these sales,' cautioned William Croft, 'you are sure to repent of your bargain.'[122]

Charles Dickens' creation, Tackleton, appears to have been a fictional equivalent of W. H. Cremer, who owned two substantial retail outlets in Regent Street and Westminster As well as buying in from overseas and from small makers, Cremer was also a direct employer of labour. He operated his own manufacturing premises and there was a factory, or at least a proto-factory, side to the industry as well. Factory is perhaps too grand a term for the small units that were typical of the London trade, although it might be appropriate for some of the units operated by the Birmingham tinmen. In the capital, however, the two makers of dolls' eyes employed two and six men respectively. But for those journeymen who did work in the larger enterprises wages could be much higher than the incomes received by the independent garret masters or the doll makers. Mayhew cited sums as high as thirty shillings a week for those engaged in making dolls' eyes and rocking-horses. On the other hand, the eight women and girls employed on piece rates by a substantial manufacturer of papier maché models, could receive as little as four shillings.

This particular individual was one of an elite of master craftsmen standing at the very apex of the manufacturing network and producing expensive toys of the highest quality for a select range of customers. He personally carried out the skilled process of dressing the animal skins from which the coverings were produced and he was adamant that he would not reveal its secrets to Mayhew. A Frenchman, he was proud of the fact that his goods, which sold for as much as £5 a piece, outdid his countrymen's for quality. A High Holborn man who made speaking dolls was able to charge six guineas a time, while the wax dolls exhibited by the London-based Montanaris at the Great Exhibition sold, undressed, at anything between ten shillings and five guineas. An Italian, the only commercial producer of detonating crackers in Britain, found his business so lucrative that he was able to invest in a parlour full of 'old foreign paintings, religious, mythological, or incomprehensible, unmistakable Hogarth prints'.[123] An English maker of top quality magic lanterns estimated that his income in 1849 had been almost £1470, while the inventor of the toy theatre reckoned that at the peak of their popularity in the 1840s they had brought him in £30 a week. At that time, he had been turning out about fifty models each week, the most expensive costing £20.

How can these wide-ranging changes in both the nature and scale of toy manufacturing in Britain after 1750 be explained? It is possible that they reflected a fundamental shift in parental attitudes towards children, although the extreme version of that hypothesis – that parents now began to invest emotionally in their offspring, showing them affection and love where none had been risked before – has been much criticised.[124] It has encountered the obvious and instinctive objection that the withholding of parental affection is biologically and psychologically unlikely. One detailed critique has attacked the historical integrity of the thesis, noting the inability of its advocates to agree about its timing, and referring also to the cavalier way in which evidence has been freely transposed both across space and time.[125] On the other hand, this critique itself is unduly, if understandably, reliant on evidence drawn almost entirely from the experience of upper- and middle-class children.[126] Whatever the truth, there is no disagreement that from the middle of the seventeenth century onwards there was a growing recognition of childhood as a distinct stage of human development, with its own needs and activities which were different from those of adults.[127]

Health was one area of concern. Thus the caption accompanying one illustration of children playing with whips and tops in a compilation of short moralistic tales urged that

> this is good exercise, and we know of no reason why girls should not use it, in moderation as well as boys, for when they have been working with a needle for some time in cold weather, the exercise will tend much to promote their health.[128]

But it was children's education that attracted most attention. In Europe, Froebel (born 1782) encouraged the use of toys for child development while in England the Edgeworths' interest in toys was derived purely from their educational objectives, as the title of their work, *Practical Education*, indicates. Similarly, J. A. Paris, whose three-volume work of 1827 provides one of the earliest, albeit indirect, insights into the widening range of toys, also had an educational intent, made explicit in the subtitle of his book – 'to illustrate the first principles of Natural Philosophy by the aid of popular toys and sports'.[129] John Spilsbury's jigsaws were certainly marketed with an educational appeal while the titles of the earliest board games reveal a similar purpose – 'A Journey Through Europe' (1759); 'Royal Geographical Amusement' (1774); 'Royal Genealogical Pastime of the Sovereigns of England' (1791); 'Arithmetical Pastime' (1798); 'Game of Life' (1790). Most of them can be fitted easily into categories such as moral improvement, geographical, historical or instructional. Pure amusement is underrepresented, although it might adequately describe the function of Overton's 'Royall and Most Pleasant Game of Goose' (1750).[130]

Although one early nineteenth-century periodical lamented the passing of 'intellectual toys' such as dissected maps and chess, which had 'now long since given place to the elegant accomplishments and varied resources of modern youth', the notion that amusement was a legitimate

occupation for children took a long time to struggle free from the
strait-jackets imposed by puritanism, the evangelical revival and utilitarianism.[131] A quarter of a century later another journal averred that
most conscientious parents 'hesitate to place in the hands of their
children works of mere fiction, calculated only to amuse the imagination'.[132] 'We noted fifty English games,' reported another, 'some of
them with titles of fearful dryness.'[133] Although there was perhaps a
hint of regret in this last comment, the conviction that toys, properly
used, were a potent medium of education remained an ever-present
theme in the first half of the century. Toys were to stimulate, train,
excite and even to inspire, according to one writer who concluded by
recommending not only the more conventional items now available,
but also reading spectacles on the grounds that they constituted a toy
'of great power . . . for a child over-flowing with intellectual life' because
they could be swung, polished, worn, and moved into a variety of
positions.[134] Tongue in cheek it may have been, but *Punch*'s hope that
children's nurseries would be transformed by appropriate toys into
miniature laboratories, staffed by lambswool dogs barking chemical
formulae or speaking dolls conversant with ten foreign languages, struck
many a receptive chord in more serious-minded contemporaries.[135]

Gender stereotyping was perceived as an important aspect of toys'
educational functions. In contemporary children's fiction, for instance,
dolls were frequently used for such purposes. Reviewing Dorothy
Kilner's *Dolls' Spelling Books* (1803), Mrs Trimmer noted with evident
satisfaction that

> in this pleasing volume we find a little girl acting in the character of a
> mamma towards her family of Dolls . . . all little mammas of the same
> description will find much to amuse, and many things to improve them
> in the lectures which this young lady gives to her wooden and wax
> children.[136]

Clearly, however, the implications for toy manufacturing of any
growth of interest in children and their activities depended also on
supply and demand; toys could be adopted for educational, health or
recreational purposes only if parents could afford to purchase them
and if there existed a capacity to produce them. On the supply side
several developments may have been important. First, it is possible that
manufacturers may have diversified into producing for children because
of adverse trends in the market for their usual products. As early as
1702 it had been suggested that the abolition of the duty on tin for
export would prove 'vastly prejudiced to the Pewterer's Trade'.[137] It may

be, therefore, that the establishment of a successful tinplate industry in England by the end of the century gradually pushed displaced pewterers towards producing miniatures for children.[138] This particular instance may be speculative but the principle is sound. Mayhew interviewed at least one worker who entered toymaking in the 1820s when his skills as an optical glass grinder were rendered superfluous by the advent of steam machinery.[139]

Secondly, the economic effects of political disturbance in Europe may have exerted some influence. Certainly when France's revolutionary government banned the import of toys, it specified exactly the sort of trinkets in which some branches of the Birmingham toy makers specialised, 'little works in tortoise shell, ivory, mother of pearl, horn, and fancy woods'.[140] Sir Francis Eden noted in 1797 that the midland trade in buttons and buckles had been badly affected by the outbreak of war, while changes in fashionable taste had also reduced the demand for buckles.[141] The dislocation of these specific trades may have been essentially short term and to some extent offset by increased demand from the British military establishment, but in other commodities it may have encouraged some diversification, including a move into children's playthings. Whittock's book may have exaggerated in claiming that the disruption of the Napoleonic War led to the creation of innumerable toy makers, but a number of toymaking manufactories did appear in the Black Country at this time.[142] They turned out a huge range of tin toys:

> miniature drums, trumpets, whistles, popguns, soldiers, sailors, elephants, lions, tigers, racehorses, pigs, spotted dogs, sheep etc. together with the numberless gimcracks which were the joy and delight of the children.[143]

A similar process of diversification was also occurring in Nuremberg where by 1853 all but three of the sixty-four masters in the tinsmiths' guild were dependent on the production of tin toys.[144] Prominent among the newly-emergent English producers of such items was the Wolverhampton firm of Evans and Cartwright, established in the first decade of the nineteenth century and destined to become one of the largest producers in the country.

Another result of the general upheaval caused in Europe by the long period of war was migration. It is possible that the British industry received something of a fillip from the arrival of a number of foreign craftsmen. The dollmaker Pierotti arrived in London in the 1780s while Crouchet started work in London in 1815. William Cremer junior, who by mid-century owned two of the most fashionable and best known toy houses in London, was sufficiently well established to refer to himself as an Englishman in the 1870s.[145] His father, however, was a German woodcarver who had settled in England earlier in the century. It is clear, too, that there was a strong European influence on the distribution side. Among the owners of fancy repositories in Newcastle, for example, were Signors Grassi and Rampoldi, Mastaglio and Molteni, Origoni, and Antonio Tarelli.[146] A similar Italian presence was apparent in Leeds where those listed as toy dealers included Luvoni and Pusinelli, and Pellegrino Vassalli.[147] In London, German toymen were building upon the trade links established over several centuries by the merchants of the Hanseatic League. The bulk of imports in the eighteenth century were German goods imported mainly through what had been the Hanse ports and individuals such as Cremer capitalised on these connections. In London German traders were instrumental in organising Christmas trade fairs and their influence was equally apparent in the arcades and bazaars.[148] 'The shrines to which the London children make such constant and willing pilgrimages', it was reported in 1854, were 'mostly inhabited by Germans and French, the former in the greatest number . . . the Arcades are their colonial settlements.'[149]

While such supply side changes may well have been influential in determining the quality, range and even availability of toys, in the last analysis none would have been manufactured had there not been a sufficient demand to guarantee the possibility of a living to the producers. The major impetus to the spread of the toy industry came from the growth of effective demand. The precise role of demand and consumption in stimulating Britain's industrial revolution has been intermittently disputed ever since Dr Gilboy complained so forcefully that classical economists tended to overlook it.[150] In identifying new patterns of economic growth in the eighteenth and early nineteenth centuries some recent studies have tended to play down the impact of rising consumption in driving the economy forward.[151] It is difficult to reconcile this conclusion with the claims put forward by the enthusiastic advocates of a consumer revolution in the eighteenth century.[152] One recent analysis of inventories left by London's middle income groups certainly indicates a consistent growth in the value of their domestic possessions (even excluding plate and jewellery) during the course of the eighteenth century.[153] The annual profits of the jewellers and toymen, Haynes and Kentish, rose from £1846 in 1798 to more than £4000 in 1819 before falling back again.[154] Nor was this merely a metropolitan phenomenon. Dr Lorna Weatherill's study of eight English regions has revealed comparable growth in the provincial ownership of material possessions, justifying her contention in a later, though narrower, study that many Britons came to expect to own a much wider range of furniture and household goods.[155] By the early nineteenth century observers of the middle classes were frequently to be found discussing the growth of consumption, one commenting, for instance, 'on the vast increase of superfluities which of late years have become primary necessaries in the appointment of the well appointed furnished house'.[156] Such evidence certainly seems to square with developments in the indigenous toy industry, where both diversification and expansion were evident from the 1750s onwards in London. From the 1780s the pace of change quickened and affected the provinces, a trend which must have reflected the fact that a growing number of people, mainly from middle income groups, were able to spend money on children's toys.

From the start of the nineteenth century toy buying seems to have spread even further down the social scale. In the absence of anything more than the odd, isolated statistic, this cannot be quantified and it must be conceded that the evidence is not entirely unambiguous. What, for example, should be deduced from the fact that Gaskell's survey of the manufacturing population, which included a lot on children's conditions, health and upbringing, made no mention of toys?[157] Were the children of the industrial working classes to be equated with the armies of ragged urchins noted by another contemporary, children 'whose cheap playthings are nothing more than mud, snow, sticks, or oyster shells'?[158] Or was it rather that the ownership of commercially made playthings was now so commonplace among the children of the labouring classes that it did not merit particular reference?

Mayhew is helpful here. Although he was writing in 1850, his surveys of the various branches of toy manufacture frequently ranged back to the early years of the nineteenth century. In this context, therefore, it is significant that he introduced the second of his pieces on the toy trade by reminding readers that the first had dealt with toys produced for the 'children of the poor'.[159] His original article, four days earlier, appeared to equate the poor with the working classes. 'The principal division', he wrote 'is into the toy-makers for the rich, and those for the poor. I shall deal in the present article with those who principally supply the children of the working classes with toys.'[160] Whether there was a fine distinction in his mind between the poor and the working classes is not relevant here.[161] What is important is his suggestion that at least some of those for whom commercially made toys had been out of reach in the eighteenth century could now afford them. This is a clear indication that, even in the short term, industrialisation brought economic gain to some workers, the main beneficiaries being those whose skills had been created by the new technology or whose older craft skills had not yet been overtaken by it. The real wages of male workers do appear to have risen quite significantly between 1781 and 1821.[162]

This of course is not entirely consistent with the view that living standards deteriorated or at best were stable during the industrial revolution. Indeed, there is some evidence that for working-class women things got markedly worse, although this is not universally accepted.[163] It has also been proposed, for instance, that the downward spread of consumption was facilitated by the earnings of women and children, which, although low in absolute terms, boosted family income.[164] It might also be argued that the growth of child labour during the years of industrialisation deprived youngsters of any sort of childhood during which toys might be enjoyed. The decade upon decade growth in the number of children (i.e. persons aged under fourteen years) after 1740 produced a steady increase in the crude dependency ratio, which accelerated from the 1780s and peaked in 1826.[165] Theoretically, this should have pushed per capita income down, depressing living standards. The crude dependency ratio, however, is not a realistic guide to what actually happened. For one thing, by working themselves, children made some contribution to aggregate economic output. For another, it has been argued that, far from representing the immiseration of children, this was a rational adult decision to put them into the labour market in order to increase family income which in turn improved the well-being of the children.[166] The general point still stands, even if, as seems likely, family incomes generally rose less significantly than male earnings and in times of slump the wages of women and children were worst affected.[167] Finally, whatever view is taken about its underlying motivation or its impact, the extent of child labour during the industrial revolution was quite limited. Only 2 per cent of boys and even fewer girls between the ages of five and nine were at work by 1851. For those between ten and fourteen, the percentages of those classified as being gainfully employed were 36.6 for boys and 19.9 for girls.[168] In other words, the overwhelming majority of children up to the age of fourteen did have the time to enjoy toys. The evidence of a burgeoning toy industry and growing imports in the first five decades of the century further suggests that a growing number of parents had the resources to provide them.

Chapter 3

Adolescence, 1850–1914

A few years after Mayhew's articles appeared in the *Morning Chronicle*, another observer of the London scene, John Hollingshead, noted children in Whitechapel whose playthings consisted merely of 'oyster shells and pieces of broken china'.[1] In nearby Shoreditch the broken china was supplemented by 'rusty old saucepans . . . stones. . . or cinders'.[2] At roughly the same time in Scotland, the young James Keir Hardie was growing up in circumstances which later caused him to suggest that he had been 'one of the unfortunate class who never knew what it was to be a child'.[3] Hollingshead was, however, writing about the inhabitants of some of London's worst slums, while Hardie's capacity to sentimentalise the past was matched only by his ability to romanticise about the future. Most contemporary commentators supported Mayhew's contention that by the middle of the century commercially made toys were within the reach of a growing number of working-class families. One side-effect of the rising real incomes generated by the mid Victorian boom, limited though the increases were, was to extend such toy buying even more widely. London carmen and coal-heavers were able to afford tiny shovels and little waggons filled with coalsacks for their children.[4] Thomas Wright described how children of *The Great Unwashed* anticipated the arrival of Saturdays, for it was on that day that new Sunday jackets and frocks are forthcoming and father's 'big brother' and lodgers, or 'mates' . . . are liberal in the bestowal of odd

> coppers upon the 'young 'uns' and toffy, cake, and toys, as a natural consequence, abound.[5]

Even the son of a rural wheelwright, George Sturt, was quite well provided for, his best items consisting of some carved animals 'smelling divinely of mountain forests . . . clean and whitish from Swiss or Norwegian chiselling'.[6] For the rest, however, his toybox contained mainly cheap and 'broken toys – a wooden Punch short of arm or leg, a Jack-in-the-box, a monkey-up-a-stick from Farnham Fair'.[7]

Nevertheless, the contents of Sturt's toybox were modest compared with the wide range of commercially manufactured toys, particularly those of a more expensive kind, now being acquired in increasing quantities by children of the middle classes. It is true that some, like Alice Pollock, daughter of a magistrate, still made do in the main with home-made toys.[8] On the other hand, Molly Hughes's playthings included bricks, soldiers, 'several remains of ninepins, and plenty of marbles'. For her fifth birthday she received a large and resplendent wooden horse and cart.[9] Similarly, the daughter of a prosperous barrister remembered an outing with family cousins which culminated in the purchase of a doll's perambulator and a toy farm.[10] Although this particular family was not in the habit of exchanging Christmas presents, a legal friend always marked the festival by providing copious quantities of toys.[11] The writer E. E. Nesbitt noted in 1913 that the toys of her childhood had included a substantial rocking-horse, a large dolls' house, a Noah's Ark and a considerable number of bricks.[12] Esther Stokes, who enjoyed a standard of living appropriate to her father's status as a Chancery barrister, recorded memories of generous gifts for birthdays and Christmases.[13] She was one of those relatively wealthy children for whom, it was proclaimed, Christmas 'blooms into a rich luxuriance of toys'.[14]

Further insight into the extent of middle-class toy consumption in the third quarter of the nineteenth century can be gained by perusing the contents of the numerous juvenile magazines and books, whose own existence was further testimony to increased purchasing power, and also perhaps to a growing army of lower middle-class suburban toy buyers. *Peter Parley's Annual* for 1863 contained a substantial advertisement from W. H. Cremer, 'Manufacturer and Importer of Toys and Games to Her Majesty and all the Royal Family, the Courts of Prussia, France and Austria'. The same publication advertised games made by Asser and Sherwin of the Strand and ranging in price between 7s. and 31s. 6d. Darton and Hodge offered games of skill between 1s. 6d and 15s. In *Routledge's Magazine for Boys* George Richardson of Liverpool advertised himself as a manufacturer of and dealer in a wide variety of mechanical toys, including boats, telescopes, model telegraphs and tool chests.[15] Another very popular juvenile periodical was *Boys of England*, which appealed in the main to male adolescents from the new lower middle classes as well as to the sons of skilled workers. The contents of its regular exchange column provide a revealing catalogue of toy ownership as it existed in the 1860s. Scattered among the more obvious detritus of fading boyhood aspirations – collections of butterflies, stamps, coins and redundant sports equipment – are to be found demands for, or offers of, items such as steam yachts and engines, model sailing ships, chemical apparatus, cameras, microscopes, assorted musical instruments, clockwork trains and boats, several toy theatres (one complete with eight plays), puzzles and a magic lantern.[16]

Another, even more tangible indicator of growth in the third quarter of the century is provided in Table 9, which, whatever the limitations of directory evidence, reveals a marked increase in the number of repositories, warehouses and dealers. Only in London did the number of dealers appear to have decreased, which may have been the result of some attempt by the *Business Directory* to define its categories more tightly. Readers searching for toys were advised to look also at the entries under archery warehouses (twenty-two), as well as makers of backgammon boards (eight), balls (ten), cricket bats (twenty-eight) and fishing rods (fifty-five). It is perhaps significant that C. E. Turnbull, the largest specialised toy wholesalers in the country by the early 1890s, first entered the toy business in 1872.

Table 9
Toy Dealers, Makers and Repositories, c. 1870[17]

Birmingham	1847	1872	1900
Toy Dealers	13	25	19
Bristol	*1848*		*1900*
Toy Dealers	21		
Toy/Fancy Dealers			65
Fancy Importers			4
Cardiff	*1848*	*1873–74*	*1900*
Toy Dealers		2	
Toy/Fancy Dealers			30
Toy Warehouses	2	5	
Dublin	1849	1870	1906
Toy Warehouses	8	51	14
Fancy Goods Warehouses			19
Toy Makers			2
Edinburgh	*1850*	*1875–76*	*1899–1900*
Toy/Fancy Warehouses	6	41	46

Glasgow	1857	1870–71	
Toy Warehouses	31	53	
Leeds	1853	1872	1901
Toy Dealers	9	26	18
Toy Makers	4	3	2
Liverpool	1853	1870	
Toy Dealers	30	37	
Fancy Warehouses	28	38	
Fancy Goods Importer		7	
London	1846–47	1864	1894
Toy Dealers	252	210	
Fancy Goods Importers			141
Toy Makers	46	47	38
Doll Makers	12	27	16
Magic Lantern Makers		10	
Puzzle Makers		10	
Rocking-Horse Makers	5	9	6
Manchester	1850	1876	1901
Toy Dealers	30	48	65
Toy/Fancy Warehouses	6	137	44
Fancy Goods Importers			60
Newcastle	1847	1865	1900
Toy Dealers		8	24
Fancy Warehouses	3	3	16
Games Makers			2

But if ownership of toys (and for that matter of an expanding range of consumer goods both large and small) was spreading and deepening in the third quarter of the nineteenth century, it was commonly assumed, as the *Graphic* put it, that 'Englishmen are too much engaged in the solid business of life to find employment for these trifles'.[18] Two years later W. H. Cremer set out in his *Toys of the Little Folks* to take issue with the widespread belief that the 'English don't profess to do much in this line'.[19] The same assumption also provided the starting-point for George Bartley's 1876 essay on toys. There was, he wrote, a general tendency to ignore the extent to which toy manufacture was carried out England.[20] He concluded by claiming that 'as far as I am aware, no attempt has hitherto been made to bring this subject before the public, it probably having been thought too insignificant and un-important'.[21] This may have been less than fair to Mayhew but it is easy to see why the quiet progress made by the indigenous industry during the middle years of the century should have gone largely unremarked by the public at large. For one thing, it was still of only peripheral economic significance compared with the staple industries whose rise to international prominence had made Britain into the workshop of the world. Furthermore, its own development during the years after Mayhew wrote was completely overshadowed by the expansion of heavy industry, construction and, above all, the railways, which characterised the great Victorian boom.[22]

It was also the case that British toy makers presented a very low profile at the various international trade fairs organised in the aftermath of the Great Exhibition of 1851. That had been bad enough from the point of view of British participation. Asked if he intended to show any of his toys, one of Mayhew's interviewees, a pewterer, gave a revealing reply. 'I don't know much what it's about but mine's too small a way.'[23] True enough, when the Crystal Palace opened its doors on the great celebration of (mainly) British industrial achievement, the twenty-one British toy makers who showed 'manufactures relating mainly to amuse-ments', were completely outclassed by the thirty foreign exhibitors. All three of the French entries were awarded prizes, as were four of the nineteen from the various German states. Even two of the three British award-winners were in fact foreigners resident in London. Furthermore, as the *Official Report* made clear

> as the greater part of their productions consists of large models and other objects, the United Kingdom is scarcely represented in Toys prop-erly so-called . . . None of the ordinary strong toys of English manu-facture are contributed, probably on account of the makers of these sorts being generally poor.[24]

It was perhaps not surprising, therefore, that the British makers did not avail themselves of the opportunities afforded by the New York Exhibition in 1853. There was not a single toy maker among the thirty-three entries in the class for miscellaneous manufactures and small wares. By contrast, rather more than twenty of the seventy-four exhibitors from the German Zollverein displayed toys.[25] So profuse and diverse were they that one visitor described the whole section as one vast toyshop.[26] Predictably, there was a better British presence in London nine years later, although even then the various makers of parlour games, dolls, dolls' houses, mechanical toys, rocking-horses and rubber balls listed among the thirty-nine home entries were rather overshadowed by a block of eleven British manufacturers of cricket and sports gear and outnumbered by another impressive range of toys made by German firms, many of them with well-established national agents in London, including Mittler and Eckhardt; Zimmerman; Krause and Nuerbach of Basinghall Street; Killy, Traub and Company of Cheapside; and Meyerstein of Friday Street.[27] When it came to the Paris Exhibition in 1867, George Sala noted that Cremer was the only British manufacturer who bothered to show.[28] Once more, it was the European entries which most caught his eye, particularly the military toys produced by some of the German firms.

The prominence of foreigners in the toy trade was further confirmed by the import statistics, which showed a huge jump after the final abolition of the remaining duties in 1853 (Table 10). In the space of fifteen years between 1855 and 1870 imports more than quadrupled. Contemporary references to the decline of the Birmingham toy industry, which was virtually moribund by the 1860s, may have further strengthened the impression that British toy making was undeveloped and unimportant, although of course it was to the trinket industry that such comment mainly applied.

Table 10
Toy Imports to Britain: Selected Dates, 1853–1914[29]

Year	Value £	Year	Value £
1853	18,011	1885	572,792
1855	49,789	1890	748,113
1860	70,541	1895	997,647
1865	116,004	1900	1,187,773
1870	238,879	1905	1,179,662
1875	392,149	1910	1,292,723
1880	577,397	1913	1,452,723

The most recent official survey of occupations, published for 1871, also appeared to provide yet further confirmation of the position (Table 11). With hindsight it is apparent that the fall in the number of toy makers between 1851 and 1871 was more apparent than real, the product of the defective and changing classification system used by the census-makers. Even as they stood the published figures would certainly not have impressed themselves upon the general public as indicators of a dynamic and expanding industry.

Table 11
The Toy Making Population of Britain, 1851–1911[30]

Occupation	1851	1871	1891	1911
Toy Dealer				7,672
Toy Maker	2,539	2,502	6,776	11,152
Ball/Bat Maker	294	439		
Figure/Image Maker	378	187	383	
Fishing Rod Maker	376			
Modeller	583	336		
Pewterer		289		
Wax Modeller	56			
Total	4,226	3,753	7,159	18,824

Yet that is exactly what *was* developing as both Cremer and Bartley sought to show. From their different perspectives, the one intimately involved in the trade, the other an experienced industrial journalist, both provided important correctives to the prevailing popular misconceptions about British toymaking. Cremer began by conceding that French toys, especially dolls and mechanical items, were the best on artistic and technical grounds. Germans toys were the most commonly purchased, however, partly because they were cheaper and partly because they were aggressively marketed.[31] After describing at some length the main centres, products and processes of German toy making, he focused on the British industry. Significantly, his praise was unqualified. What the British made, he wrote, was

coveted in every nursery that has ever had the good fortune to become acquainted with their sterling qualities . . . Of course, I am not referring to the penny Jacks in the box, mangles, bedsteads, stoves, and windmills which are hawked about the streets by their makers, or their makers' wives and children – often enough, however, marvels of workmanship at the price . . . I allude to our large wheel barrows, our carts, drays, and cart-horses, railways and such like . . . wax dolls that can move their limbs . . . we excel in other branches . . . mechanical toys . . . We are, moreover, great in traps, bats and ball, croquet sets . . . ships, drums, rocking-horses . . . and in educational toys.[32]

This positive, if rather generalised, picture was more fully fleshed out three years later in Bartley's survey. Cremer was doubtless right in maintaining that a great many toys were still provided by small makers – makers carrying on their trade in cul-de-sacs and attics.[33] On the other hand, the output figures cited by Bartley and the adjectives he used certainly appear to bear out his claim that the industry was now 'very large', verging on a mass production enterprise and almost certainly utilising interchangeable parts. Edwards' doll factory in the Waterloo Road, for example, was making 'thousands of dolls' a week; more than 10,000 model boats were being launched annually from Sanderson's factory in Oxford Street; another establishment was turning out no fewer than 20,000 toy theatres every year; the production of rubber and gutta percha toys was now a 'large and important industry'; Messrs March and Sons manufactured a million packs of toy playing cards a year; small wooden toys were being made 'in very large quantities'; London alone possessed three substantial makers of pewter toys, with even larger producers situated in Birmingham.[34]

These claims can be verified from other contemporary evidence. Doll ownership in London was sufficiently widespread to support the opening of the first doll's hospital in the Fulham Road.[35] From the middle of the century onwards British dollmakers began the commercial production of the rag (i.e. fabric) dolls, known for centuries as a home-made item but now possessing printed features. As for model boat manufacture, one paper claimed that it was now so extensive and fine that it threatened the 'use of the boy's clasp knife in the occupation to which he most loves to put it – the cutting out of his model ship'. The same paper added that in steam engines, and doll making, Britain 'beat the world'.[36] In rubber, vulcanisation had been patented in Britain in 1843 and several specialist toy manufacturers were among the twenty-seven new firms entering the rubber trade in the 1850s and 1860s.[37] In the making of tin toys the Wolverhampton firm of Evans and Cartwright certainly had more than fifty employees by the 1860s.[38] These were what C. L. Mateaux had in mind in 1881 when she wrote that 'we, too, have certain specialities – toys in which we are not to be equalled by the workers of any other country, and therefore which are readily sold at home and largely exported to other lands'.[39] Significantly, a considerable number of important prewar firms had their origins in these years. They included William Lindop, the Manchester maker of indoor games; fellow Mancunians J. and T. Thorp, who made heavy wooden toys; Bell and Francis, composition doll makers from the 1860s; Ridingbery and Company, the Bristol manufacturer of wooden playthings (1850s); Peacock and Company, the Islington-based maker of nursery blocks, model buildings and furniture (1853); and Simpson, Fawcett and Company in Leeds.

All in all, there was plenty to justify Bartley's assertion that, in their own particular areas of expertise, British toys 'cannot be equalled by any other country, and are preferred, not only in this country, but also on the Continent, to which they are largely exported'.[40] His conclusion was well founded, and (although his geography was awry) Table 12 shows he was correct in drawing attention to the growth of a healthy if sometimes erratic export trade, once it recovered from the disruptions caused by the Crimean War. When they topped the £100,000 mark for the first time in 1869, exactly two-thirds of Britain's toy exports were going to Australia, Canada and India.

Table 12
British Toy Exports, 1853–70[41]

Year	Value £	Year	Value £
1853	46,825	1863	82,316
1855	26,007	1864	83,360
1856	34,666	1865	84,890
1857	40,616	1866	74,770
1859	42,554	1867	85,258
1860	50,557	1868	79,216
1861	48,818	1869	101,475
1862	68,965	1870	98,028

Bartley went on to observe that the amendment of the Patent Law in 1852 had resulted in a veritable flood of applications from toy makers. Numerous patents had been sought on devices designed to bring movement to dolls and animals, or to improve the working parts of toys such as pistols and kites. Others had sought to protect new chemical toys or new materials, particularly rubber compounds and pastes. From the 1870s onwards some London doll makers began to copy the German technique whereby composition doll heads (made from papier maché) were coated with wax, giving a superior finish at a cheaper price. 'From what I have stated', Bartley concluded, 'it will be obvious that the manufacture of toys has long since ceased to be carried on exclusively on a small scale and by such men as Caleb the toy maker'.[42]

Still further confirmation for Bartley's claims was provided by a comparatively stronger British showing at international exhibitions in the 1870s. It is true that they were generally lukewarm towards the Philadelphia Centennial Exhibition in 1876, but that was a reaction common to most British industries, arising partly from doubts about its organisation and partly because of annoyance with current American trade policy. As a result, no royal commission was established to coordinate

British participation.[43] At Paris in 1878, however, six British exhibitors got awards. They included honourable mentions for the games submitted by H. Driscoll of Pentonville, for the boats from Hanks and Son of Walthamstow, Montanari's wax dolls, and for Hamlet Nicholson's cricket balls (to go with his prize from Philadelphia). Bronze medals were won by Mead and Company's boats, and by the various games shown by the Scientific Toy and General Novelty Company of London.[44]

If British toymaking had been in its childhood in the first half of the nineteenth century, the mid Victorian boom nurtured its early adolescence by providing some further increase in personal disposable incomes for sections of the middle class and for some skilled workers. Just like the Germans and the French, the British had their own specialities and their exports were growing. There were some isolated indications, too, that units of production were already beginning to get larger, although toy making, like most other consumer industries, was still predominantly a matter of small scale enterprises. Progress continued through the years of the great depression and the following Edwardian boom, for children were among the chief beneficiaries of these economic fluctuations. 'It is a commonplace of the day', wrote A. I. Strand in 1896,

> to congratulate our children on their singular good fortune in having been born some sixty years later than their grandparents. If comparative luxury with far greater indulgence be an unmixed good, there is no denying the proposition.[45]

By the last quarter of the nineteenth century children were firmly fixed at the centre of public interest and concern. This was evident in several consumer industries. Food and medicine manufacturers emphasised the benefits of their products for children, while both furniture and clothing were increasingly made specifically for the juvenile market.[46] Few would have disagreed with the suggestion made in *Chamber's Journal*, that contemporary society was 'distinguished from all that have preceded it by the intensity of its interest in and regard for children'.[47] In part, this was both a cause and a consequence of a general upsurge of interest in social conditions, dating back to the 1830s and beyond. As far as the young were concerned, this now expressed itself at one level in a plethora of organised youth movements. At another it produced numerous angst-ridden investigations, both official and private, into a whole range of related social issues, including boy labour, juvenile delinquency, child prostitution and sweated industry. To some extent as well this interest was fuelled by changing demographic patterns. The proportion of the population aged under fourteen in England and Wales fell slightly between 1850 and 1901 from 35.4 to 32.4 per cent. Over the same period there was a corresponding drop in Scotland from 35.6 per cent to 33.4 per cent. However, child mortality was also declining, falling successively among those over ten from the 1850s and those over five from the 1870s. Deaths among infants finally turned down after 1900. Overall deaths among children under the age of fifteen decreased from around 300 per 1000 in 1850 to 230 in 1900, with the result that there was a significant increase in the actual number of children in Britain. A total of 7,380,000 in 1850 grew by about 50 per cent to 10,550,000 by 1900.[48]

Market size was never simply a matter of sheer numbers. Other variables were important, although their impact on toy buying is not always easy to define. For instance, because their schooling generally lasted longer, children from middle- and upper-class backgrounds usually experienced a more protracted childhood than their social subordinates. It is conceivable that this reinforced the propensity for toy buying, initially engendered by rising real incomes and the falling family size, which first showed itself among the professional classes.

The formal identification of adolescence in the late nineteenth century may have offset this – to some extent at least – in the sense that adolescence seemed to imply the laying aside of all the artifacts and icons of childhood.[49] A hint, no more, of this is perhaps apparent from a poem published in the *Girls' Realm Annual* for 1900:

> The Rocking horse is banished to a corner of the garret,
> And noone comes to comb his tail, or offer him a carrot;
> The India rubber Ball has quite forgotten how to bounce
> But Betty's last new party frock has got another flounce . . .
> The skittles and the Dominoes are tumbled on the floor,
> The Skipping rope is hanging on a nail behind the door.
> The Toys and Hoops and Bats and Ball all wonder what it means,
> They've each good reason to regret that Betty's 'in her teens'.[50]

On the other hand, some of the newer toys appearing for boys by this time clearly had an appeal which could last well beyond conventional definitions of childhood. Public school boy Paul Jones was fifteen when he recorded triumphantly in his diary the purchase in January 1912 of a yellow and red Bassett Lowke railway wagon, a 'splendid model'.[51] At the other end of the social scale, a child like Ralph Finn, born in one of the poorest parts of London, maintained his passion for Meccano well into manhood. 'Most of all I remember my Meccano box . . . to which, over the years, I had added part after part until it had become quite some set.'[52]

Finn's experience might seem to confirm that for many working-class children the implementation of factory legislation and the gradual extension of formal education after the 1870 Act were effectively extending the length of childhood, making them as dependent upon their parents as middle- and upper-class children had long been. In the 1840s Mayhew had turned up a seller of water-cress who obviously did not consider herself to be a child, despite the fact that she was only eight years old. She was momentarily flummoxed when he asked about her toys, although she finally admitted to having some at home, given to her at a Jewish club.[53] By the 1890s children were not legally permitted to work at such tender ages, full-time work being barred until they were twelve or thirteen years old. But the law was sometimes more honoured in its breach than in its observance. Nettie Adler's 1908 study of *Child Employment and Juvenile Delinquency* found that, while they may not have been regularly or formally employed, numbers of working-class children still had paid jobs. She reckoned that, not counting the half-timers still common in Lancashire, 9 per cent of all children worked outside school hours.[54]

The Times drew attention to a second implication of the Education Act of 1870 when it suggested that children would have less time to make their own toys and would thus become more dependent upon those commercially produced for them by adults.[55] It is a moot point as to whether the first part of this claim was true, but there is no doubt that the extension of formal educational provision did serve to revitalise the debate about the role of toys in education. It was not mere whim, for example, that caused the organisers of the 1871 exhibition to classify toys under the heading of educational works and appliances. As a manufacturer and seller, Cremer's was not a disinterested testimony but his view was widely shared:

> Stocked with a goodly selection of toys, the nurseries of the rising generation may be made not only the enchanted and picturesque domiciles of happy boys and girls, but the most entertaining of preparatory schools of natural history, science and art.[56]

His advice that the elementary schools created by the 1870 Act should provide educational toys for those whose only playground was the gutter, was apparently followed – at least in spirit – by some teachers. Ernest Shepard's recollections of school in the 1880s included 'the grand toys' reserved for wet days, fighting cocks and feathered birds operated by wires – 'a special treat and only allowed out under strict supervision'.[57]

Others (in the spirit of John Locke) questioned whether such manufactured toys were in fact beneficial, arguing that their growing sophistication tended to stifle those crucial ingredients of the educational process, imagination and curiosity. Toys, it was suggested, had become 'so superior that they risk eliminating the important role of fancy and imagination which sometimes permitted yesterday's children to forget all toys from the shop and use beads, furniture etc., to create worlds of make-believe'.[58] The trade press was not slow to rebut such criticisms:

> In the progress made in toys and games for children it is noticeable that those which have a distinctly educational purpose, and which give to the little ones not only something to admire, but also something to put together or to invent, are increasing, relatively in numbers and apparently in popularity.[59]

Thus miniature printing presses were recommended as a means of encouraging accurate spelling and punctuation.[60] By 1914, claimed *Games and Toys*, most manufacturers had accepted that there was a strong link between toys and education:

> next to the parents comes the toy dealer as a factor in the education of the youngsters. It is certain that the realisation that this is so has only recently come to the toy manufacturer, the distributing agent and the dealer. The last twenty years have seen it accepted as an axiom.[61]

One company which took it as axiomatic was Bedington Liddiatt, a Birmingham-based producer of novelties dating from the 1830s. Towards the end of the century the firm turned to toymaking and importing, trading under the slogan of 'Toys that Teach'. Notions and concepts such as these also received a certain amount of academic backing. In 1908, for example, the Sociological Society organised an exhibition on toys and their role in education. The Grote Professor of Mind and Logic at King's College, London, James Sully, was not convinced, registering his dissent from prevailing wisdom. 'The idea of transforming play into an educational instrument', he wrote, 'has been carried quite far enough already.'[62] His was an isolated voice, however, washed aside by the tide of contrary opinion.

Equally marooned were the proponents of rational recreation, whose voices, powerful in the first half of the century, could still be heard in the 1870s, albeit mainly from the sidelines, warning about the potentially corrupting effects of the growing availability of playthings. 'It has generally been considered desirable that public amusements should in some way conduce to edification', suggested the *Dublin University Magazine* in 1874.[63] Recreations, agreed another periodical,

> should not only be compatible with the business or duty of life but absolutely and far subordinate; and this, not only in kind but in number and quantity. Their utility and, sometimes, even their only justification is that they may increase the power and readiness for work; beyond this they should not be allowed to pass.[64]

More specifically, the Reverend Lord Sydney Godolphin Oliver informed readers of *The Times* that, while it was better to give children toys rather than tit-bits of food, excessive generosity in this respect was 'apt to create an unhealthy appetite for artificial amusement'.[65] W. H. G. Kingston, whose book, *Infant Amusements: or How to Make a Nursery Happy*, was both chronologically and philosophically a sort of hybrid between utilitarianism and Dr Spock, agreed that children were given too many useless toys. He was also doubtful about placing a toy theatre in the playroom. 'I should particularly object to running any risk of giving a child a taste for theatrical amusement.'[66] But by the end of the century the twin forces of commercialism and the greater consumer choice conferred by rising incomes had rescued a lot of recreational activities from hands such as these.

Toys were also being freed from some of the stricter religious conventions which had governed their use earlier in the century. Most memories of early nineteenth-century childhood note that there were special toys, if any were permitted at all, for Sundays. Only those with suitably pious or high-minded connotations, such as religious books and games or Noah's Arks, were permissible. Miss Lyall noted simply that 'we mayn't have our dolls or toys on Sunday'.[67] Alison Utley was allowed only her best doll while her brother's Sunday toy was a Noah's Ark.[68] In the countryside, the Sabbath for George Sturt meant only 'quiet toys', although these were deemed to include his model farm.[69] Encompassing as it did religious reading, Bible pictures, exercise (preferably combined with pastoral visitation), sick visiting, singing to the aged and playing at Sunday School, Kingston's 1867 recipe for a happy Sunday would scarcely have recommended itself to a more amusement-conscious society thirty years later.[70] True, the son of one semi-skilled Primitive Methodist remembered that even on the eve of the First World War Sunday still remained the day when 'all your toys, tops, balls and everything else, was put away . . . until Monday'.[71] More generally, however, sabbatarianism and the religious beliefs and practices in which it was rooted were both losing something of their hold in these years, with a consequent relaxation of the domestic rules applying to children's play.

If espousers of rational recreation and upholders of the evangelical Sunday were to some extent being marginalised, other threads of social control were very strongly woven into the debate about toys. Pretty well everyone agreed, and autobiographies largely confirm, that the play-things of childhood were a crucial determinant of adult character. Most famously, Winston Churchill noted that his decision to enter Sandhurst had been influenced by his childhood passion for toy soldiers, which 'turned the current of my life'.[72] A. E. Wilson recalled that his patronage of drama grew out of his boyhood love for the juvenile theatre.[73] It then became a matter of which personal attributes were deemed desir-able. Aesthetic appreciation was thought by some to be a worthwhile aspiration for adults, and E. E. Nesbitt spoke for many in railing against the ugliness of commercial toys, 'vulgar and foolish. . . ugly toys, monstrosities . . . impossible . . . trivial, unsatisfying things, the fruit of a perverse and intense commercial ingenuity . . .'[74] H. G. Wells had more martial traits in mind when he noted that appropriate toys and games could build up 'a framework of spacious and inspiring ideas in them for after life. The British Empire will gain new strength from nursery floors'.[75] His thoughts were further amplified by a later writer on toy soldiers, A. J. Holladay. 'Try and realise what Lord Roberts and Lord Kitchener felt when in command of all those men in South Africa.'[76] It was precisely her belief that such thoughts were socially undesirable that led to Mrs Oscar Wilde's plea, at a women's meeting of the International Arbitration and Peace Society in 1888, for the banning of toy soldiers.[77]

Behind this lay broader issues of gender roles, although this was perhaps not something on which the wife of Oscar Wilde was best qualified to speak. One of the strongest themes in the education debate concerned the ways in which toys should and could serve to reinforce sexual stereotypes. This had always been inherent in discussion about the use of playthings but it became increasingly common as a more rigorous gender separation emerged after mid century, especially among middle-class families. Mechanical toys, board games, cheap novelties and many other types of toy were sexually neutral, at least in terms of their users. Others were not, being clearly intended for one sex or the other. Predictably, girls were directed towards gentle and domestic activities such as sewing and flower-pressing. Dolls were recommended as a way of fostering motherly skills. It was also urged that doll play provided 'a good text for various lessons in domestic economy, especially the great clothes philosophy, and the art and mystery of gussets, tucks, and herring-bone hems'.[78] Boys were encouraged in appropriately robust and manly activities like carpentry, construction and games playing. War toys were justified on the grounds that they were necessary for the survival of an imperial nation. 'They probably serve as a sort of elementary training to fire the war spirit of the nation.'[79] Cremer, who as frequent visitor to his father's homeland knew what he was talking about, observed that with all their toys the Germans had worked up the instructive element. As far as military toys were concerned, he said, it was deemed

> important that every child of the new royal empire should be well acquainted with the customs of the soldiers of other countries against whom he might one day have to stand, face to face, in mortal strife, and therefore very good copies of possible antagonists are prepared for his instruction.[80]

While nothing as blatant as this was apparent in Britain, the rise of imperial rivalries in the late nineteenth century provided further ammunition for both sides of the argument.

Demographic and social change, then, lay behind much of the interest that late Victorians developed in issues concerning children and their toys. More important than either, however, was the marked rise in the standard of living which occurred from the 1870s onwards. Several overlapping developments in the world economy worked to produce a consumer boom in which most industrial countries shared. The spread of cheaper forms of transport combined with technological advance and an expansion of aggregate productive capacity to create a much more highly competitive environment for industrial manufacturers. The resulting downward pressure on prices benefited consumers, who in Britain were simultaneously enjoying a fall in the cost of food, consequent upon the opening up of major agricultural resources in North America and parts of the empire. Conventional indices show that, allowing for unemployment, average real wages rose by more than 75 per cent between 1867 and 1900. Even though their rate of growth fell back slightly during the Edwardian period, wages were still very much higher in 1914 than they had been even in 1880.[81] Both the desire and ability to acquire non-essential items seeped ever more deeply into British society, while the potential for consumption was carefully converted into actual expenditure through the channels of mass advertising, popular magazines, the expansion of credit facilities and changes in the pattern of retail distribution.

These developments had predictable consequences on the toy market. 'The ingenuity in providing pastimes and the ardour with which they are followed, have never in any former age been exceeded', ran one report.[82] As a result, said another, 'the toy industry is making itself felt in the world of commerce'.[83] Nor was this expansion of benefit only to children, for one characteristic social change of the late nineteenth century was the appearance of the adult hobbyist on a significant scale, mainly but by no means exclusively amongst the middle classes and skilled workers. Collecting, whether of pictures, books, furniture or other valuables, had long been an aristocratic activity – witness the earlier fads for dolls' houses and silver miniatures. The first literary use of the word 'hobby' in the modern sense occurred in 1816. By the end of the century the notion was sufficiently well established to prompt the publication not only of *Hobbies* magazine, but also a host of journals dedicated to specific interests such as fretwork, model engineering and cycling.[84]

Toys, too, became an important part of the world of adult hobbyists, further boosting the demand for them. G. K. Chesterton reckoned that in his childhood it was not a matter of a single hobby but of 'a hundred. . . piled on top of each other', although he confessed to a particular weakness still for the toy theatre.[85] Mrs Nevil Jackson collected toys of all descriptions, exhibiting in a toy pageant in 1909 some of those about which she had written so lovingly in the previous year.[86] Others were more focused, like the author Kenneth Grahame, who had a penchant for mechanical toys. His work room, it was reported by one visitor, was more akin to a nursery than a study, the books being outnumbered by toys. Grahame's forays back into childhood were not confined to his story writing. Once he told his wife that he and a friend had 'found a drore [sic] full of toys wot wound up, and we ad a great race tween a fish, a snaik, a beetle wot flapped is wings, and a rabbit'.[87] Similar items found their way into the collection of some 1700 penny toys bought from London street-sellers by Ernest King between 1893 and 1918. At his peak period of interest, 1904, he bought something two days in every three. Although his acquisitions included flags, pocket books, badges and brooches he also purchased many children's playthings, such as a mouse in a matchbox, dolls' cutlery and squeaking frogs.[88] Model railways provided another pastime capable of spanning the generations. Cheap tin trains had been widely available for many years but it was the scale models produced by the firm of Bassett Lowke after 1901 that really caught the adult imagination, initiating what was to become arguably the most important toy-based hobby in the first half of the twentieth century. Finding their host deeply engrossed in a model-railway system, guests at the home of the politician, Hugh Arnold Forster, were promptly assured that the toy belonged to him rather than to his children.[89]

Above all, it was the toy soldiers produced by William Britain after 1893 that became a major craze. Their cheapness, derived from the fact that they were hollow, made them easily accessible, while their very appearance harmonised exactly with the tones of aggressive and martial imperialism apparent in contemporary Britain. 'Of the various kinds of present that I received during the birthdays and Christmases of my childhood I can recall none', wrote C. W. Beaumont, 'that afforded me greater delight than a box of toy soldiers, especially those of Britain's make.'[90] Henry Sweeting got his first box in 1906 and had 500 figures by the time his mother sold them in 1914.[91] At about the same time the young Julian Symons was playing intricate and elaborate games with his collection of 300 men.[92] H. G. Wells was the best-known publicist of miniature war games but he was only one of a number of leading literary and political personalities who maintained an interest in toy soldiers well into adulthood. Chesterton, Jerome K. Jerome, C. P. Trevelyan, Winston Churchill, Sidney Buxton and C. F. G. Masterman were among the others.

There can be no doubt that children were the main beneficiaries of rising living standards. To varying degrees and at different rates the falling cost of living benefited most income earners, whatever their social class, and this provided the main impetus to the development of the domestic manufacturing industry. It is therefore puzzling to find some modern historians playing down the availability of toys for working-class children in the late nineteenth century.[93] Jeremy Seabrook is probably the most dogmatic, claiming that when the old working class talk of childhood, they speak of 'circumstances that tended towards the effacement of children's needs'.[94] Other oral investigations of working-class childhood, however, have yielded more positive impressions.[95] Much, of course, depended on the attitudes and rituals of individual families. As small shopkeepers, Robert Roberts' parents were certainly not wealthy but they could have afforded toys had they so wished. But, wrote Roberts, his was

never a gift-minded family. Mother was unenthusiastic about presents as a way of demonstrating affection. On birthdays and Christmas she hugged us and wished us happiness of the day . . . it seemed ample. They bought us no toys.[96]

A similar family was observed by Walter Besant in 1903. Although not among the poorest, their children's playthings were simply bits of wood and bones and oyster shells, 'transformed by the imagination of childhood into heaven knows what of things precious and splendid'.[97]

It is also the case that to a considerable extent the different judgements reflect the variable economic circumstances in which working-class children lived. In E. J. Urwick's famous study of urban working-class juvenile males, Reginald Bray reckoned that there were at least three different sub-groups. Children of the better off workers with regular incomes naturally enjoyed a higher standard of living and a richer home life, in which neither toys nor hobbies were lacking. One boy, for example, utilised a surplus bath in his back garden as a miniature lake for his model boats.[98] Interviewed in old age, the son of another skilled worker, a Lancashire iron moulder, recalled that Christmas had been especially gay 'with presents such as dolls, toys, sweets, games and once even a watch'.[99] This contrasted quite sharply with childhood among Urwick's unskilled labourers, where limitations of space dictated that most playing had to be done outside. Even so, there was still evidence of some limited ownership of games and toys. He did not mention such possessions in the context of his third group, the children of the poor. Mrs Pember Reeves' contemporaneous study of Lambeth confirmed this lack of indoor amusements: 'No books, no games, nor any place to play the games should they exist'.[100] A similar opinion came from a district nurse who claimed that she had never seen an indoor game of any type played in the homes of the poor.[101]

The various social surveys published by Charles Booth and Seebohm Rowntree at the turn of the century suggested that about a third of the urban population was living on or beneath the poverty line. Rowntree spelled out the implications of this in unequivocal terms. Such families, he said, could purchase nothing save that which was absolutely necessary to the maintenance of physical health. 'The children must have no pocket money for dolls, marbles or sweets.'[102] He made a similar claim in his slightly later study of rural labourers. Calculating that the average family had a disposable income of about sixpence a week and setting aside just over a half of this for tobacco left twopence halfpenny. This implied, he went on, that toys and dolls and picture books, even of the cheapest quality, should never be purchased; that birthdays should be practically indistinguishable from other days. It means that every natural longing for pleasure or variety should be ignored or set aside.[103]

Yet it did not follow automatically from such findings that the children of poor families had no commercial toys.[104] By no means all placed a higher priority on tobacco and drink than on their children's pleasures. Many a mother went short of necessities in order to save the pennies necessary to celebrate Christmas, although Easter went unheeded. The revival among higher social groups of the custom of giving eggs was an aspect of social behaviour that relatively few working-class parents bothered to emulate, even when they could afford to.[105] Equally, working-class birthdays often, though not always, went uncelebrated. Fred Mills, son of a farm labourer, recalled presents of fruit and nuts at Christmas but added that birthdays passed without presents. On one birthday he 'went to bed and cried, I hadn't got no presents'.[106] Clifford Hills, whose father was a thatcher, agreed in saying that there 'was no particular celebration for birthdays. There wasn't too much money to celebrate, only Christmas'.[107] But he added that his mother's former employer used to call at Christmas 'with the gifts, sweets, and little trains and things like that as kids had in those days, little engines and little motors. Nearly always . . . there was a little box of soldiers'.[108] In similar fashion every child on the Corsham estates received an annual Christmas gift from the landlord, Sir John Poynder, 'an orange and some sweets and a toy'.[109] Such philanthropic gestures, whether private or institutional, further brought toys into the hands of children who would not otherwise have had them. Regular attendance at the local Ragged School brought due reward to the young Richard Morgan at the annual Christmas treat. 'As each child came out through the door they'd be given a present . . . A little girl gets a doll. A boy'd get a wooden fire engine or a wooden train. Everybody got something.'[110] From 1879 onwards *Truth* magazine organised an annual display of homemade and other toys for distribution to children in London's hospitals and workhouse institutions. There were 27,000 such inmates in 1893, but thirty years previously Dickens had described how on each bed in a children's hospital ward there were 'little platforms whereon were to be seen little dolls' houses, woolly dogs with mechanical barks . . . tin armies, Moorish tumblers, wooden tea things . . .'[111] This was a more generous provision than that recalled by one inmate of a convent orphanage in Aberdeen at the turn of the century. She had only a single toy, a wooden horse on wheels.[112] Even police stations sometimes provided a toy or two. At least this was why one boy, reared in the Jago, probably London's most notorious criminal slum, did not mind being arrested.[113]

The growth of purchasing power also had far-reaching implications for the organisation and nature of distribution in Britain. Primed by the removal of taxes in 1853 and 1855, advertising was well placed to benefit and the growth of commercial promotion was itself a potent indicator of the developing significance of the industry. Articles on toys, their uses, their makers and the trade appeared with growing frequency in the periodical press and, even more so, in children's magazines. To give just one example, the *Strand Magazine* carried four pieces on toys in 1895–96, covering penny toys, outlandish toys, the manufacture of games, and one on a dolls' hospital.[114] Major toy manufacturers increasingly advertised in the national press and some also provided material for comics such as the *Boys' Own Paper* and *Chatterbox*.

Toys themselves were also used as advertising gimmicks. Charles Brett was one of the first to appreciate their potential in this respect, giving away free sheets of model theatre characters with the inaugural issues of the *Boys of England*. In 1897 Bissells, the American manufacturer of carpet sweepers, produced 'Little Bissells', utilising the waste from the adult version. Although originally intended as nothing more than an advertising medium for both the manufacturer and the local retailer, they generated such a huge demand that they became toys in their own right, available in five sizes. At about the same time the Ulster firm of William Barbour was distributing small, dressed dolls as a way of drawing attention to its main product, linen thread.[115] Lever Brothers had a similar idea in 1896, offering paper toys in return for wrappers collected from their soaps. In a foretaste of what was to become a major issue for the trade in the twentieth century, it was suggested by *Athletic Games, Sports and Toys* that such schemes were hardly fair to retailers, although of course to the manufacturers they represented extra business.[116]

First issued in the autumn of 1895, *Athletic Sports, Games and Toys* was the harbinger of the new toy trade press, yet another measure of the industry's progress in the last quarter of the nineteenth century. Prior to the 1850s, it was claimed, only two trades had their own journals, even though by the time the first of the toy papers appeared there was scarcely a commercial activity left unprovided for.[117] *Athletic Sports, Games and Toys* was accompanied by the *Games Gazette* and also the *Fancy Goods and Toy Trades Journal* which first appeared in March 1891, its editor proclaiming that 'those who have not looked into the figures would scarcely conceive the growing importance of the trade in toys, home and foreign'.[118] A similar justification was offered for the publication of *Games, Toys and Amusements*. The trade 'is very large and steadily increasing. Within the last ten or a dozen years these trades have assumed big proportions, and the market was never so active as at present'.[119] As it happened, few of these early publications lasted for very long and by 1908 J. D. Kiley of toy importers and wholesalers Whyte, Ridsdale and Company, was complaining about the lack of a journal to represent the interests of what was now a large and flourishing trade. W. B. Tattersall, proprietor of the *Sports Trader* (1907), took the hint and started the *Toy Trader* in 1908, a paper destined to enjoy a long and informative life.[120]

Retailing was also changing, although the essentially seasonal nature of demand meant that toys were perhaps less affected in this respect than some other consumer goods. The evidence of Table 9 suggests that in a few cities, especially the traditional wholesale centres of Manchester and London, competitive pressures produced some consolidation of business with a consequent reduction in the number of outlets. Elsewhere the general growth in the number of repositories, dealers and warehouses appears to have sustained its momentum through to the turn of the century.

Despite the development of a commercially aware and aggressive retail system, represented by the emergence of the department store and multiple shop organisations, the number of itinerant traders working in Britain actually increased from 25,747 in 1851 to more than 69,000 by 1911. They certainly remained an important source of toy supply, especially for the cheaper items aimed at the lowest income groups. It was to Petticoat Lane that Grace Foukes' wharfinger father went just before the First World War in order to buy the dolls which she and her sister were given for Christmas.[121] Another Edwardian child recalled that the Caledonian Market was a similarly 'wonderful place for toys'.[122] In London, particularly, penny toys continued to form the main stock in trade of hawkers. Gavarni had commented on their numbers in 1859. 'As day advances, the loquacious vendors of cheap toys . . . take up their places. Some of these have been in St Paul's Churchyard and Leicester Square for years, altering their wares as public taste was satiated or changed.'[123] Another observer watched a man making halfpenny flags from bits of stick and odd paper cuttings and then disposing of his entire stock in a couple of hours. 'Here, by the outlay of a little time and by the aid of a few bits of cast away wall-papers, a grown man was actually making a living, though certainly not a large one.'[124] Such street-sellers remained so prominent a feature of the London scene, especially around Holborn and Ludgate Hill, that in the years before 1914 increasing demands were made for their prohibition, mainly by local shopkeepers. Fred Willis said they were so numerous that in some streets they stood virtually shoulder to shoulder.[125]

For other classes of toys, street-selling was in decline from the 1860s as the retail revolution gathered pace. In the 1860s one hawker, known locally as Dick the Dollman, told Mayhew that the proliferation of bazaars and shops was already destroying his trade.[126] He was not referring primarily to the development of specialised children's toy shops. Rather he had in mind the growing tendency for shops of all types to carry toys, either on a regular or a seasonal basis. Stationers, newsagents and post offices, whether rural or urban, all stocked children's playthings on their shelves.[127] The *Graphic* even identified a somewhat bizarre fashion among opticians for selling steam-powered engines, locomotives and fire engines.[128] The converse was also true, except in the wealthiest parts of the large cities. J. K. Cliveden's father ran a toy retailing business in a poor part of London before the First World War. 'It was impossible', he recalled later, 'to run a shop on toys alone: every shop had sidelines.'[129]

Most of the newly-established department stores also branched out into toys, if only at Christmas time. Lewis's Bon Marché in Liverpool introduced its first Christmas fairyland in the 1870s. While it may be fiction, Arnold Bennett's account of Bostock's in the Potteries captures the atmosphere well. He describes it as

> a blaze of splendour and electric light, a glitter of gilded iridescent toys and knick-knacks . . . the cashiers in their cages gathering in money as fast as they could lay their tired hands on it! Children dreamt of Bostock's. Fathers went to scoff and remained to pay.[130]

By the 1890s Father Christmas had become a regular seasonal recruit to the sales forces of most major shops. Others established toy selling as a permanent feature of their operations. The toy section in A. W. Gamage's 'People's Emporium', for instance, carried such a huge range of the new model soldiers produced by William Britain that the store was popularly described as the 'Aldershot of the Toy Soldier World'.[131] Similarly, when William Whiteley reopened his department store in 1887 after it had been gutted by fire, he established a toy section that was sufficiently successful to make sales worth £12,000 in 1888.[132] Others enjoyed more modest returns. Emboldened perhaps

by a successful Christmas season in 1901, Cockaynes of Sheffield tried
selling toys all year round, but the experiment was quickly abandoned.
It was revived in 1910, but the largest annual profit recorded was only
just over £89 in 1912 and the department more usually ran at a loss.[133]

For a combination of reasons, – economic, social and demographic
– toys therefore became a much more prominent feature of childhood
at all levels in British society in the years after 1870. The view common
at the time, and one still repeated by many modern observers, is that
foreign manufacturers, particularly the Germans, were the main beneficiaries of burgeoning British demand. Certainly, as Table 10 indicates,
imports rose continuously, more than quadrupling between 1870 and
1895, passing the £1,000,000 mark for the first time in 1896, and then
growing a further 46 per cent by 1913. Nor were these toys merely
brought into Britain as a prelude to being reexported. In the middle
1880s about 15 per cent of imports were reexported but the figure fell
off thereafter. By 1914 more imports were being retained than had
earlier been the case.[134]

Combined with the increased quantity of German toys being imported, the decline of reexports may have served to fuel the notion
that the domestic market was virtually a Teutonic monopoly. Yet these
trends must be seen against the general patterns of contemporary
international trade. One feature of the very intense foreign competition
which characterised the two and a half decades prior to 1914 was that
Britain received a greater increase in foreign manufactures than any
other industrial nation. As for the source, it was the practice of British
customs to classify imports not by their country of origin but according
to the location of the ports through which they were shipped. As a lot
of German toys still travelled their long-established routes to Britain
via Holland, the true extent of the German contribution is best estimated by adding together the German and Dutch figures. These certainly show a consistent rise. Imports of toys valued at some £45,500
in 1855 had grown to reach almost £236,000 in 1875. By 1900 the
total had climbed to more than £800,000, passing £1,000,000 in 1907
and standing at almost £1,200,000 in the last full year of peace. If,
however, these figures are expressed as a proportion of all toy imports
(Table 13) then a modified picture emerges. On average between 1870
and 1913 about 77 per cent of the toys imported into Britain were
German. Although in terms of value they stood at an all-time high in
1913, this still represented just over four-fifths of total imports, about
the same proportion as had been common in the years between 1850
and 1865.

Table 13
Origins of British Toy Imports[135]

Year	Germany %	Holland %	France %	USA %	Japan %
1855	82.0	8.4	7.5		
1860	79.8	9.2	7.9		
1865	45.0	23.2	30.7		
1870	43.4	28.8	5.0		
1875	58.6	1.5	22.1		
1880	18.8	57.1	13.8		
1885	43.2	26.9	16.3		
1890	53.6	28.6	11.1		
1895	46.1	33.8	16.6	1.5	
1900	54.3	14.2	12.5	2.5	
1905	60.5	13.5	9.6	4.1	0.4
1910	77.9	0.5	10.7	6.1	1.8
1913	81.5		9.6	3.6	2.8

In the light of this, how should contemporary views about German dominance of the British toy market be interpreted? To some extent no doubt they reflected the hold which German traders had established on the distribution trade in earlier years. It was German merchants, for example, who from 1860 had organised the trade fairs that were to grow into some of the most important buying events in the toy industry's calendar, the Manchester Toy Weeks. The number of Germans settling in England increased quite noticeably after 1880. While most attention has been focused on their commercial travellers, clerks and waiters, their prominence in the toy trade should not be overlooked.[136] By the 1890s about a half of the 141 fancy goods importers listed in one leading trade directory were German.[137] Zimmermans, responsible for bringing in huge quantities of imports, had been established over a century, although many of the major German makers were represented in Britain by a relative newcomer, Stahlecker and Company of Christopher Street.

The toy trade was particularly vulnerable to the waves of xenophobic hysteria periodically whipped up about the threat presented by the expansion of German military and commercial might. *Fraser's Magazine* had drawn attention to the economic danger in 1877, warning that Germans were 'possessing themselves of the advantages previously monopolised by Englishmen'.[138] A similar point was made some years later by a writer recently returned from visiting Germany. He attributed its prosperity to the fact that Germans, 'when they are once convinced that money is to be made in a given locality, lose no time in making it possible'.[139] Such fears were heightened by German naval policy and German sympathy for the Boers during the South African War. 'All England', Edward Goschen wrote in his diary, 'is bitter against everything German.'[140]

Rather complacently perhaps, *The Times* dismissed such concerns as another example of the

> tendency to overrate and to misinterpret. It is no exaggeration to say that the 'German danger' spread dismay and alarm through a considerable section of mercantile Britain. It was distorted and exaggerated in those newspapers which are given to sensationalism; it was impressed into. the service of those who believe the best way to rouse their country is to send a shudder through its nerves.[141]

Even such a careful statistician as Charles Booth could claim in his survey of London industries that little toymaking was done in the capital because nearly all toys came from Germany.[142] This notion was fed most avidly by supporters of the powerful protectionist lobby, for whom truth was sometimes less important than the wider political agenda which they espoused. The main perpetrator of myths about the toy industry in this respect was E. E. Williams, whose book, *Made in Germany*, deliberately played up the German industry, damning the British makers both implicitly and explicitly. 'To a large and an ever-increasing extent', he thundered, 'our children's playthings . . . are made in Germany.' As a nation, he went on, Britain had quite failed to look after toy manufacturing and, as a result, London toy making was 'well nigh at the point of death'.[143] The doll market had gone to the continentals because the English makers were too conservative in sticking to wax, which was breakable, scratchable and unwashable.[144] Mechanical toy manufacture had quite expired, he added and, although the major English producer (by which he meant William Britain) had recently gone over to lead soldiers, 'the solitary instance of English success in toys', he insisted that they, too, were quite inferior to the German products.[145] Yet there were several who did not share this opinion, stressing that Britain's attention to detail and anatomy produced accurately attired and less simian-like figures than those originating in Germany. Britain's soldiers, exclaimed one enthusiast, 'conquered the world' precisely because the 'men are nobly built, their uniforms resplendent'.[146]

In fact, the marketing skills so much vaunted by Williams had not prevented the appearance of many German anomalies. From the stable of Heyde, the world's largest toy soldier maker, had appeared representations of the British household cavalry mounted on brown horses. Miniature London buses had been driven out of the tin toy factories of Biberach en route to destinations such as 'Bimlico' or 'Peckam'. Nuremberg makers set up models of British army encampments labelled 'Aldershott' and manned by soldiers wearing Prussian-style helmets.[147] To these and other solecisms, Williams apparently closed his eyes. He was no more clear-sighted when it came to the export figures. 'You may search the Board of Trade Export Returns in vain for any mention of any export of British Toys to anywhere, he proclaimed.'[148] This was disingenuous to say the least. No official statistics had been *published* after 1873 but Williams's implication that there were no exports was quite wrong. One journalist valued the export trade at about £60,000 a year in 1889.[149] When the figures were made public again in 1900, four years after Williams' book appeared, they stood at almost £352,000, hardly consonant with his portrayal of a decayed and dying industry (Table 14).

Table 14
British Toy Exports, 1900–14[150]

Year	Value £	Year	Value £
1900	352,000	1908	532,000
1901	368,000	1909	588,000
1902	452,000	1910	707,000
1903	429,000	1911	716,000
1904	440,000	1912	811,000
1905	455,000	1913	886,000
1906	479,000	1914	837,000
1907	534,000		

There was no doubting Williams' fundamental premise that German trade was expanding very rapidly in the last years of the nineteenth century, as accelerating exports showed. Three-fifths of the increase in the value of German manufactured exports to Britain before 1896 were in the category of miscellaneous manufactures, mainly light consumer goods, which included toys.[151] But it did not follow, as Williams apparently believed, that the British industry suffered as a result. His portrayal was a travesty, distorting or overlooking truth, and drawing general conclusions from isolated examples, despite the fact that it was only in particular categories that German toys were doing well in the British market. The highest quality miniature theatres, larger in scale and more visually attractive through the use of colour lithography, were now certainly coming from Germany, pushing British products into the cheaper end of the market. In similar fashion, the trade in wax dolls had been much reduced by French and German success with bisque, although one French contemporary still believed that 'Londres et Birmingham ont une superiorité bien connue pour la poupée de cire'.[152]

More important still was the manufacture of metal and mechanical toys which had taken off in Nuremberg following a near tripling of the number of masters between 1844 and 1873. The progressive introduction of mass production techniques combined with wages that were low, even compared with those of other workers in the city, to give the Germans a marked advantage in such goods. Although Barringer, Wallis and Manners used the latest techniques of lithography to produce colourful containers for major confectioners, an expertise which encouraged them into toy production once the First World War broke out, British makers could not generally compete with German tin toys. In Wolverhampton, Evans and Cartwright closed down about this time. The pressure of competition forced William Britain to turn to toy soldiers as an alternative to his business in mechanical and metal-cast toy manufacture. 'There came a time', Alfred Britain later told a journalist, 'when we were in a difficult position. Something had to be done.'[153] It is significant that when the American consul in London informed an American trade journal that the Germans outdid the British by better business practices and superior selling techniques, he made it clear that his remarks applied only to tin toys.[154]

Other parts of the home industry, most of them ignored by Williams, were still thriving, prospering on those items which Mayhew, and after him Cremer and Bartley, had identified as characteristic of British expertise. Writing at about the same time, Whitfield Crofts could see few of the defects apparent to Williams. Despite the growth of foreign competition, he maintained that there was still 'wide scope for the English maker in the costlier and better kind of playthings, in the making of which we can confidently hold our own'.[155] Even a protectionist journal like *Athletic Sports, Games and Toys* had to agree, conceding that in the area of heavy wooden toys of the sort made by G. and J. Lines 'neither the German nor the American can beat us'.[156] Model boats, educational toys, dolls' prams and other wheeled toys, as well as boxed games, the latter associated particularly with Roberts Brothers of Gloucester, were also consistent strengths in the British industry. So, too, were rubber toys. When the New Eccles Rubber Works opened in Manchester in 1895 its first target was to double its initial production of 70,000 to 80,000 rubber balls a week. In the paper toy sector Raphael Tuck patented an improved printed cardboard doll with paper clothes in 1893. R. H. Journet, who had opened a couple of toy and fancy goods shops in the late 1870s and early 1880s, started to manufacture high quality jigsaws and other puzzles on his own account in 1891. It was also the case that if Britain's wax doll makers had lost something of their standing, her makers of glass eyes for dolls still dominated the world market.

To these should be added the newer toys and firms whose collective emergence from the 1890s onwards has sometimes tempted writers on the toy industry to play down the strengths of what already existed. Certainly by no means all were successful. Keen and Company, self-proclaimed pioneers of a new method of making jointed dolls, do not appear to have survived the outbreak of the First World War. Yet the two decades before hostilities began did see the substantial development of several companies which were to dominate the British industry for much of the twentieth century. Britains was so successful that about a dozen other new toy soldier manufactories were established before 1914. Most of them, it is true, were very small-scale operations but at least two, Reka and Johillco, did sufficiently well to threaten Britains' dominance. Britains' equivalent in the field of scale model ships and railway stock was the Northampton engineering firm of Bassett Lowke. In Liverpool Frank Hornby was perfecting his Mechanics Made Easy which, as Meccano, promptly established itself as the world's premier construction toy. It, too, spawned a host of imitators like Structator, Ereklit, Mysto-Erector, Metallo-Trigon, Anchor Blocks, Meta-Loxo and Kliptiko, which between them made construction toys a major growth area in the Edwardian trade. Just before the war Ralph Dunn came up with the idea of selling miniaturised packets of real foods. His Pets Stores were particularly successful in Germany and sold 9,000,000 sets in six years. Other manufacturers established international reputations for soft toys, which, in the persona of the teddy bear, were also a major seller in the prewar years.[157] This was a particularly creditable achievement since German competition, in the form of the huge Steiff factory, was formidable. In the opinion of one trade journal 'the progress we have made is really very good and does great credit to those manufacturers who were the pioneers, and who had the pluck, perseverance, and belief in their work'.[158] The establishment of Dean's Rag Book

Company in 1903 marked another new area of British enterprise within the industry, as did the first production of Harbutt's Plasticine, the revolutionary, if somewhat odiferous, modelling material. In Birmingham Joseph Johnson set up the Chad Valley Company in 1897, building upon an existing national reputation for boxed games. Small wonder, then, that the British Consul at Nuremberg reported in 1911 that local makers were increasingly viewing Britain as a serious competitor in some categories of toy production.[159]

Most of these new firms were much larger than had customarily been the norm in British toymaking. The persistence of small-scale manufacturing in the industry was part of a general tendency in consumer trades such as clothing, leather, shoes, cutlery and domestic hardware. But the intensity of competition, and the low prices which marked the great depression years, put small manufacturers under intense pressure to expand investment in order to reduce costs. A desire to lessen their reliance upon wholesalers, who dealt with increasingly distant and cost-conscious markets, worked in same direction. Although it is possible to find an occasional example in the 1860s of toy firms employing fifty of sixty workers, Evans and Cartwright or G. and J. Lines for instance, there were many more by 1914. The statistics have survived only randomly but Britains were employing 270 workers when the war began. Bassett Lowke had 300 employees by 1914, although some of these staffed the firm's retail outlets.[160] Information presented to a Board of Trade Committee just after the war revealed that in 1913 the soft toy makers, Farnell, employed 189 factory workers and fifty outworkers, Roberts Brothers had 201 employees, while sixty men and 220 women worked for Chad Valley.[161] Bedington Liddiatt employed at least sixty in 1911. Beechwood, a brush manufacturer dating from 1876, turned to toys in 1909 and had between 100 and 150 workers in 1913. At the same date Parker Brothers, established in London in 1852, had about 100, while the workforce at John Dore, a Glasgow toy maker, fluctuated between 150 and 200.[162]

A similar expansionary trend was apparent in capitalisation values, although here the information is even thinner. The legislative recognition given to private limited companies in 1900 and 1907 led to the proliferation of relatively small companies, as private partnerships sought to get the advantages of limited liability. Raphael Tuck became a private limited company in 1895 with capital of £110,000, a figure which had risen to £500,000 when the company went public six years later. This is misleading, however, since Tuck had only just moved into toy making, having built up a successful printing and publishing business over the previous half century. Britains was incorporated in the same year with a capital worth £18,000, although it, too, was a relatively long-established company. More typical of the newer firms perhaps was Meccano, set up in 1908 with a capitalisation of £8000, or Reka, valued at only £2000 when it was incorporated in 1914. Multum in Parvo, a games manufacturer, had an equally small capitalisation, £2000, when it was established in 1896, although only £1400 was actually taken up.

In every case the success of British firms like these was built upon some combination of technical skill, innovatory products, aggressive marketing and exploitation of publicity. Indeed, many sought to capitalise on the prevailing impressions of German dominance by emphasising their own Britishness. Britains' products, for instance, were advertised as the work of English workpeople, designed 'to take the place of the wretched caricatures . . . modelled and manufactured abroad'.[163] Bedington Liddiatt's Joiboy range went out under the slogan of 'British Toys for British Boys'. This may have made commercial sense but it did history a disservice by further reinforcing a myth.

More specifically, William Britain ousted the Germans from the domestic market by perfecting a new technique of casting hollow figures, thus greatly reducing their manufacturing and transport costs. He also brought to the process his own version of the interchangeable parts technology characteristic of some parts of American industry. Various sections of the moulds could be screwed off. An alternative head or a change of limbs meant that a completely different figure could be produced at very little additional cost. Subsequently, the firm patented a new design for fastening moveable arms on to the models. Britains exploited all opportunities for publicity, emulating continental practice by producing catalogues, and providing plenty of material and interviews for the trade press and boys' comics. This was combined with a sure feel for the nature of demand. On being shown Heyde's version of a British lifeguard riding a brown horse William Britain responded confidently that 'the English boy knows better than that'.[164] Similarly, Britains appreciated the appeal of their redcoated regiments in an age of imperialism, even to the extent of leaving their model highlanders in kilts, rather than dressing them in the combat khaki adopted by the War Office at the time of the Boer War. Abroad, Britains invaded the lucrative American market, initially by signing an agreement with an American businessman who used the soldiers in a game which he was selling in the United States. In Europe the company opened a factory in France just prior to the outbreak of war and its products were selling well in Germany, the traditional home of the toy soldier industry.

Bassett Lowke followed a similar recipe. Wenman Lowke, son of the proprietor of J. T. Lowke and Sons of Northampton, was interested in model-making and appreciated that there were few domestic sources of materials, castings and parts. 'Here was an idea!', he wrote. 'Why not start selling small fittings and parts that I made in my spare time, to other enthusiasts, who needed them for their model making?'[165] The first catalogue appeared in 1899 and by 1910 had grown to some 476 pages. Links with Europe were established, initially through the importation of some models made by the German firm of Bing, but in 1904 Bassett Lowke produced a German-language catalogue and by 1914 the company had appointed agents in both Paris and the Hague. Like Britains, Bassett Lowke took full advantage of the advertising opportunities provided by the expanding press, buying space not only in hobby magazines like the *Model Engineer* but also in more populist papers like *Captain*, *Boys' Own Paper*, and the *Strand Magazine*. The company was also a regular participant at the Model Engineers' Exhibition organised annually from 1905 onwards. While there may be some doubt over Bassett Lowke's claim to have been the first European firm to market a scale model of an English railway locomotive, another innovation, the launching of an OO gauge table railway, was frustrated only by the outbreak of war.

Frank Hornby was equally resourceful. Meccano was the most commercially successful construction toy yet manufactured. It was initially slow to sell, a reflection perhaps of Hornby's lack of familiarity with the toy business, his early career having been in the grocery and meat trades. He learned very quickly. Advertising costs appear in some of the first balance sheets and the acquisition of a London showroom gave easier access to the major domestic market. Quite soon he decided to eschew the wholesalers altogether, opting instead to sell to selected retailers. In effect, therefore, he was creating Meccano franchises. Hornby was similarly energetic in the overseas market. An exclusive agent was appointed to handle American sales in 1909 and three years later an independent manufacturing facility was opened in France. Foreign language instruction manuals were provided for the overseas market; perhaps as a result, an international model building contest organised in 1913 attracted plentiful entries from several European countries as well as from the Americas.

Although there is rather less information available about other companies, similar strategies and ideas were apparent. Chad Valley games, for example, were made available with instructions in French, German, Spanish or Italian. The firm also produced cheaper versions for the colonial markets in order to minimise the impact of transport costs. Again, the company was willing to sell its goods in unmarked boxes so that wholesalers and other middlemen could market them under their own names, if they so wished. Farnell and Company, originally silk merchants, went into soft toy production in 1897. It was the first firm in England to make a teddy bear. The company also manufactured its own plush so successfully that it was exported to Germany. Although the first of Dean's rag books appeared in 1903 with only two colours, within a year there were eight and the product was available in German, French, Swedish, Danish and Dutch. When Charles Baker assumed control of Reka in 1905 the firm was almost moribund. He opened up his own tool shops, engaged skilled tool-makers, and reorganised production on modern lines. He was, said a later tribute, 'imbued with a full share of those qualities of courage, enterprise, energy, and initiative which have brought the toy industry in this country to its present advanced stage'.[166]

'Altogether', judged a trade journalist on the eve of war, 'we have not much to grumble about.'[167] This was a revealing verdict, given the oft-expressed view that the quality of late nineteenth-century British entrepreneurship was deteriorating in the decades prior to 1914. This idea has had an enduring appeal, not least because it has been both intellectually easy and strategically convenient for politicians and businessmen alike to blame the economic ills of the late twentieth century on the failings of the late nineteenth. As subsequently elaborated in a number of studies, the thesis of entrepreneurial failure has suggested that too many British firms had grown complacent under a third generation of family owners; that they were obsessed with quality at the expense of economic realism; that old technologies were preferred to new; that there was an unwillingness to experiment; that there was a lack of aggression in exports, revealed by a bias towards imperial markets, indifferent salesmanship, poor marketing and preferences for both imperial units of measure and the English language.[168] These alleged defects are said to have originated deep within the value system perpetuated by British culture, although few would now go quite as far as H. G. Wells in attributing them to the malign influences of the Church of England and Oxford University.[169] The whole issue has been clouded by methodological and conceptual difficulties. Entrepreneurship has been confused with management, while the technique of juxtaposing examples of worst British practice against the best of the foreign is unsatisfactory, partly because of the danger of arguing from the particular to the general, partly because it ignores the different national economic contexts. The effort to put the debate on a sounder methodological footing has led to the development of econometric techniques designed to define and measure the performance of entrepreneurs in quantitative terms. The outcome has been the establishment of a new orthodoxy which suggests that, in the circumstances facing them in the late nineteenth century, British managers and entrepreneurs responded rationally and successfully.[170]

As far as the toy industry is concerned, the available statistical information is sparse, even by the occasionally undemanding standards of some econometricians. As small-scale enterprises, the majority of toy makers left at best only the barest trace of their existence. Although rather more is known about the larger companies emerging around the turn of the century, the quality of entrepreneurship in the toy industry has perforce to be judged primarily from more traditional types of qualitative evidence. It would be idle to maintain that the industry exhibited none of the defects alleged to be characteristic of British industry as a whole. The bulk of exports certainly went to the imperial market, while most firms were small and tended to be controlled by single family interests. Although a few larger enterprises appeared, British toy makers did not share in the merger movement characteristic of other British industries at this time, and which in France produced the Societé Française de Fabrication de Bébés et Jouets, an attempt to compete with booming German doll imports.[171] It is also possible to find contemporary complaints that products were poor in quality, made by outmoded methods of production, carelessly packed and delivered late.

Most of these criticisms, however, date from the war years and there is little to suggest that in these respects the majority of British companies were any worse than their overseas competitors. Claims of German supremacy in design, machinery and processing were certainly not universally applicable.[172] The British were increasing their sales to both the domestic and overseas toy markets. In some goods they were markedly superior, the most notable exceptions being wax dolls and mechanical and tin toys. Furthermore, the industry was attracting a number of new, dynamic and innovative entrepreneurs who exhibited few of the weaknesses alleged to characterise British enterprise at this time.

Even so, the impression of foreign supremacy was further strengthened by the findings of the first Census of Production, taken in 1907. It valued the total output of British toys at only £265,000, a figure which was well under a third of German imports in the same year.[173] On a priori grounds alone this estimate seems unlikely. It is true that the statistical assumptions and methods employed by Mayhew and Whittock's anonymous contributor in the 1840s were questionable but, for all that, their calculations do provide some sort of production parameter. Relevant information may have been more readily available by 1907 but the result implies, contrary to all the evidence, that there had been virtually no expansion in seven decades; years during which the aggregate output of British mining, building and manufacturing had more than quadrupled, and per capita income had gone up two and a half times.

There are, however, some quite specific reasons for doubting the accuracy of the census so far as toy production is concerned. For one thing, there was still no agreed official definition of what actually constituted a toy. Even ten years later when the Toy Trade Board was set up to monitor wages, the members 'spent days discussing what is a toy'.[174] Thus the 1907 production estimate of £265,000 was made up of £216,000 of goods manufactured by toy firms and £51,000 declared by firms returning toys on schedules submitted for other trades. From this was subtracted £2000 to eliminate a certain amount of double counting. Not allowed for, however, were £437,000 of miscellaneous rubber goods, some portion of which consisted of toys. It is also clear that a lot of toy production was allocated elsewhere and not transferred, simply because what the manufacturers made was a smaller version of an adult article, or something not described as a toy. Trades in which this was particularly likely to have happened included paper and printing, papier maché, basketware, brushes, carpet sweepers and cycles.[175] Addressing a meeting of the Central Committee of Toy Industries in 1915 the politician, Gilbert Parker, was cautious in citing the census findings, warning that production was £265,000 '*as far as could be ascertained*'.[176] Walter Lines, the dominant personality in the British industry after 1918, was quite convinced that the 1907 figure was wrong. Giving evidence to a Board of Trade inquiry in 1922, he adamantly affirmed that he had 'no hesitation in saying that that entirely misrepresented the facts; in fact we knew it at the time. The turnover of the company with which I was connected at the time (G. and J. Lines) was, I think, £55,000.'[177] Since a tentative estimate of William Britains' output for 1910 gives a sum of about £70,000, these two firms between them apparently produced about half of all the toys made in Britain.[178] There is no hint of any such dominance in contemporary sources.

Lines' doubts about the output figure rested upon the fact that the

£216,000 was supposed to have been produced by a labour force of 1862 individuals. This he dismissed as 'quite absurd and I think it was generally admitted at the time it was so'.[179] He admitted that his own suggestion of 30,000 employees could well be wrong but it was perhaps not insignificant that the Board of Trade's own inspectors had reported that in 1907 there were 32,193 people working in factories which made fine instruments, fancy articles and games.[180] A slightly earlier survey suggested that these goods were also being turned out by a further 38,831 employees of workshops.[181] Even these figures may have been on the low side, as another of the Board's inspectors had noted in 1903 that 'comparatively few factories and workshops for the manufacture of such articles [toys] are to be found upon the official registers'.[182] Direct comparisons or extrapolations cannot be made, since occupational definitions do not necessarily overlap directly. Nevertheless, the 1907 census employment figure is so much smaller – less than 3 per cent of the totals reported by the Board of Trade inspectors – that Lines' doubts seem justified. At all events, the Board of Trade Committee to which Lines expressed his concerns professed itself quite unable to establish with any certainty the number of firms or persons engaged before the war.[183]

Makers of toys were specifically enumerated, although aggregated with producers of fishing tackle, in the occupational returns included in the 1911 Census of Population. Inevitably some proportion of the 11,152 individuals who assigned themselves to these occupations were retired or unemployed.[184] The compilers of the production census in 1907 had reduced their total labour force estimate by a maximum of 9.6 per cent to allow for these eventualities. Applying this proportion to the 1911 estimate of toy makers, and allowing a further 0.4 per cent to allow for some growth of the workforce between 1907 and 1911, leaves 10,037. Taking away the 1832 who were counted in 1907 leaves 8175. Thus the total number of games and toy makers whose output was missed in the 1907 Census of Production was 8175 less the unknown number of fishing tackle makers.

The 1907 estimates were based on returns which were legally required from all those to whom the Factory and Workshops Act of 1901 applied. Not included, therefore, were employees in all-male workshops and those working on their own account or in family units making and selling their own goods, whether on a regular or intermittent basis. Families like those described in 1907 by O. C. Malvery were not counted. In one, the father carved white wood animals which were painted by a disabled son and sold in the streets by his wife. In another, six tubercular children were occupied in making toy table tennis bats.[185] At the same time Clementina Black warned readers of her influential study on sweated industry against assuming that all home workers were female. She drew particular attention to men who made various types of toys and trifles for hawking in the streets.[186] One such hawker, whose output certainly did not get into the census, was the young Charlie Chaplin. Having learnt how to make cheap boats from two itinerant Scottish toy makers, Chaplin set up in business on his own account. For the outlay of sixpence he was able to turn out three dozen penny boats in a week, securing a 600 per cent return on his capital. His career was diverted to other and ultimately more lucrative ends when his mother complained that his habit of boiling up horse-glue in the family laundry bucket was having a deleterious effect on her blouses.[187]

By itself of course Chaplin's contribution was merely transitory and utterly insignificant. But despite the changes of the previous years the toy industry was still predominantly a small-scale one, in which such activities loomed relatively large. There were 800 individuals in London alone who made a living by selling cheap toys in the streets. If some bought their stock from the commercial warehouses of Houndsditch, perhaps as many as a half of them made their own, selling as many as six dozen items on a good day.[188] They also have to be included in any recalculation of the aggregate output figure.

The 1907 census itself estimated that there were up to 1,250,000 workers of this type in the United Kingdom's total labour force. This represented about 15 per cent of those whose output was recorded in the census. In the toy industry the ratio of homeworkers to factory and workshop employees was larger than this, and using this average proportion undoubtedly introduces an upward bias in the calculations which follow. On the other hand, this may perhaps be allowed to offset the amount of toy production that was allocated to other industries but for which no figure can be derived. Although no detailed information on the productivity of homeworkers was collected, it was assumed by the census makers that the annual value of their production was £50 each. This compares with the £116 a head produced by the 1862 toy workers whose output was registered in the Census. A more accurate output figure for the British toy industry in 1907 can thus be calculated by adding together the gross output as published, the uncounted output of factories and workshops, and the uncounted output of homeworkers.[189] Revised total output clearly hinges on assumptions made about the number of fishing tackle makers included in the occupational returns of 1911. The range of possibilities is tabulated below.

Table 15
Estimated British Toy Production, 1907

Fishing Tackle Makers	Census Output	Factory Output	Workshop Output	Total
%	£	£	£	£
20	265,000	586,177	44,588	895,765
30	265,000	476,139	36,218	777,357
40	265,000	366,200	27,855	659,055
50	265,000	256,262	19,493	540,755
60	265,000	146,322	11,130	422,452
70	265,000	36,383	2,768	304,151

None of the estimates comes anywhere near Walter Lines' over-enthusiastic suggestion that total production before 1914 was about £3,000,000.[190] But figures closer to £1,000,000 seem plausible, given the progress made since the 1840s. Certainly the proprietor of Hamleys, who as the biggest single purchaser of toys in the country should have known what he was talking about, affirmed that, while tariff policy and cheap labour had enabled the Germans to muscle in at the cheaper end of the market, he 'had no doubt whatever as to the prosperity of the English toy trade'.[191] The editor of *The Times* agreed, suggesting that except for the very cheapest toys London 'has no need to seek help from Germany'.[192] Although of course he did not realise it, on the eve of the First World War, this was a reassuring assessment.

Chapter 4

Coming of Age, 1914–1922

In August 1914 two sets of British soldiers passed each other in the English Channel. One consisted of composition model figures, imported by Seelig and Company from the Viennese firm of Pfeiffer. The other was their real-life equivalent, en route to France to turn back other and more lethal manifestations of Germanic militarism. Set against the waves of unprecedented human misery and loss which engulfed most of the civilised world following the assassination of the Austrian Archduke Franz Ferdinand on 28 June 1914, the development of a single, small-scale British industry seems trivial. Yet the war years were crucial in the long-term evolution of the industry, for they created fresh opportunities and threw up new challenges which did much to set the pattern of British toymaking for the rest of the twentieth century. Even in the midst of momentous events, *The Times* found space to point out that war provided indigenous toy manufacturers with a unique chance to undermine the German hold on parts of the British market.[1]

The industry was not unaffected by the frenzy of anti-German feeling which accompanied the formal declaration of hostilities. Several manufacturers urged the public to ensure that they bought only British-made toys. Advertisements announced bluntly that customers wanting toy books printed in Germany or Austria need not bother to seek them from Messrs Dean. The makers of Compocastles stressed that 'You must have British made toys . . . British Made by British Labour with British Materials – British Throughout'.[2] *Little Folks* took up the theme with rather more subtlety in its 1914 Christmas number.

> Little girls and little boys
> Never suck your German toys
> German soldiers licked will make
> Darling Baby's tummy ache.
>
> Parents, you should always try,
> Only British toys to buy,

Though to pieces they be picked
British soldiers can't be licked.[3]

Although widespread, this sort of comment was not universally acceptable to the trade. A few firms like Bassett Lowke found that their
German supplies (in this case from Bing Brothers) did not arrive, but
many wholesalers and retailers had already ordered and taken delivery
of considerable quantities of German toys before the war broke out.
They made an effort through the trade journals, therefore, to impress
upon consumers that there was nothing unpatriotic about buying such
toys, as they had long since been paid for and their purchase in Britain
would do nothing to assist the German war effort.[4]

Certainly there was no shortage of toys for the first Christmas of the
war, producers of war-related items such as lead soldiers, forts, boats,
aeroplanes and uniforms, doing particularly well. Hanks Brothers built
a new factory, twice the size of their previous premises, to meet the
expanding demand for toy soldiers. Erector, best known for its construction toys, also opened a new factory in Tottenham to turn out
soldiers and wooden playthings. By February 1915 Charles Baker had
laid down new plant doubling the size of Reka's casting room and
establishing a permanent showroom in a hotel. H. G. Wells caught the
mood exactly when he described how the coming of war spurred on the
sons of his fictional hero, Mr Britling, to mobilise 'with great vigour
upon the play-room floor'.[5] Christmas reinforcements for their metal
armies were slow to arrive, however, as the boys discovered that their
price had risen considerably.[6] Once again, Wells proved to be an acute
observer of the contemporary scene, for toys, like everything else, were
quickly affected by the price distortions characteristic of the early months
of the war.

By 1915 stocks of imported toys had largely been sold, although in
practice German products continued to find their way to Britain. For a
couple of years at least rumours were rife of toys arriving from neutral
countries. One such consignment was landed in April 1915, having gone
via Italian ports to the United States. From there these toys were shipped
to Britain – ostensibly as American goods – by one of the big German–
American toy houses. A few others were taken as part of prize cargoes
and were periodically sold off by the Admiralty. But with official German
imports down to about £1000 in 1915, a major gap appeared in the
British market, opening the way for other sources of supply. The main
foreign beneficiaries were the United States and Japan, as the trade
figures in Table 16 indicate, but French imports also held up surprisingly
well, considering the disruption caused by the German invasion.

Table 16
Main Origins of British Toy Imports, 1914–18[7]

Year	Total £	Germany £	France £	USA £	Japan £
1914	700,421	484,741	89,057	55,729	50,105
1915	534,325	1,012	200,774	140,119	168,228
1916	533,918	548	195,636	73,411	245,600
1917	258,434	674	220,010	14,304	21,363
1918	447,439		426,079	3,779	15,306

The store-owner, A. W. Gamage, was almost alone in arguing that in the postwar years the Americans would pose the major threat to the British because they appreciated the power and potential of advertising.[8] Most observers, however, were much more taken with the threat from the Far East. Even in the late nineteenth century trade journalists had been predicting that it was only a matter of time before the Japanese gained the greater part of the Asian toy market currently supplied from Europe.[9] Now the outbreak of war gave them a sudden and unexpected opening into a major European market as well. It was an opportunity they were not slow to seize. Japanese imports into Britain more than tripled between 1914 and 1915 and as early as Christmas 1914 eight Japanese demonstrators were working at London's Bon Marché store. Their celluloid dolls were particularly successful, being both well designed and finished. The *Toy and Fancy Goods Journal* had no doubt that in the long run Japan would be a far deadlier rival than Germany.[10] A similar sentiment was reported from a meeting of the Liverpool Branch of the Incorporated Association of Toy Manufacturers and Wholesalers, where the audience was warned that unless they were very careful the Japanese 'might jump into Germany's place'.[11]

The danger was averted, at least in the short term, very abruptly. Japanese producers had been able to overcome the economic costs incurred by their distance from the British market, even though freight space grew both more scarce and more expensive as the war proceeded. They could not, however, avoid the impact of the severe restrictions on toy and game imports imposed in March 1916 by the Board of Trade. Thanks to the system of licensing the French escaped relatively lightly, but the effect on Japanese and American imports was severe. As Table 16 shows, American toy imports fell by some 90 per cent between 1915 and 1917, Japan's by rather more over the year 1916–17. These measures came totally out of the blue and provoked particular anger among wholesalers and importers, who promptly deputised Walter Runciman, the President of the Board of Trade. It was to no avail, however, and they were left with nothing more effective than personal abuse. One outraged individual suggested that only a member of the British Government could be such a fool as to allow the import of golf club shafts while prohibiting the dowels vital to toymaking.[12]

The imposition of import controls provided a further incentive to domestic manufacturers who had already responded enthusiastically to the opportunities provided by the elimination of effective German competition. It seems odd that, when Britons were being slaughtered in unprecedented numbers across the Channel, the production of items so identified with childhood and innocence should have continued at all. But as a commercial enterprise toymaking was thought to have a part to play in the economic war against the Central powers. The industry was one of a number identified by the Board of Trade as having considerable development potential in the enforced absence of German products from the home market. As early as September 1914, the Board organised an exhibition of German toys which it believed could be manufactured in Britain. As an incentive, it released to the trade details of German toy patents which, under the terms of emergency legislation, British firms were now permitted to exploit. A similar intent lay behind the Board's decision to make available to the manufacturers its collection of almost 300 German toy trade catalogues. Toy businesses were also encouraged to participate in another government initiative, the British Industries Fair, first held in 1915. This they did in reasonable numbers, despite some envious carping from the editor of the *Toy and Fancy Goods Trader*, who had first suggested the idea of a toy trade fair in 1914 and actually organised one the following year.[13] Initially, entrepreneurs were understandably somewhat sceptical about the viability of producing mechanical tin toys, dolls, dolls' heads and other items in which the Germans had had particular prominence. They feared that once hostilities were concluded the wholesalers would revert back to their original German suppliers. It was in an attempt to allay such fears that, at a specially convened meeting held early in 1915, Board of Trade officials apparently made some commitment to maintain import controls when peace was restored. This was subsequently denied and became a matter of major dispute after the war ended.[14] Whatever the truth, there is no denying that the first year or so of the war did see a considerable number of new firms entering the toy business.

A few of these, it is true, were not strictly commercial enterprises at all, being more in the nature of relief works designed to provide for those whose livelihoods had been directly interrupted by the war. The East London Federation Toy Factory, which made soft toys, was the brain-child of local suffragettes and conceived as a way of providing employment for women whose usual sources of income had dried up. Deprived of their seasonal custom, Isle of Wight landladies also turned to soft toys as an alternative source of revenue. Toymaking appeared to offer a particularly suitable form of employment for the disabled servicemen whose numbers mounted remorselessly as the war got bogged down in the Belgian mud. By October 1916 eight Lord Roberts Memorial Workshops were open or planned and a further four were under active consideration.[15] These enterprises were expected to be self-supporting after the initial equipment had been supplied. Most charitable forms of toymaking, however, were deplored by commercial manufacturers as sources of unwelcome competition, even if patriotism sometimes dictated that such sentiments were not openly expressed.

In the main, though, the commercial sector itself responded vigorously to the opportunities provided by the war, so much so that by the autumn of 1916 it was claimed that 1500 types of toy, previously imported from Germany, were now being made at comparable prices by British firms.[16] 'Toy factories and workshops', reported one of the Board of Trade's inspectors, 'are springing up through the Midlands. China manufacturers are attempting to make dolls' heads, and a workshop in the Potteries has been opened where dolls' bodies and limbs in composition and papier maché will be made.'[17] Elsewhere, Lotts Bricks began to produce stone bricks to replace lost German imports. Hawksley and Company of Liverpool, long-standing importers, exploited the prevailing war fever by manufacturing forts and battleships, while Oliver Harper and Company launched the Unity range of toys and games in 1914. Most of the new initiatives were concentrated in four particular categories of production. Doll and tin toymaking were both specifically targeted by the Board of Trade. Spencer and Company started dollmaking in Cardiff almost as soon as war was declared. In Sheffield, the All British Doll Manufacturing Company began work in the following year. So, too, did the Elite Doll Company and the Dura Porcelain Company A prewar manufacturer of dolls' wigs and hair, Speights Doll Factory in Dewsbury, responded directly to the Board of Trade's injunctions by starting to make the actual dolls. Others tried to manufacture the china dolls' heads formerly imported from Germany. It was in anticipation of being able to obtain such heads from new manufactories in Staffordshire that the Dolphitch Manufacturing Company of Shoreditch, which had begun life in 1909 as a doll-dressing establishment, started to produce its own composition bodies. As for mechanical tin toys, F. A. Selle took up toy piano making in the early autumn of 1914, while British Metal and Toy Manufacturers Ltd was registered in September 1914 with capital of £35,000, making it one of the six largest such firms in Britain. Frank Hornby's Meccano made its first tin railway engines in time for the inaugural British Industries Fair in 1915. Another exhibitor at this venue was Whiteley, Tansley and Company, a firm which, again acting on Board of Trade promises, increased its labour force to one hundred by September 1915 and moved into larger premises to facilitate an expanding tin toy operation.

Other newcomers looked to those products in which British toy makers already had a proven track record, such as soft toys and wooden items. Swayed perhaps by talk of a war ending by Christmas, the Birmingham gunmakers Scott and Walker started to manufacture heavy wooden toys and games in September 1914. A producer of office furniture, W. H. Norman of Leeds, also switched to toys when the war started. The South Wales Toy Company began in 1915 as a soft toy maker. Another 1915 debutant was the Emell Toy Manufacturing Company, which diversified from jigsaw puzzles into dolls' houses and shops. Other companies launched in the aftermath of the Board of Trade meeting included the Parkstone Toy Factory and the Happy Day Toy Company (wooden toys), the British Indoor Games Company and Sanderson and Company (both indoor games), Scott and Walker (games), Watford Toy Manufacturers (stuffed toys), and Atlas Manufacturing, which transferred from sports goods to soft toys. Harwin and Company began making stuffed toys in November 1915, under the expert scrutiny of a sales manager recruited from Steiff's sales force. Almost two years later, the *Toy and Fancy Goods Trader* was still reporting the creation of new toy companies, listing in December 1916, for instance, All British Toys Ltd with capital of £600, the Bricks, Toy and Furniture Company, capitalised at £500, the Alliance Toy Company, Ashton and Company and the Terminus Emporium, the last two each with capital valuations of £2000.[18]

Quite evidently, the chance of a quick profit was sufficient to tempt many to try their hand at commercial toymaking, even though the long-term prospects were never very good. Limited capital resources meant that they could usually produce only in small quantities. They had high unit output costs which would make them uncompetitive once the normal market was restored. Many did not even survive the war. In 1916 the British Indoor Games Company was declared bankrupt with assets of only £25 standing against liabilities of £1099. Substantial sales of the firm's first board game, 'Dash to Berlin', in September 1914, had encouraged it to take larger premises; but its original capital of £155 had proved insufficient to sustain further expansion, hence the bankruptcy. It was ironic that the company's initial success should have been based on exploiting the widespread anticipation of a very short war, for it was this very expectation, coupled with the associated prospect of renewed German competition, which made the banks reluctant to advance funds to newcomers in the trade.[19]

Such capital shortages may have tempted the *Toy and Fancy Goods Trader* to exaggerate when it claimed in May 1915 that the industry was in a bad way.[20] On the other hand, its analysis was shrewd in pin-pointing a number of other difficulties that would increasingly dog commercial toymaking as the war dragged on into its third and fourth years. First, there were chronic problems with distribution. Even in the first year of war, the initial disorganisation of goods traffic made it hard for toy makers to get their products to the shops and wholesalers. One of the largest dealers in the north, Overtons of Leeds, said in September 1915 that, while they were buying toys from everywhere, the English makers were bottom of their list because their deliveries were so deplorably bad.[21] By the time of the Manchester Toy Week in January 1916 it had become the case, as a visiting journalist pointed out, that the major concern of potential buyers was not with prices but rather with securing guaranteed deliveries.[22] Limitations on transport also made it extremely difficult to sustain exports, which fell, though not evenly, throughout the war (Table 17). A leading Australian importer complained in December 1916 that, although their freight rate was about twice that charged by the Japanese, the English suppliers could never guarantee delivery dates.[23]

Table 17
British Toy Exports, 1914–18[24]

Year	Value
	£
1914	836,636
1915	641,558
1916	700,403
1917	527,550
1918	401,295

Secondly, the cost of raw materials escalated. All prices were given an upward thrust by the outbreak of war. Sauerbeck's overall index shows a rise of 23 points between 1914 and 1915, slightly lower than the increase registered over the same period by the Board of Trade's wholesale price index.[25] Almost as soon as the opening shots of the war were fired, toy prices rose between 10 and 50 per cent, a reflection of the upsurge in their raw material costs.[26] By October lead prices were up between 40 and 60 per cent, while the acceleration in the cost of bronze powder was sharper still at between 300 and 400 per cent. Over the same period the cost of strawboard, used in making games and also a major component of packaging material, rose by 75 per cent. In January 1915 one leading London manufacturer advised against investing in new plant because fluctuating raw material prices would eventually lead to a slump.[27] Another staple material of the industry, wood, was equally affected. By March 1915 the price of timber shelving was up from a penny three farthings to twopence three farthings per foot. This raised the costs incurred by manufacturers of heavy wooden toys. More generally, the relative dearth of wood also pushed up the price of the packing cases in which toys traditionally were transported. The material used for Noah's Arks and other smaller wooden toys followed a similar price curve, quadrupling to sixpence a foot by the autumn of 1916. Nor did soft toy makers escape, the cost of plush doubling in the twelve months from October 1915. Two years after the war began the price of tin plate stood at three times its level of August 1914, making it even harder for tin toy manufacture to establish itself on a sound financial footing. Small firms, lacking capital resources, found it particularly difficult to offset rising raw material prices by bulk buying, with the result that their manufacturing costs and product prices rose disproportionately.

As the war progressed, proving to be a far more significant drain on national resources than anyone had anticipated, so these price pressures were reinforced by growing government intervention in the allocation of materials. The laisser faire approach favoured by the Asquith administration was progressively abandoned when Lloyd George took over in 1916 and imposed a far more dirigiste style on the conduct of the war. As a result, toy manufacturing was relegated to a more appropriate place in the nation's scale of priorities. In the spring of 1917 an Order in Council gave the Army possession of all soft wood stocks of 230 standard and upwards while sales of timber were subjected to strict licensing. By this time, too, paper was becoming scarce. Early in 1918 paint supplies for the trade deteriorated as government restrictions were imposed on essential ingredients such as lead and turpentine. Strawboard prices had climbed to £85 a ton by June 1918 while from

1917 metals were released only to strategic industries, although the manufacturers' representations did succeed in gaining some small concession on this score.

Labour was affected in similar ways, growing progressively more expensive and scarce. Although it was protected to some extent by the fact that adult men made up only about 60 per cent of its labour force, the industry suffered, like most others, from the enthusiastic volunteering characteristic of the first year and a half of conflict. The heavy wooden toy firm J. and T. Thorp of Manchester was soon struggling with the adverse impact of voluntary enlistment from among its 870 strong workforce. Furthermore, as a low-wage industry relying mainly on unskilled labour, toymaking was particularly vulnerable to the impact of the disproportionately large rises which occurred in unskilled wages over the course of the war, and also to the movement of workers to more lucrative employment in munitions. With the introduction of conscription and the transfer of both male and female workers to better paid and more strategic work, labour shortages became acute. When it was established in 1914 the British Toy and Metal Company had work for 100 toolmakers but, so attractive were the wages available in the expanding war industries, it could recruit only twelve. The same lure produced a very high turnover among the women who made up the majority of the company's workforce. The soft toy and doll manufacturers did rather better in this respect since, unlike most other toymaking activities, they could utilise the labour of those women who, for whatever reason, were tied to their own homes.

When conscription was introduced some toy makers tried to resist enlistment by claiming that they were fighting the battle for British trade. Such appeals usually fell upon deaf ears. The toy works of Collins and Cosens at Thatcham, for example, was wound up at the end of 1916 when both partners were called to the colours. Just occasionally, however, a recruitment tribunal took a more liberal view. A High Wycombe company, which had invested £1000 in order to start up a business making toy ships, secured three months exemption for the skilled toy maker on whom the enterprise depended. Another individual successfully argued against his obligation to military service on the grounds that his newly-formed toy business would otherwise have to close down. But such cases were exceptions rather than the rule. When the government cancelled all remaining exemptions in the spring of 1918 the trade press was not unduly concerned, taking the view that the toy industry had already been quite thoroughly combed out and

the number in it who were still liable for military service was consequently negligible.[28]

The broad picture was well summed up in 1917 by Sidney Stowe,
managing director of British Metal and Toy Manufacturers Ltd. In the
course of the previous year, he said, his company had been faced by
four particular problems. First, there had been a shortage of working
capital caused partly by escalating labour costs which had raised his
pay bill from £19,500 in 1916 to almost £52,000 in the current year.
He also noted that, while production was up from the previous year,
£2237 had been invested in extra plant. Secondly, the material for
clockwork springs, which had cost almost £74 a ton in 1915, had been
unobtainable in 1916 and the company had had to resort to imports.
Four orders had been placed at £130 a ton, only one of which was
finally delivered, and that at a price of more than £191 a ton. Dutch
strawboard, at £5 a ton in 1915, had risen to £9 in 1916 but the ban
on imports had forced to him to order an inferior quality product at
£63 a ton, though it had originally been offered at £15. In this case,
however, the increase proved irrelevant since the supplier had failed
to deliver anything at all, citing war work as the excuse. Thirdly, he
drew attention to labour shortages, stressing that the loss of skilled
men to the services had had an adverse effect on labour efficiency.
Finally, he noted that while the company had managed to secure orders
from the colonies and other overseas customers, little had actually been
exported because of the shortage of shipping space.[29]

The results of these various pressures on the toy industry were
manifold. Many of the smaller operations disappeared altogether, with
bankruptcies accelerating in number through the war years. Both the
Wychwood Toy Company and Britannic Toy Works went to the receivers
in the spring of 1917. They were followed into oblivion shortly afterwards by Hockley Toy and Fancy Goods Industries, closed because of
labour and raw material shortages. A related fatality was the *British
Toymaker* which went into what it called 'suspended animation' at the
end of 1915 because so many staff had enlisted. It had proved impossible to generate sufficient revenue to offset the rising costs of paper,
print and postage.[30]

For customers prices rose, partly because of increased labour and
material costs, partly because supply could not match demand, which
despite the hardships of war remained surprisingly high. By the second
Christmas of the war domestic manufacturers were struggling to keep
up, while the public was complaining about the relative dearth of
clockwork toys and high prices. While some of the new doll factories

had succeeded in supplying both china and stuffed dolls they were, at 24s. a dozen, considerably more expensive than the German models they replaced. *The Times* suggested that Christmas prices in 1916 were about 50 per cent up on the previous year.[31] Early in 1918 Autoscooter of Stockport, who made a wide range of scooters and wheeled toys, raised prices by between 5 and 11 per cent, because over the previous twelve months the cost of wood parts had risen 385 per cent, wheels 85 per cent, iron castings 60 per cent and wages 33 per cent.[32]

Rising prices were accompanied by deteriorating quality as makers lacking both capital and skill were attracted into a seller's market. The decline was so marked that it could be recalled almost half a century later by Mary Clive, who particularly remembered dolls lacking separate fingers and moveable joints.[33] A similar lowering of standards was also noticeable in a lackadaisical approach to packing. Wholesalers complained that English makers 'practically throw them at you in any kind of packing'.[34] Among the worst examples were white soft toys wrapped in old newspapers and thus bearing the imprint of current events in unexpected places. The buyer at one of Chicago's major stores was similarly dissatisfied: 'The way the English manufacturers are packing their toys for our market is very disappointing and absolutely discourages any attempt at re-orders.'[35] Of course, not all of this was the fault of the manufacturers, as a 1917 Chad Valley catalogue sought to convey. 'We reasonably expect to be in a position to supply', it stated, but added that specifications might have to be changed according to the availability of materials. Furthermore, purchasers were reminded that all goods were sold subject to cancellation or reduction of quantities in the event of difficulties in obtaining raw material or labour. Finally, the firm informed customers that it could not be held responsible for the delay of goods in transit.[36] But if some of these deficiencies could be blamed on the exigencies of war, wholesalers and buyers were generally agreed that British firms had failed to produce anything comparable to the quality of the missing German toys, particularly in dolls and tin work. The chief buyer for Bon Marché, for example, conceded in February 1915 that British makers had filled some of the gaps left by the Germans but not in dolls.[37]

Ultimately, the supply of British-made toys fell away as major firms, especially those with metal-working capacities, increasingly switched to war production after 1915 at the behest of the Ministry of Munitions. Wallis Bros and Wicksteed went over to munitions work in July 1915. William Bailey of Birmingham, makers of the construction toy, Kliptiko, had just received £20,000 of orders for another building idea, Wenebrick, when the firm shifted over to war work in 1915. In Liverpool, most employees at Meccano and Whiteley, Tansley and Company, were engaged on the war effort by the end of 1915, as also were a growing number at Britains Ltd in London.[38] Another firm of tin makers, Paton and Calvert, largely abandoned their range of Happynak Toys in favour of military work. Bassett Lowke's suppliers were diverted to making master gauges for the munitions industry and training models for the Admiralty. Harbutt's plasticine did continue to appear but almost exclusively for military purposes, as it was used by the War Office for making map reliefs and also carried in armoured cars and transport waggons. By Christmas 1917 stocks of toys were in short supply and prices rose still higher in consequence. Many of the 163 manufacturers exhibiting at the British Industries Fair the following spring had virtually no toys to sell, putting in an appearance simply to keep their names in the buyers' minds.

All of these problems, common to most non-essential industries during this prolonged period of what finally became total warfare, took a steady toll of the manufacturers. When Tattersall produced the first trade directory in 1912 he had listed 1248 manufacturers and wholesalers. H. Richard Simmons' 1920 directory of manufacturers, wholesalers and agents contained 1326 names, an increase of only about 6 per cent. Neither guide can be regarded as totally reliable. Tattersall's was described after the war as most unsatisfactory because it contained so many whose interests were at best peripheral to the toy trade, including Cadburys and the Religious Tract Society, as well as makers of electric batteries and roofing slates.[39] Equally, however, the 1920 directory contained charitable toy makers such as the Burgess Hill Women's Institute, the Dundee Women's War Relief Committee and the Primrose League Junior Branch Toy Industry. More indicative perhaps of the unsettling effects of the war is the fact that only 268 of the names listed in 1912 appear to have survived until 1920. Almost a thousand had vanished, although rather more than a thousand new organisations had appeared to take their places. 'The manufacture of toys', proclaimed W. H. Nicholls, 'has assumed an importance which did not exist at any other period in our history.'[40] In 1921 J. T. Makinson wrote what he described as the first book to offer information on commercial toymaking because the upheaval of war had transformed it into one of Britain's standing industries.[41] 'The British toy industry as we know it today', commented the *Morning Post* in 1931, 'may be said to date from about the beginning of 1915.'[42]

Substantial diversification had occurred both in location and product. Tattersall had shown significant concentrations only in London, which accounted for 49 per cent of entries, and Birmingham which, with its smaller satellite towns, accounted for 29 per cent. Industrial counties like Yorkshire had only 3.4 per cent, Lancashire 4.6 per cent of firms. Interestingly, a book issued under the auspices of Lancashire chambers of commerce in 1912 contained no references to toy making, whereas a similar publication of 1918 described Liverpool as the most important toy manufacturing location in Britain.[43] Liverpool and Manchester, along with Leeds and Glasgow, were both added to London and Birmingham as major centres in the survey taken by the Board of Trade in 1918 as the preliminary to creating a trade board.[44] The same document also underlined how diverse the industry had become. Apart from miscellaneous goods, the main categories of production were wooden toys (23 per cent), light metal (18 per cent), dolls (16 per cent), stuffed toys (7 per cent), cardboard (6 per cent), toy prams (4 per cent), heavy metal (3 per cent), books (3 per cent) and metal soldiers (2 per cent).[45] More than a third of output was in dolls and light metal goods, the two areas previously dominated by German producers. This compared with an encyclopaedia article, published as recently as 1906, which had identified only six important British toys.[46]

War work also kept most of the major firms intact, raising their levels of skill and capital equipment. Sufficient profitability had been maintained to provide the resources necessary for further expansion. Significantly, the trade was well represented at a meeting organised in the summer of 1920 by the National Union of Manufacturers to protest against a government proposal to reintroduce an excess profits duty of 60 per cent. This may have reinforced the suspicions, voiced in the press, that some toy makers had done very well out of the war. On the other hand, raw material costs had risen enormously and the accounts of a major producer like Meccano certainly show little in the way of profiteering. In the years between 1914 and 1919 Meccano's successive net profits to 28 February were respectively £54,000, £7930, £8340, £41,535, £29,169 and £13,745.[47] If anything, it was the importers who had done well. Faudels' net profit for 1918 was £120,435, not far short of Meccano's five-year total.[48] In the spring of 1917 the wholesaler Whyte, Ridsdale and Co. registered as a private company capitalised at £40,000.

Another outcome of the war was that the industry now had the backing of a more substantial trade press. Prewar journals had led a somewhat precarious existence and some were early victims of the war. *British Toymaker*, first published in October 1914 to assist the British industry and characterised by repeated appeals to 'Buy British', closed after two years. Others, however, proved more resilient. *Games and Toys*, edited by H. Richard Simmons, first appeared in 1914 and was to prove as durable as Tattersall's longer established *Toy and Fancy Goods Trader*. Another newcomer made its debut in December 1916 with a clear editorial line. Edited by George Kipling and, as its name suggests, directed primarily at retailers, the *Toyshop and Fancy Goods Journal* advocated the prohibition of all enemy toys and fancy goods and the imposition of a heavy tariff on such goods from neutrals. It further argued for a similar duty on Japanese goods to offset the advantages of cheap oriental labour and for a strengthened Merchandise Marks Act to compel the marking of goods with their country of origin.

Not only did the war see the emergence of a healthy and viable press, the industry's interests were much better organised than they had previously been, a development which occurred throughout British industry.[49] Compared with their overseas rivals, British manufacturers had largely eschewed cooperation in the prewar years. By contrast many of the biggest firms in Germany had belonged to the Metal Industrialists Association. Only the absence of the country's largest maker led to the collapse of a thirty-seven strong American cartel in 1907. In France, a trade cooperative of some 400 producers, the Syndicat des Fabricants de Jouets et Jeux, came into being in the late nineteenth century. In Britain, however, only a few manufacturers belonged to the Toy and Fancy Goods Section of the London Chamber of Commerce, a body primarily representative of the wholesale, merchant and import interests. Not until June 1913 was any effort made to bring together the British manufacturers, when the All British Toy Association was formed. But by no means all felt able to support a body whose policies included the promotion of British goods, the exposure of sweating, the elimination of illegal commissions and financial support for the Union Jack Industries League. About a year later, the British Toy Association was formed but it had little to do with commerce, being concerned rather with the development of toy making for the unemployed and underemployed, particularly rural workers, the disabled and the infirm.

It was really in the aftermath of the meeting with Board of Trade officials early in 1915 that consideration was given to the establishment of a single organisation to represent the combined interests of the manufacturers, wholesalers and retailers. The initiative appears to have come from W. B. Tattersall, proprietor of the *Toy and Fancy Goods Trader*, although the editor of *Games and Toys* was less than enthusiastic.

It was, he suggested 'a quaint scheme . . . difficult to grasp the exact objective'.[50] But Tattersall's view that government tended to ignore representations made by individuals or single companies was a persuasive one. There was some general agreement within the trade that a corporate expression of opinion on relevant matters, such as fiscal policy, transport and the marking of foreign merchandise, would carry more weight. In the event, the retailers did not get involved, as the name of the new body, the Incorporated Association of Toy Manufacturers and Wholesalers, indicated. A year later the first provincial branch was formed in Liverpool, with Manchester following suit in October 1916. Lancashire firms accounted for about a half, London slightly more than a third, of the total membership which stood at 111 in March 1917. By early the following year further regional offshoots had appeared in Birmingham, Yorkshire and South Wales.

Labour, too, came out of the war better organised and protected, although in its case government influence was much more direct. Prior to 1914 toy workers had not attracted much interest from the state. They had not been covered in an inquiry into the use and effects of noxious materials, for example, despite the claim of one unhappy customer that a four-foot doll purchased in the Lowther Arcade had its intestines half eaten, the doll being more alive than dead.[51] Workers in the burgeoning toy soldier manufactories had not been included in a survey of the lead industries in 1893–94, and the toy industry was involved only very marginally in the 1914 investigation into the use of celluloid. More significantly, the workers had not figured at all prominently in the various public and private surveys of wages and sweating which were so marked a feature of the Edwardians' newly articulated social conscience.

This was not because their wages or conditions were particularly good. Indeed, one writer in the *Manchester Clarion* had claimed that 'the toy makers of England are living in a state of chronic pauperism'.[52] Charles Booth's survey of the London trade in the late nineteenth century suggested that 30 per cent of workers in toymaking and related miscellaneous manufactures received less than 30s. a week. But his calculation was based on figures provided by a few relatively large manufacturers, only one of whom made toys, and Booth warned his readers that 'account must be taken of a considerable number of persons working in small toy industries etc. in East London, for whom we have absolutely no wages returns'.[53] These would have included the female outworkers being paid to stuff dolls at the rate of 3s. a gross in 1903, as well as the male woodworkers observed in 1906 by Clementina Black.[54] One of these, who provided his own materials including cast wheels, got 22s. a gross for wooden engines which were retailed at 6d. each. The other made go-carts at between 3s. 3d. and 6s. 6d. a dozen depending on their size.[55]

If wages could be low they were not uniformly or distinctively so. Doll stuffing and making up at between one and two shillings a day, said one writer in 1897, was often better paid than other work.[56] No mention was made of toymaking in R. H. Sherard's *White Slaves of England*, a study of England's worst paid and most arduous trades.[57] As for conditions, they too were not noticeably worse than those in many other contemporary trades. Very few toy manufacturers appeared in the factory inspectors' annual lists of those summonsed for keeping unsafe or unhealthy premises.[58] Although George Moore had child toy makers in his novel *Esther Walters* (1894) they were conspicuous by their absence from F. Hird's *The Cry of the Children* (1898). Similarly, despite Kropotkin's claim to the contrary, various government inquiries revealed no evidence of serious sweating in the industry and it was not, therefore, included in the 1909 Trade Boards Act.[59]

As the war drew to an end, however, the government was determined to provide wage-bargaining mechanisms that would reduce the potential for conflict in trades, like toymaking, where workers lacked any strong organisations of their own. Before 1914 there had been no unionisation in the industry at all, unless one counts the Amalgamated Society of Cricket Ball Makers (1898). The general increase of union membership during the war inevitably involved some toy workers. By 1918 the National Union of Warehouse and General Workers reckoned to have about 2000 toymakers in its ranks. Lesser numbers were claimed by the National Federation of Women Workers, the Workers Union, the National Amalgamated Union of Labour, the Dock, Wharf and Riverside and General Workers Union, and the Amalgamated Society of Woodcutting Machinists. Although 80 per cent of the workforce was female, 60 per cent remained unorganised.

The case for a trade board rested partly on this lack of effective organisation among the workers, partly on the low rates of pay still typically offered for some kinds of work. Although the NUWGW reckoned 25s. to be the average wage in the industry, there was in fact a bewildering variety of wage rates and arrangements. Pay for trained women ranged from 14s. to £2 a week. In one Worthing firm no female piece-worker received less than 30s. a week. Toy workers employed by Deans got the rate agreed by National Union of Printing and Paper Workers. The weekly earnings of adult male woodworkers at Chesham varied from £2 18s. 0d. to £3 10s. 0d. a week. Just before they went bankrupt in the spring of 1921 Fry and Company were paying £4 to £4 10s. 0d. a week to adult metal workers. It seems that a top skilled man could earn as much as £4 10s. 0d. whereas his unskilled colleague made about 30s. There were only two negotiated wage agreements in the entire trade, both purely local in scope. Elsewhere, it was clear that the exigencies of war demand had fostered some sweating. In Dublin female wages as low as 3s. 6d. to 13s. 0d. a week were reported.[60]

For their part, the manufacturers were initially suspicious and, in March 1918, the Incorporated Association rejected a suggestion that the Ministry of Labour be requested to create a trade board for the industry. As war drew to an end and wages started to move upwards the notion became more attractive, appearing to offer a means for controlling increases and preventing internecine competition for labour. This sort of problem was apparent in Liverpool, where female piece-workers at Meccano struck work to demand conditions and wage rates comparable with those available in other Liverpool toy firms. In September 1918, therefore, the employers invited the Minister of Labour to address a meeting on reconstruction and the function of industrial councils in the context of the toy trade. When the conference met, on 4 April 1919, the employers supported the proposal to create a trade board, Mr Speight saying that he had had a very successful works committee for twelve months at his Dewsbury factory. It 'had kept the workers from joining other Unions by enabling them to ventilate their grievances. He would encourage a Toy Trade Union, but objected to the Workers joining other Unions, and thus being involved in other trades' quarrels.'[61] Shortly afterwards notice was given that a Toy Trade Board was to be created with effect from 23 March 1920.

If the trade thus emerged from the war on a sounder institutional footing, its economic prospects when the guns finally fell silent in November 1918 also appeared to be very good. Business at the Manchester Toy Week in January 1918 was brisk in anticipation of the war's end. The number of orders taken at the 1918 British Industries Fair was also a promising augury, eclipsing previous records. The imminent release of pent-up wartime demand seemed likely to provide a further boost for the domestic manufacturers. During the war toymaking capacity had certainly developed overseas in Japan, the United States and Canada, and even in Spain, where £200,000 of prewar toy imports had been converted into £50,000 of exports by 1917. But it appeared unlikely that German goods would be immediately available. Within three weeks of the Armistice, *The Times* reported that even shopkeepers were astonished by the amount of money that was changing hands for toys, a state of affairs it ascribed to a combination of high raw material prices and heavy demand.[62] 'The British Toy Manufacturer', it was suggested elsewhere,

> need have few qualms as to the future. In a very little time now the markets of the whole world will be open to him, and the demands from overseas will dwarf into insignificance the business he has been doing during the past four years.[63]

Certainly the outlook was sufficiently promising to encourage existing firms into expansion. In Liverpool Hornby increased the capitalisation of Meccano from £5000 to £100,000, moved into new premises twice the size of his existing ones and extended his advertising in various directions, including the publication of the short-lived *Meccano News* in November 1920. It was, he wrote, a critical time.

> The only right course, as I see it, is to produce goods of the best possible type and to give a square deal to the trade, the public and our employees so that when the nation sails into calmer waters Meccano Limited will take the high place in British industry which I am convinced is its natural destiny.[64]

In the same issue he announced his commitment to producing clockwork trains and steam engines of the sort which in prewar days had been imported. Another established toymaker who moved quickly to take advantage of the favourable economic climate was Walter Lines. Lines and his brothers had all previously worked in the family business of G. and J. Lines but they returned from the war with a desire to strike out on their own. With a loan of £28,000 from Lloyds Bank they purchased a woodworking factory in the Old Kent Road.[65] A new workforce was recruited, obsolete plant sold off and the first range of toys designed by Walter himself. An initial order was secured from an acquaintance in South Africa, to be followed quickly by another from Harrods. After that, Walter wrote later, he was 'flooded with orders from customers of the old firm who were thoroughly fed up with the poor stuff they'd been forced to buy during the war'.[66] Net profits in the first year of business reached almost £9000.[67]

Relatively old hands like Hornby and Lines were joined in the trade in the heady postwar days by scores of others, attracted by the favourable outlook. Even an engineering giant like Vickers was said to be considering toymaking as a way of providing work for its hugely swollen labour force. A cursory glance at the trade press reveals that new companies were being formed virtually every week. In the course of 1922 alone, by which time the postwar boom was faltering, sixty-seven public and 190 private companies with a combined capitalisation of almost £1,300,000 were registered for the manufacture and sale of sports goods and toys.[68] Most were quite modest. Typical enough was L. E. Feeny, a West India merchant with no previous knowledge of factory management. With his brother, he began making model boats in 1919 because, as he put it, they were 'looking for a business and this appeared to have considerable prospects'.[69] Another aspiring entrepreneur converted a house into a small factory in 1918, and took on fifty workers to produce toy tennis rackets. The metal toy company set up in Islington by A. W. J. Wells, a toolmaker, was destined to become a major force in the interwar years, but it was launched on a capital of only £50. Wells made his own tools and did his own selling – so successfully that in 1921 he was able to move into larger premises.

The boom which followed the ending of the First World War lasted for about two years. Consumer expenditure rose 21 per cent between 1918 and 1919 and the removal of wartime controls in the spring of 1919 gave it a further impetus. But as the economy's productive capacity could not meet the demand, prices rose faster than output. In turn, this pushed up wages and thus costs. By the middle of 1921 Britain was in the grip of severe depression with 2,400,000 workers unemployed. The slump took its inevitable toll of the toy industry. In November 1920 one of the charitable toy enterprises, the Primrose League Toy Industry, collapsed. The following month T. A. Dixon, a Worcester doll maker, closed, adding a hundred people to the local unemployment register. As Christmas 1920 approached the *Toy and Fancy Goods Journal* warned that it would not be a happy festive season because rising labour costs, falling consumer demand and inadequate financial backing were causing many toymakers to fall by the wayside.[70] By early 1921 a hint of panic had appeared, the same journal referring to the 'closing down of hundreds of firms'.[71]

The impact of the faltering economy on the industry was all too apparent in the evidence presented to a Board of Trade Committee early in 1922. It has been partially tabulated in Tables 18 and 19 below.[72] Most types of toymaking were hit, as unemployment rose steadily. Things were so bad for the English Novelty Company that by 1922 its twelve remaining employees were reduced to chopping firewood. Fry and Company, lead soldier makers, ceased trading in May 1921. Lines Brothers also suffered, taking only £5000 of orders at the British Industries Fair in 1921, compared with £40,000 in the previous year. Other leading companies whose businesses were affected included Chad Valley and Roberts Brothers of Gloucester. Although wages were three times their prewar level, Roberts managed to maintain a workforce but only by dint of half-time working throughout 1921.

Table 18

Orders in Hand and Employment: Selected Toy Companies[73]

Company	Date	Orders in Hand £	Employees
Chad Valley			
	1919	16,500	
	1920	21,000	
	1921	6,600	
	1922	4,700	
Feeny Brothers			
	1920	1,500	43
	1921	87	13
	1922	17	
English Novelty Company			
	1919		120
	January 1920		140
	June 1920		80
	October 1920		50
	November 1920		43
	February 1922		12
J. H. Glasman			
	1918		50
	1922		5
Nunn and Smeed			
	1920		260
	1921		12
Roberts Brothers			
	1920	24,022	
	1921	3,989	
	1922	2,131	
Wolstan Doll			
	1920		80
	1921		10

It was the doll makers and metal toy companies which bore the brunt of the economic downturn. H. J. Hazell, a doll-dresser, who had employed between forty and fifty girls in 1920, was reduced to twelve by early in 1921. In December of the same year Roberts Brothers closed down the doll making department which they had opened during the war. The Wolstan Doll Company, first registered in 1915, told the Board of Trade Committee that it could not compete against German dolls which were 20 to 30 per cent cheaper. The Liverpool firm of Nunn and Smeed gave up the struggle, abandoning the doll making taken up in 1914 and reverting to its original import business.

The situation was equally disastrous for the metal toy makers. In 1921 the receivers were called in to Whiteley, Tansley and Co. who claimed that 'not a single toy of this class [mechanical metal] has been manufactured by us during 1921'.[74] Another major casualty liquidated in 1921 was British Metal and Toy Manufacturers, notwithstanding its annual turnover of £75,000 in 1919 and 1920. The firm founded by Hone Pierce suffered a similar fate, despite the fact that his labour force, a hundred strong at the end of 1918, had been equipped with brand new machines and worked only on scrap metal. Barringer, Wallis and Manners survived, as did Meccano, to take advantage of the upturn of trade after 1923 but only, as Table 19 shows, after severe labour cutbacks.

Table 19
Production and Employment: Metal Toy Makers[75]

Company	Date	Export £	Home £	Workforce
Whiteley,	1920	13,043	62,184	301
Tansley, Co.	1921	3,384	2,353	54
Barringer,	1920	7,987	19,108	200
Wallis, Manners	1921	2,098	3,732	49
Hone Pierce	1919	12,000		84
	1920	7,000		
Meccano	1919		955	
	1920			1,207
	1921			1,454
	1922			453

A few attributed their difficulties to the workings of the new trade board, which had begun work in September 1920. The workers' side had proposed a general minimum rate for women of 44s. 6d. for a

forty-four hour week to which the employers responded with an offer
of 24s. for forty-eight hours. Deadlock was resolved eventually at eight-
pence halfpenny an hour, but only because the independent members
sided with the employers. A similar process of accommodation produced
a male rate of 1s. 5d. an hour. Barely had these rates been implemented,
however, than the employers successfully pressed for a reduction to
sevenpence halfpenny for women and 1s. 2d. for men, again with the
support of the independents.[76] Even this was not deemed adequate by
many employers. At a meeting of the Incorporated Association in September 1921 their representatives on the Trade Board came in for some
strong criticism. A Chad Valley spokesman said they had been weak,
while another speaker described the new rates as prohibitive. James
Renvoize agreed, claiming that his firm had been compelled to lay off
women even though they had agreed to work at lower rates.[77] Similar
views were put to the Board of Trade in 1922. One doll-dresser blamed
the trade board for the fact that he was now forced to sell at 10s. a
dozen items formerly available at 3s. 9d. each because he could no
longer get them made at low wages by girls coming straight from school.
Such complaints were supported in the press by Tattersall, whose initial
sympathy for labour had quickly evaporated in the heat of depression.
The very notion of a trade board was, he declaimed, 'part of the process
by which the State Socialists hope in time completely to subdue industry
to their will'.[78] On a subsequent occasion he complained about 'the
tender mercies of the Trade Board, who have helped on the work of
destruction so well started by the British Government'.[79]

On the whole, however, most of the blame for the industry's predi-
cament was heaped, not on the trade board, but on the Government
for permitting the unexpectedly early renewal of German competition.
It was always believed likely that wholesalers and importers would revert
as soon as they could to German toys, particularly dolls and metal
items, where it was generally agreed that the new British producers
had failed to match German quality.[80] But the process was unexpectedly
accelerated when, early in 1919, the Government announced that it
would let in imports immediately at 20 per cent of their 1913 levels
and then in unrestricted quantities from 1 September. This gave very
little time for consolidation and development to those firms established
during or immediately after the war, especially as some were still
suffering from labour and raw material shortages. *The Times* called the
announcement a bombshell, adding that

it is not a pleasant thought that thousands of British boys and girls who have become orphans during the war will, unless something is done at once, be playing next Christmas with toys made by the men who were responsible for the deaths of their fathers and brothers.[81]

The manufacturers were still enjoying the boom when the announcement was made and did not bother to support the protest made against it by the National Union of Manufacturers.

The situation was dramatically altered, however, by the collapse of the German mark, which conferred huge price advantages upon German manufacturers. The Board of Trade Committee was told of metal tea sets available from Germany at 5s. 6d. a dozen to wholesalers whereas the comparable British item cost 7s. 6d. J. K. Farnell, the major soft toy maker which had competed on equal terms with Steiff before war, also found prices considerably out of line. In 1921 a 22cm. Farnell bear was 23s. 4d. as against the equivalent German item which was priced at 12s. 5d. A 60 cm. bear cost £9 14s. 5d, over three pounds dearer than the same sized animal from Germany. The wholesale price of British-made tin motor cars was 21s. a dozen, almost twice the price of virtually identical German toys sold at 11s. Ernest Whiteley of Whiteley, Tansley and Company told the committee that his factory was efficient, geared to continuous production, and supported by a research department. With overheads working out at 21.9 per cent of production costs, profits of 7.5 per cent had been, he believed, sufficient to sustain his company. He attributed the demise of its toymaking activities wholly to the unfair price advantage enjoyed by the Germans. The owners of British Toy and Metal Manufacturers also pointed to the exchange rate difficulty, arguing that without it they would have been competitive. Even a survivor like Frank Hornby attributed his declining profitability to the falling exchange rate. In a letter to *The Times* another manufacturer claimed that, unless exchange rates were rectified, 1921 would see the funeral of the British toy industry, German dumping having already cost the jobs of 22,500 British toy workers.[82]

One by-product of tumbling German prices was the very rapid evaporation of any lingering prejudice against 'enemy' toys. In the first flush of peace many voices had been raised in support of British industry against that of the country's erstwhile foes. Even in 1920 both Lines Brothers and Patterson Edwards expressed confidence in the long and patriotic memories of the British consumer. For a time, it is true, retailers and wholesalers resisted the attractive offers being made by German firms anxious to reestablish themselves in Britain, but there was a cautionary note in a statement made by the managing director of Hamleys to *The Times*. He would give no orders for German goods, he said, unless others did so first, in which case competitive pressure would force him to follow suit.[83]

Within a year this is exactly what had started to happen. As the new Christmas toys began arrive in London shops towards the end of 1920, *The Times* suggested that even those who had held out longest against German toys would now have to stock them because of the strong competition from those whose patriotism had given out first.[84] In London, only Harrods, the Army and Navy, Woollards, and Shoolbreds refused to take German toys that Christmas. Thereafter resistance crumbled quite quickly with the German manufacturers' export efforts deriving a further impetus when the loss of the Rhineland in 1921 served to weaken their own domestic market. It had always been apparent that shopkeepers would take whatever maximised their profits. Even during the war A. W. Gamage had had no qualms about acquiring quantities of the German construction toy, Structator, when Bing's London business house had been wound up in the autumn of 1916. Gamage sold it despite its adverse effect on British products such as Meccano. Along with Selfridges and Julius Kohnstamm, Gamage had also been quick to buy up a quantity of German toys made available at auction by the Admiralty in 1917 after the capture of a German prize ship, SS *Frisia*. Such actions created profound disgust in the trade.[85]

With gloom mounting, demands for protection grew. The artificial circumstance of the war had of course given the British toy makers de facto protection from foreign competition and several of the more farsighted had called for some form of tariff once peace was restored.[86] Lancashire tin toy makers whose trade had really taken off during the war had been particularly vociferous on this score. Some Liverpool members of the Incorporated Association who debated this issue in September 1916 wanted a five-year ban on imports from present enemies. Others demanded even longer periods. A few, mindful perhaps of Japanese and American success, wished to extend the ban to all foreigners. In January 1917 the Manchester branch also agreed to press the Board of Trade for a tariff.

Almost as soon as peace came questions were asked in the House of Commons, although initially they were put by Members concerned to protect the toymaking activities of disabled servicemen. This was the purpose of one request, made in November 1918, for a ban on toy imports. At that time, distracted by the rush to revert to peacetime production in order to cash in on booming demand, manufacturers themselves were generally deaf to the alarms being sounded in the trade press.

> We cannot too strongly urge the toy manufacturers of Great Britain that to a large extent the prosperity which they are enjoying today is an artificial one, the absence of competitive lines has created the demand for those of home production, but unless steps are taken to organise the methods of production so as to ensure increased output and a reduction in costs it will require a very big tariff to enable manufacturers to hold their own against foreign competition.[87]

Six months later came a similar warning, with the further admonition that even protection would not help the industry in the export markets and that the Toy Association was growing rather too self-satisfied.[88]

The announcement that import restrictions were to be lifted did, however, galvanise the trade into action. When the *Toy and Fancy Goods Journal* circularised the trade on the subject, in August 1919, it found that protection was favoured by eighty-four manufacturers, including old, established firms such as Johnson Brothers of Harborne; Patterson Edwards; Renvoize; Roberts Bros; and Whiteley, Tansley and Co.[89] In the same month the Incorporated Association took a deputation to the Board of Trade whose President, Sir Auckland Geddes, abruptly told his interlocutors that the toy industry was not a key one and that in any case it had nothing to fear from its crippled German rival. In short, noted a trade journalist with a nice line in mangled metaphors, the toy trade 'and all that therein is melts into a very small potato when looked at through his spectacles'.[90]

With restrictions lifted and exchange rates plunging, the results were all too predictable. German imports worth £72,575 in August 1919 became £106,977 by September and £159,475 by October. Despite this evidence, the editor of the *Toy and Fancy Goods Trader* was initially sceptical, denying that there was any flood of German toys getting into Britain.[91] The London branch of the association had no doubts, however, launching a campaign fund which was well supported by several of the larger companies. The press was bombarded with correspondence from manufacturers and dealers with the result that supportive leaders appeared in several of the national papers, including *The Times*, as well as in a number of leading provincial dailies.

The case for a tariff was set out in a letter signed by employers and workers and sent to all MPs in October. Not all were sympathetic, though few were as brutally direct as Josiah Wedgwood. He told executives of the Wolstan Doll Company that he wanted cheap toys, not protection. 'Tell your workers to go elsewhere and close down.'[92] But others were sufficiently concerned to raise the matter in the House of Commons. Geddes stood by his opinion, telling a variety of questioners that German capacity was currently so small that even if its entire output came to Britain it would not seriously damage the British trade.[93] The parliamentary campaign was sustained throughout 1920, questions being put in February, July, August, November and December. It was effectively orchestrated by George Terrell, a Unionist who was President of the National Union of Manufacturers, and J. D. Kiley, a member of the Incorporated Association who had been elected the Liberal Member for Tower Hamlets in 1916. Feelings frequently became heated and more than once the Speaker had to intervene to prevent Members turning Question Time into a debating session. In November the Parliamentary Secretary to the President of the Board of Trade told the House rather wearily that 'I only wish a repetition of questions would increase the Parliamentary time at my disposal'.[94]

By the middle of 1920 it is clear that the manufacturing members of the Incorporated Association were pinning their hopes on the forth-coming Safeguarding of Industries Bill, designed to afford protection to selected trades. They were perhaps encouraged when Kiley's question about the scope of the measure received an equivocal answer. Sir Robert Horne, who had replaced Geddes at the Board of Trade, replied that he did not consider toymaking a key industry but that did not mean that it would be excluded.[95] With the depression deepening, the asso-ciation circularised MPs again in February 1921 with details of the industry's deteriorating plight. In March it organised a special meeting to consider the future. The Government's disdain was perhaps evident in the fact that it was represented only by the Parliamentary Secretary to the Minister of Transport. Undeterred by his firm statement that they were not to be included in the Safeguarding of Industries Bill, the employers' section of the Incorporated Association went ahead and submitted an application for inclusion. This required the preparation of a very detailed submission concerning the types of toys involved and the countries supplying them, and statements of comparative prices, including costs per unit of production. It proved difficult to collect this information. As one member of the association pointed out, segments of the industry had virtually disintegrated. It was also the case that not all members were willing to provide the necessary information. For some, self-interest and an inordinate desire to protect trade secrets were stronger than any sense of corporate identity. Nevertheless, in December 1921 the Board of Trade did instigate an inquiry as to whether the association's application for inclusion under the act should be entertained.

The submission was straightforward. It was claimed that the government had encouraged the industry's development during war and that Geddes had promised action if there was a flood of imports. If protection was not granted then three-quarters of works would close, with a consequent loss of 20,000 jobs. The investigating committee was highly critical of the association for failing to provide much of the detailed information for which it had been asked. 'No attempt has been made to prepare a general statement on the lines of our memorandum.'[96] Consequently, the committee concluded that the supporting evidence was 'very indefinite and falls far short of what has been considered in previous applications to be sufficient to establish a prima facie case'.[97] On this occasion, however, the preliminary inquiry ignored the Civil Service's obsession with red tape and requirements for full compliance with all the detailed and obscurely written small print of its procedures. In view of the level of agitation the association had sustained, the constant references to Board of Trade promises, and the very high levels of unemployment allegedly due to German competition, a full hearing was recommended to consider the industry's case.

Under the chairmanship of Arthur Balfour, a steel manufacturer, the full committee heard submissions in February and March 1922. On behalf of the association, Mr Bernard Faraday relied heavily on evidence from a succession of employers about the impact of cheap German competition on output, prices and employment. Some of this has been summarised above in Tables 18 and 19. The nub of his argument was the conviction, widely held among the manufacturers, that the government had encouraged the industry to expand. In general terms, certainly, politicians had made encouraging statements during the war; only hindsight suggests that these should not have been taken too seriously. There was, for example, Lloyd George's ringing proclamation of February 1917 that 'new industries have been set up and we are not going to drop them after the war'.[98] On the other hand, the manufacturers had shown a certain capacity for self-delusion. It was quite frequently claimed that a 1916 Board of Trade paper on postwar trade had recommended a 25–30 per cent tariff for general toys and a prohibitive one on mechanical toys. These suggestions had, in fact, been put to the committee respectively by a representative of Dean's Rag Books and by Frank Hornby, the only two witnesses who had given evidence on behalf of the toy trade.[99] While the final report itself mentioned these suggestions, it had not specifically recommended such a step, merely commenting that certain goods of vital national interest which were in foreign hands 'should be afforded sufficient tariff protection to enable them to maintain such production after the war'.[100] Not for the first time, representatives of the toy trade were guilty of an over-inflated sense of self-importance in assuming that this included their trade.

They were on much stronger ground, though, in stressing to the Balfour Inquiry the very specific commitment which, it was claimed, had been given at the meeting held in the spring of 1915. A document submitted independently to the inquiry stressed that, on that occasion, Board of Trade officials had 'promised every possible support and backing . . . They would, in future, receive every consideration and practical help from the Board of Trade and would not be allowed to suffer from German competition in the future.'[101] The manufacturers were initially so sceptical that Dalton had reiterated his statement. This was why employer after employer presented the same story to the 1922 inquiry. The spokesman for Chad Valley conceded that although 'no pledge was given in writing; we relied upon the verbal promise which was made to us'.[102] That promise had been sufficient to encourage his company to invest £20,000 in new plant. Roberts Brothers had also increased investment during the war, in their case by £15,000, and J. O. Roberts had a similar recollection of the 1915 meeting. 'We were certainly led to believe that if we laid ourselves out to capture this trade . . . the country would afford us protection, and as a consequence of that we went ahead.'[103] The experience of the English Novelty Company as recounted by Mr Tiley was identical – heavy wartime investment made in the light of Board of Trade statements. Whiteley, Tansley and Co. had progressed from making press tools for German toy manufacturers to making toys on their own account on the strength of a 'definite assurance' given at the Board of Trade meeting.[104] Barringer, Wallis and Manners also claimed that they had diversified into tin toys for the same reason. In the Potteries, the Mayer and Sherratt China Manufactory started making dolls' heads 'at the instigation of the then Board of Trade'.[105]

Significantly, perhaps, the opposition hardly referred to this aspect of the association's application. Only one witness mentioned it and then in very guarded, even ambiguous terms. C. H. Riley of J. Riley, Liverpool importers, had been at the Board of Trade meeting but 'I would not like to say that they promised protection'.[106] On the other hand, he admitted that everyone had believed that a tariff would be imposed, even if that belief seemed subsequently to have died away.

The committee's final report seemed to accept that promises had been made.

> No doubt an enormous number of people did take to it. It is very difficult to know why. However, it is not for one to criticise the Overseas Trade Department here, but it is an extraordinary idea that people should have troubled themselves with a trade of this character.[107]

The final report did not, however, support the manufacturers' plea for inclusion in the Act. The committee was apparently convinced by the eloquence of Sir Arthur Colefax, appearing on behalf of the London Chamber of Commerce to oppose the application. He introduced a string of buyers and importers, all of whom suggested that the problem was one of quality, the new British products being inferior in style, construction, finish, packaging and delivery. Nor did they give any credence to the applicants' claim that falling exchange rates had anything to do with domestic problems. One manufacturers' witness had pointed out that the internal value of the mark was a fifteenth of the prewar level but that externally it was worth only a fortieth of the prewar mark. While German workers were paid on the same scale as in 1914, in terms of sterling they were getting only a third as much. British manufacturers on the other hand were paying twice their prewar rate because of the rulings of the Toy Trade Board. Another claimed to have sold nothing for two years because the wholesalers and factors could 'make more money on the German imported stuff than they can out of ours'.[108] Faraday suggested that the profit margins on imported toys were between 40 and 50 per cent, more than twice that on British made goods. A. C. Janisch of Farnell alleged that there was a combination of German makers pledged to break the British manufacturers. Hone Pierce went further, claiming that this ring, organised by Bing Brothers, had institutional links with British wholesalers and importers. He named a company called Concentra which, he insisted, was headed by Leon Rees of Eisenmann and represented in the House of Commons by J. D. Kiley. He further charged that Rees and Kiley had each invested in the other's business. The threat of legal action was sufficient to secure the withdrawal of these unverifiable claims, although they do indicate the depth of despair felt by some of the manufacturers.

For the rest, Colefax's witnesses simply dismissed suggestions of profiteering. Although one or two witnesses said that they had increased their profits by buying in marks rather than in sterling, the Whyte, Ridsdale representative denied that exchange rates had affected prices very much. For Isaacs and Company, Mr G. Isaacs claimed that the

British makers had got work during the war only because of the lack of competition. This was echoed by Harry Brown, another importer. Faudel's chief toy buyer said that he bought German goods on the grounds of their superior quality, not their lower price. His counterpart from Bon Marché went even further, averring that 'if the war had gone on a few years longer the toy dealer would have been knocked out of existence because both the trader and the public were so dissatisfied with the toys which they supplied'.[109] Ernest Hall of W. H. Hall of Birmingham agreed that the British manufacturers had forfeited the chance they had had during the war to corner the domestic market.

In presenting his case, Colefax completely ignored the matter of Board of Trade promises and concentrated instead on the relative efficiency of British firms. Those established before 1914 he averred were doing well. Then he went for the newcomers' collective jugular, describing Hone Pierce's products as 'badly made', British Metal Toys as 'grossly over-capitalised', and finished by suggesting that something was 'radically wrong' with the 'absurd' business run by another applicant.[110] It was powerful advocacy which bore little relationship to the evidence, not least because his contention that the successful prewar manufacturers were still performing well was hardly borne out by the testimony of J. O. Roberts, Walter Lines or A. C. Janisch of Farnells. But Colefax was not the Solicitor General of the County Palatine for nothing. Rhetoric swept aside the evidence for all but one member of the committee who, however, declined to submit a minority report. The final report rejected the application, suggesting that unemployment was caused not by the fluctuating mark but by a combination of economic inefficiency and the current depression, since rates were not out of line with those prevalent in other parts of the manufacturing economy.

These conclusions and recommendations effectively ended the manufacturers' struggle for protection. Walter Lines, already beginning to emerge as the dominant figure in the industry, felt that the campaign might have fared better if it had been better supported. This was perhaps intended as a rebuke for companies like Britains and Bassett Lowke. Fred Britain had told Lines that he did not intend to waste his money on behalf of other firms, while Bassett Lowke representatives had actually appeared at the inquiry to oppose the association. In part this was because they relied to some extent on imported parts but it is also clear that they were quite pleased on aesthetic grounds to see some of the new, low-quality producers go to the wall.[111]

B. G. Arthur, secretary of the Incorporated Association, described the outcome as 'a severe blow'.[112] Its seriousness was perhaps underlined by the contrasting experience of the American Association of Toy Manufacturers. As in Britain, the domestic industry came under strong pressure from cheap German exports which combined with a minor depression in 1921 to wipe out many new firms founded in war. The American trade lobbied for a 60 per cent tariff and was eventually given a 70 per cent one. For the British industry, however, there was little alternative now but to accept the reality of foreign competition, although one trade journalist could not resist a final savage swipe at the government.

> No more concrete example of the ruin of an industry by Government ineptitude could be instanced than that of the toy trade, which, after being deliberately asked and encouraged to develop, given definite promises of protection during its development period, was ruthlessly denied even consideration, was openly flouted and insulted by the President of the Board of Trade.[113]

At the British Industries Fair that summer there was no shortage of foreign toys on display. Bedington Liddiatt showed a big range of German toys and some best sellers from Japan and USA. Hamley Brothers also arranged a display of English and continental toys, while Kleiner showed Structator, an ingenious German construction toy. Quite soon the pages of the trade press filled up again with advertisements from agents and importers offering German toys on advantageous terms. A. J. Holladay, for instance, stressed that all consignments of toys ordered from one of the four German firms he represented would be sold free case and free delivery.[114] The *Toy and Fancy Goods Trader* carried a puff for the miniatures made by the Nuremberg firm of Marx and Jondorf. 'Imported, of course, they are, for it would be quite beyond our people to compete successfully in their manufacture . . .' Despite his initial scepticism, Tattersall had finally accepted the existence of a German threat, but now there was a brisk note of realism now in his tone.

> We excel in Britain in making certain goods so let us boldly recognise the fact that we must look to Germany for the best and cheapest mechanical toys . . . and console ourselves with the fact that for heavy toys we have obtained an unassailable position . . . the sooner we in Europe settle down to a more amicable life among ourselves the sooner will world conditions readjust themselves to prewar conditions.[115]

Such a stance was rendered somewhat more plausible when in the course of 1922 the German makers decided to sell only in sterling. This was believed to be the only realistic chance they had of maintaining viability in the international market. The threat to the British manufacturers was further diminished by the deteriorating economic and civil situation in Germany, which meant that importers could not guarantee deliveries.

The association's campaign for protection may have failed in its immediate purpose but it was not without significant results of a different sort. For one thing, there is no doubt that both sides made claims that helped to perpetuate the notion of prewar German dominance. The association's deputation to the Board of Trade in August 1919 argued that the prewar trade 'was almost entirely in German hands'.[116] Statements of this sort, backed up by assertions in the *Toy and Fancy Goods Trader* that the British industry 'is less than two years old', served the manufacturers' cause because they could then present themselves as pioneers of a new British industry.[117] For the importers and wholesalers, the same allegation was used to justify their argument that in the postwar period the level of German competition faced by British manufacturers was merely a reversion to the prewar status quo, owing nothing to the fluctuating exchange rate. Both Colefax and a number of his witnesses, most notably Herman Koewi of Marks and Spencer, exaggerated wildly in stressing that 90 per cent of prewar trade had been German.

More significant in the short term was the reorganisation of the trade association on federalist lines. Tension between the manufacturers, on the one hand, and importers and wholesalers with strong overseas connections, on the other, had never been far below the surface during the war. It was interlaced, too, with elements of anti-German feeling directed particularly at their strong position in the distributive side of the British trade. While the English branches of German houses closed down during the war, the rest of the distribution chain, including agencies for German and Austrian firms, English branches of Austro-German manufacturers and the import houses, some of which were German, remained intact. The *British Toymaker* had been particularly vocal in drawing attention to the potential dangers arising from such enemy influences. It alleged, for example, that German importers were behind the American decision to import German toys via Rotterdam in 1915, thus allowing small Germans firms to survive and be in a position to rival the United Kingdom after the war.[118] Hostility hardened considerably in the aftermath of the sinking of the *Lusitania*. The Toy and Fancy Goods section of the London Chamber of Commerce discussed a motion in the summer of 1915 that naturalised Germans trading in Britain should be barred from changing their names in an

1. Caledonian Road Steam Works, the original Lines factory.

2. Lambton Road, Hornsey, Britains' original premises, in 1912 (*Britains Petite*)

3. Britains' painting room in 1923 (*Britains Petite*)

4. Britains' painting room in 1923 (*Britains Petite*)

5. Britains' casting shop in 1923 (*Britains Petite*)

6. Painting cats' eyes at Merrythought (*Merrythought*)

THE HORNBY CLOCKWORK TRAIN

With the introduction of this toy railway system commences a new era in clockwork train construction. Engine, tender and trucks are put together on the Meccano principle. The whole system is built up from standard units, and if one of the parts is lost or damaged, a new part may be purchased and fitted by the user. The engines and trucks are supplied in complete outfits ready built up for instant use, but much pleasure can be derived from taking them all to pieces, and refashioning them. The standardisation is the same as in the Meccano system, and the Hornby train may be looked upon as a Meccano model of an altogether new and delightful type.

The clockwork mechanism is of the finest quality, all the gears being accurately cut, ensuring smooth running.

One size only, Gauge 0, in three different colours, to represent the London and North-Western, Midland, and Great Western Railway systems. Each set contains Engine, Tender and one Truck, set of Rails, including a circle and two straights. The engine is fitted with reversing gear, brakes, and regulators.

Complete set in strong attractive box ... ... 27/6 each.

Engines	...	...	...	17/6 each.	Trucks	... ...	4/6 each.
Tenders	...	...	...	4/6 ,,	Rails, straight or curved		9/- per doz.

TIN PRINTED CLOCKWORK TRAINS

Strongly built, with reliable clockwork mechanism. One size only, Gauge 0. Each set contains Engine, Tender, and two Passenger Cars, printed in close imitation of the colours of the railway companies' rolling stock, with set of Rails, including a circle and two straights. In London and North-Western, Midland, and Great Northern colours. The engines are fitted with reversing gear, brakes, and regulators.

Complete set, well boxed ... ... 22/6 each.

Engines	...	...	...	14/- each.	Carriages	2/- each.
Tenders	...	...	...	2/- ,,	Rails, straight or curved	9/- per doz.

VERTICAL STEAM ENGINE

A finely finished steam engine, superior workmanship; each one carefully tested. Oxidised brass boiler; stationary cylinder, and eccentric reversing gear; whistle, spring safety valve, etc., cast base; fittings nickelled and finely finished. Dimensions of boiler, 2¼in. diameter by 3½in. long.

Price, 27/6 each.

This device is printed or stamped on all the toys described here, and it indicates that they have been manufactured by Meccano Ltd. It is a guarantee of quality and workmanship.

7. The first known leaflet advertising Hornby Trains, 1920 (*Hornby Hobbies*)

8. The first post-war Hornby Dublo brochure, 1953 (*Hornby Hobbies*)

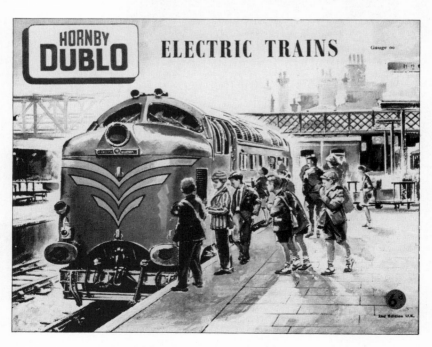

9. The *Deltic* creates interest, 1960 (*Hornby Hobbies*)

10. Melting lead at Britains , 1939 (*Britains Petite*)

11. The mould for Queen Elizabeth II (*Britains Petite*)

12. Trooping the Colour: George VI, Queen Elizabeth and Queen Mary at the British Industries Fair, 1948 (*Britains Petite*)

13. Queen Elizabeth the Queen Mother and Princess Margaret at the British Industries Fair, 1956 (*Britains Petite*)

FRANK HORNBY
1863–1936

14. Frank Hornby (*Hornby Hobbies*)

16. Dennis Britain (*Britains Petite*)

15. William Britain Jr (*Britains Petite*)

17. Oliver Holmes (*Merrythought*)

attempt to disguise their origins. 'True Britishers' demanded that action be taken against naturalised Germans in the British trade.[119] A couple of years later the *Toy and Fancy Goods Trader* attributed poor sales at the Manchester Toy Week to the fact that so many of the large buyers remained 'in the grip of the naturalised Hun'.[120] In the same issue 'Mechanical' wrote from Liverpool suggesting that the manufacturers should set up their own organisation since their interests were so different from those of the wholesalers.[121] The letter created quite a stir, so much so that Ernest Whiteley felt it necessary to issue a public denial of the rumour that he was its author, and urging that the existing cooperative organisation was the most practical.[122] But one of his colleagues took up the theme in the autumn, saying that the Japanese threat was created solely by the wholesalers' determination to buy in the cheapest markets.[123]

Once peace returned the conflicts of interest became increasingly apparent. The Manchester branch of the Incorporated Association passed a motion calling for buyers and wholesalers to buy no German toys for two years. The response from one leading firm of wholesalers and importers, Bedington Liddiatt, was to dismiss the meeting as a manufacturers' ramp. Others reacted less aggressively but their own suggestion, that it was really up to the retailers to decide whether or not German toys were acceptable, was merely another way of trying to preserve their own freedom to import them. In the course of 1920 the London branch of the Incorporated Association resolved that the manufacturers should form their own organisation. In the same year the wholesalers successfully pressed for a special section of their own to be recognised within the association which, they argued, was dealing mainly with matters of concern to manufacturers. By January 1921 the *Toy and Fancy Goods Journal* was observing that the trade was rife with jealousy and mistrust between its various sections. Its own sympathies were clear from its claim that the 'perfect flood of Teutonic toys . . . flowing unchecked into the country' had nothing to do with quality or price, but rather was caused by the greed of wholesalers and retailers to capitalise on the favourable exchange rate situation.[124] Subsequently the importers denied this vehemently before the Balfour Inquiry, many of them stating that they bought only in sterling. It is difficult to understand why they should have gone to the trouble and expense of retaining such a distinguished counsel as Sir Arthur Colefax if they were as disinterested as they proclaimed themselves to be.

Meanwhile long-term developments in retailing had created another important interest within the trade, although plans to include the retailers in the association in 1916 had not been realised. In 1918 Tattersall resurrected the idea, noting that the German trade association, organised during the war, had embraced the retail sector and that the American Association was also contemplating a similar step. He felt that their involvement in a trade organisation would give the retailers some support in resisting German goods after the war. Indeed a small retailers' organisation was set up in 1919 by W. Maxwell Lyte, proprietor of the Perambulator and Doll Hospital Ltd, with the express purpose of encouraging shops to discriminate against German goods.[125] Not everyone was supportive, one important Liverpool manufacturer saying in 1920 that he 'didn't care one bit about the retailer'.[126]

Walter Lines was more farsighted. Like Frank Hornby at Meccano, he dealt directly with the retailers, by-passing altogether the wholesalers towards whom he had never been overly friendly. They had, he believed, put little into the trade association, being too busy reestablishing links with overseas suppliers as soon as they could. Even so, a cooperative stance was likely to prove more beneficial in a time of economic difficulty. Lines was well aware that membership of the old association had fallen from a peak of 332 in 1919 to 223 by 1921. Furthermore, he felt strongly that drawing the wholesalers and retailers closer to the manufacturers would provide a greater degree of mutual protection against the domestic industry's real enemies, the importers. After all, it had been the importers who, through the Fancy Goods Section of the London Chamber of Commerce, had formed the main opposition during the Safeguarding of Industries Act inquiry. J. D. Kiley's membership of the Incorporated Association had not prompted him to speak out during the parliamentary debates that preceded the Act's passage. As an importer of fancy goods and toys, he had no desire to see them subjected to a tariff and he confined his contributions to two small interventions.

The sixth meeting of the Incorporated Association, held in March 1922, turned itself into a manufacturers' association and elected Lines as chairman. He promptly initiated discussions aimed at strengthening the organisation. By the autumn the outline structure of the new Toy and Fancy Goods Federation was public. As the name suggested, the new body recognised the diverse commercial interests of many retailers and wholesalers by embracing not only toys but fancy goods. Retailers and any wholesalers with premises in the United Kingdom were eligible for membership, ending the nationality rule used by the old Toy Association. Three sections were established, representing the wholesalers, retailers and manufacturers. Each had autonomous powers but elected ten representatives to serve on the council, which alone had power to determine policy. In this way Lines hoped to preserve some freedom of action for each section while simultaneously creating a community of interest within the toy business, restoring the spirit of cooperation which had first animated the trade during the war but which had largely evaporated when the association split into disconnected, subsidiary sections.

The TFGF held its inaugural meeting at the end of 1922. Manufacturers and wholesalers were well represented but there were relatively few retailers. They were difficult to organise because the majority ran small-scale operations which did not deal exclusively with toys. Specialist outlets had existed in most major cities by the end of the nineteenth century but a Ministry of Labour inquiry in 1921 concluded that establishments in which toys only were sold 'do not appear to be general'.[127] Most toys were sold through an amazingly wide range of retail outlets, including not only bazaars and multiples, but also sellers of cheap jewellery, fancy goods, stationery, leather, drapery, hardware, ironmongery, confectionery and artists' materials.[128] After leather handbags, children's playthings were the second most commonly stocked items, being held by 55 per cent of the shops surveyed in eighty-two reports covering the whole country. Even with a subscription set at 7s. 6d., compared with the one to five guineas payable by the manufacturers and the two guineas required from wholesalers, it was unlikely that many toy sellers would think membership of toy trade association worthwhile. As one of their number put it, the new organisation 'was of very little use to people interested in a small way but was chiefly for the benefit of the large store keepers'.[129] Only forty-eight retailers had joined by April 1923. Those elected to the federation council certainly represented only the large, London-based department stores, although they did probably account for the bulk of toy sales – Army and Navy Stores, Howard and Co., Selfridges, Ingrams, Civil Service Supply, Harrods, Whyte's Library, Gamage, Bon Marché and Hamley Brothers. The wholesalers' representatives were drawn from Abrahams (Payne, Wisbey, Turnbull), Sandle Brothers, Haywood, Faudels, Eisenman, Greiner, Whyte, Ridsdale and Co., Bedington Liddiatt, and Gray and Nicholls. Eighty-five manufacturers were in membership by the spring of 1923 and their council representatives – from Britains, Reeves and Son, Harbutts, Farnell, Patterson Edwards, Journet, Lines, Smith, Stone and Havanco – lacked only Meccano and Chad Valley of the major firms (although in March 1922 Hornby had been elected president of the Manufacturers's section and a Chad Valley executive served as secretary).

With a total membership of 185 in April 1923, the federation may be said to have represented the mature industry. On a hitherto normally developing adolescent business, the war had acted rather like an anabolic steroid, producing distortions, growths, strengths, and even frailties. The reversion to peace and the removal and subsequent denial of the comforting blanket of protection, produced withdrawal symptoms that were unpleasant and very costly for most parts of the toymaking body. The number of manufacturers contracted considerably during the depression. So, too, did the workforce, although the figures are unclear, obscured by the increasingly desperate claims made by the Incorporated Association. The petition sent to MPs in November 1920 claimed 25,000 employees, the follow-up circular letter of February 1921 mentioned 30,000, while Faraday's opening statement at the Board of Trade inquiry had 40,000. By 1922 there were certainly far fewer. Nevertheless, the long-term prognosis for the trade was beginning to brighten.

Chapter 5

Comfortable Maturity, 1923–1944

In the autumn of 1926 the *London Evening News* observed that 'in years gone by, young England used to play with Continental things. But British toy firms have now taken on the job of supplying Father Christmas with jolly playthings. They are just as good and far cheaper.'[1] This was by no means a universally shared view, however, one national newspaper suggesting three years later that the bulk of toys available in Britain were still foreign. This provoked a furious outburst from Sir William Crawford, its hyperbole predictable perhaps since he was not only a member of the Empire Marketing Board but also chief of the advertising agency that handled Meccano. The postwar success of this young industry, he thundered, 'is one of the absorbing epics of modern business'.[2]

In reality of course, few were absorbed by an achievement that was hardly epic, but by 1923 the industry did appear to have shaken off the worst effects of war-induced trauma and depression. According to the third census of production for 1924, toymaking employed some 5325 persons. Although well down on the estimate made for 1920 the increase since 1907 was the greatest achieved by any industry in the miscellaneous manufacturing sector.[3] While this may well reflect the inaccuracies of the 1907 census it was certainly the case that unemployment was falling. Between June and September 1923, for example, the number of insured male and female toy workers without employment fell from 719 to 571 and from 684 to 514 respectively.[4] Trade prospects were also picking up. The *Toy Trader* reckoned that the display of home produced toys at the British Industries Fair in 1924 had never been better and the mood of optimism apparent at the Manchester show in January 1925 was evident in the value of the orders placed, which was back to the heady levels of 1920.[5] Business continued to prosper throughout the relative boom which characterised the second half of the 1920s. The Manchester Toy Week in January 1929 was so successful that one of the promoters was inspired to prophesy, although he could hardly have been more wrong. 'Not since the War had the indications of a trade boom been so freely indicated.'[6] By 1930 average employment in the industry had risen to 6641 and output had more than doubled from its 1924 level (Table 20).

Table 20
The British Toy Industry, 1924–37[7]

	1924	1930	1935
No. of Firms	93	72	106
Gross Output	£1,468,000	£2,000,000	£2,993,000
Employees	4,992	6,641	10,907

The strength of the domestic industry was also evident from the fact that although imports rose slightly in the second half of the decade they were generally fairly stable, even in a rising domestic market (Table 21).

Table 21
Toy Imports to Britain, 1920–29[8]

Year	Total	From Germany	
	£	£	%
1920	2,586,919	1,420,235	54
1921	1,823,959	1,372,275	75
1922	2,111,802	1,630,504	77
1923	2,393,831	1,925,134	80
1924	2,312,986	1,866,320	81
1925	2,427,440	2,030,917	84
1926	2,346,038	1,878,221	80
1927	2,518,085	2,105,897	84
1928	2,465,357	2,124,053	86
1929	2,512,791	2,160,996	86

The absence of any significant import growth was partly the result of developments overseas which shaped both the volume and nature of the competition. In the United States toy makers participated fully in the consumer boom of the Roaring Twenties. By 1929 they had an estimated annual output worth $90,000,000, giving America the largest toy industry in the world. It achieved such a figure behind the shelter of a 70 per cent tariff, which allowed it to take a 95 per cent share of the domestic market. As a result, American manufacturers were relatively uninterested in exporting, sending abroad only about 4 per cent of total output in 1925.[9] Conversely, the Japanese economy grew relatively slowly during the 1920s, although manufacturing industry generally did rather better than average during the second half of the decade. With a value of £453,742 in 1920 the Japanese had accounted for about 17.5 per cent of Britain's total toy import bill. By 1929 this proportion had fallen to 5.8 percent. Although most of the major British import houses were now carrying Japanese goods, they competed only at the cheap end of the market, presenting no serious threat to the major British specialities.

As for the German industry, there is no doubt that globally it suffered from the legacy of the national currency crisis. In the early 1920s international toy merchants had reacted to almost daily price increases by turning to more reliable suppliers. Toy exports in 1925 were 20 per cent down on the 1924 level and by 1929 the German toy industry was exporting only between 55 to 60 per cent of its output compared with 75 per cent in 1913. In 1929 makers, wholesalers, exporters, retailers and department stores set up a cooperative organisation designed to discover and to remedy the causes of export decline. Nevertheless, as Table 21 indicates, Germany remained by far the most important overseas provider of toys for British children in the 1920s. Interestingly, this did not create anything like the furore that a similar domination had sparked off in the years prior to the First World War. In part this was because Germany's surrender in 1918 had diminished its status as a perceived threat to British interests. It was also the case that the prewar hysteria had developed very largely because there had been no available, reliable statistics to put the German figures into a more realistic comparative perspective. In the 1920s this was no longer the case. The 1930 census of production revised upwards the 1924 production total and added in toys made by non-toy firms to give an estimated output of £2,068,000.[10] The gap between British production and German imports therefore was nothing like as vast as it had appeared to be in 1907.

It could no longer be maintained, as E. E. Williams had tried to argue in the 1890s, that German toys were inherently superior. There is evidence that in some cases the quality of German output was affected by the country's internal difficulties. Certainly one British father told *The Times* that in his experience British railway engines, while slightly more expensive, were more reliable than their German equivalents, several of which his children had worn out within a month or so of purchasing them.[11] Any such qualitative decline was set off even more sharply by the great postwar improvement in the quality of some British products, a matter on which there was widespread agreement.[12] Visitors to the 1923 British Industries Fair were particularly taken by the high standard of the indigenous soft toys on display. For example, Chad Valley began producing quality rag dolls in the 1920s, emphasising the safe and hygienic nature of the materials from which they were made. One of the same firm's own designers, Norah Wellings, launched a very succesful business on her own account, turning out her own dolls at the Victoria Toy Works in Shropshire. At the 1929 fair, one north country store buyer told journalists that before the war he had spent his entire budget abroad, three-quarters of it in Germany. Now 70 per cent of what he bought was British because of the progress that had been made in the last few years. Not only were items like celluloid rattles and china tea sets now cheaper than the German products, but the best-quality train sets also came from English makers.[13] 'It may be safely asserted,' commented one industrial magazine in 1930, 'that the English made toys rival those of any nation, not excluding the ingenious Teutons'.[14]

This verdict was validated by the steady growth in the value of British exports from £543,590 in 1924 to £693,651 in 1929 (Table 22).

Table 22
British Toy Exports, 1920–40[15]

	£		£
1924	543,590	*1932*	378,172
1925	561,465	*1933*	419,073
1926	579,209	*1934*	397,577
1927	585,591	*1935*	419,436
1928	666,000	*1936*	439,221
1929	693,651	*1937*	436,680
1930	541,825	*1938*	454,380
1931	381,415		

This was all the more remarkable, given the general lack of interest shown in the overseas markets by the majority of British firms, an attitude which the *Toy Trader* frequently deplored. 'There is no blinking the fact that over-concentration on home trade has tended to restrict vision and to lead some folk to regard the foreign buyer as a very remote kind of customer.'[16] The British manufacturers were conspicuous mainly by their absence from major international fairs, although this was an attitude common to many British industrialists, not just toy makers. In 1926 the world's leading trade fair at Leipzig attracted 10,500 exhibitors in all classes. Only thirteen of them were from the United Kingdom, although they did include two toy manufacturers, Chad Valley and J. K. Farnell.

Complaints were also expressed in these years about the condescension sometimes displayed by British firms towards potential overseas customers. One Canadian sales manager criticised them for being content to rely on middlemen in London offices rather than sending representatives abroad. He further ventured to suggest that for every fifty catalogues sent to Canada by German and American firms he would be hard pressed to find five from Britain.[17] At the toy manufacturers' annual dinner in 1928 a director of Tan-Sad, who had just returned from a world tour, urged British toymen to seize the great opportunities existing abroad, even in the United States where stores encouraged the view that foreign products were qualitatively better than domestic ones. In both Canada and Australia, he added, there was a real danger that the prevailing pro-British sentiment would eventually be eroded by the home manufacturers' consistent unwillingness to cater for local demands by providing appropriate goods. His conclusion, that there was a need to think well ahead in order to meet delivery dates, was another thinly-disguised criticism of British toy companies.[18] 'It is repeatedly urged', agreed the *Toy Trader*, 'that our greatest weakness is on the selling side . . . We hope that in the toy trade the importance of more vigorous propaganda and sales schemes will speedily come into much wider recognition.'[19] Despite the paper's repeated calls to look further afield for markets, only a relatively small number of firms were responsible for the bulk of exports.[20] In the main they were the same small group of businesses, mostly family-owned, which effectively came to dominate the British industry after the First World War.

Table 23
British Toy Production by Sector, 1924[21]

Category	Toy Firms £	Non-Toy Firms £
Dolls/Soft Toys	271,000	
Mechanical Metal	255,000	3,000
Other Metal	161,000	41,000
Wooden	91,000	18,000
Indoor Games	241,000	46,000
Others	718,000	223,000
Total	1,737,000	331,000

The 1930 census of production assessed Britain's total toy output at £2,068,000 in 1924 (Table 23). Each sector was dominated by one or two firms, all of which had apparently taken to heart the advice offered by the *Toy Trader*. 'Old methods of doing business can no longer be relied upon, and the firms who have moved with the times, and adjusted their sales policy to the changed conditions are reaping the benefit.'[22] This involved not only expansion of the labour force but more modern methods of organisation, extensive advertising and diversification of product. It was noticeable, for example, that toy factories had become much more mechanised. By 1924 the horse power of prime movers used in the industry was more than double its prewar level.[23] In the 'others' classification the major producers were Dean's Rag Books, Sorbo Rubber and Lotts Bricks, firms which between them employed 300 workers by 1931. At Roberts Brothers almost 300 employees made a major input to the indoor games category, to which Chad Valley board games also contributed significantly. Like J. K. Farnell, however, Chad Valley was best known for soft toys. It was the first company to market toy versions of the children created by the artist Mabel Lucie Atwell, They were made of hand-painted felt and velvet and became an instant success. The Chad Valley company employed between one and two hundred (according to the season) on four sites by 1931. As with other successful consumer goods enterprises of this era, the firm was quick to appreciate the advertising potential of the popular press, then enjoying something of a boom.[24] From the beginning of 1925 the company produced *Happyland*, a comic which served as both an advertising medium and also as a vehicle for the advocacy of constructive and educational playthings. Remarkably, given the size and reputation of the Steiff factory, Chad Valley also exported quite successfully to Germany, selling £3000 of soft toys there in 1927.[25]

The dominant cast-metal toy makers was still Britains Ltd. The firm rode the inevitable postwar reaction against military toys by diversifying into the production of models connected with civilian activities, ultimately drawing inspiration from the worlds of the circus, sport, the farm and rural life in general. A new factory opened in the 1920s soon proved too small and another was acquired in Walthamstow to accommodate a workforce which reached 400 by 1931. Among the major manufacturers of mechanical metal items were Brimtoy, A. Wells and Company and Paton Calvert, who by 1932 had respectively 300, 200, and eighty workers. Meccano, however, reigned supreme in this sector.[26] Frank Hornby was assiduous in seeking out overseas markets and in utilising every medium of publicity, to the extent that his advertising literature was printed in sixteen languages. Increasing his company's capitalisation in 1921 from £5000 to £100,000, he took on a popular fiction writer, Ellison Hawks, as editor of the *Meccano Magazine*. Hawks' responsibilities also included the organisation of a specialist advertising department which had a substantial budget. He worked closely with an outside advertising agency to such good effect that by 1927 Meccano products were advertised in publications with a combined circulation of 75,000,000, including comics such as *Wizard*, *Champion* and the *Boy's Own Paper*. In addition, Hornby catered directly for the consumers of his products by providing a first-rate repair service, and excellent back-up for his selected retail dealers. Shops handling Meccano, noted a trade magazine in 1923, were particularly fortunate because the company provided ample support in the form of publicity material, including the *Meccano Magazine*, a free colour booklet on Meccano products and a trade folder.[27] Hornby was particularly quick to exploit the potential of the cinema, arranging interval showings of advertising slides which also carried the names of local dealers. In conjunction with a mass of press articles, this was the main method used in organising Hornby Train Week in 1924, a selling push described in the *Toy Trader* as 'probably the biggest that has ever taken place in connection with the toy trade in this country'.[28] It provided a very successful platform for the first of Hornby's electric trains, which became highly profitable as the sets were extended throughout the interwar years (Table 24). In 1926 Hornby scored a major coup in arranging for the child film star, Jackie Coogan, to tour one of his factories, covering the visit extensively in the *Meccano Magazine*.

Building on this domestic success Meccano also sought to protect and extend its overseas interests. In 1922 a factory was purchased in New Jersey for the production of crystal sets. A warehousing and distribution facility was acquired in France, where Hornby also conducted a successful fight through the courts against a local firm which had quite blatantly pirated the Meccano idea. It took rather longer, until 1928 in fact, before he brought to an equally successful conclusion his campaign for the restoration of his German organisation, which had been confiscated during the war and acquired by Marklin. The results of all this diversification and advertising can be seen in Meccano's returns set out in Table 24.

Table 24
Meccano Ltd: Statistics, 1926–36[29]

Net Profit to Year Ended 28 February

	£		£
1926	43,897	1933	35,184
1927	56,148	1934	51,648
1928	58,702	1935	23,449
1930	30,714	1936	40,109
1931	32,670	1937	41,262
1932	40,617		

		Sales Meccano £	Hornby £	Dinky £
1930	Home	142,282	149,338	
	Export	134,472	42,843	
1931	Home	121,673	156,668	
	Export	122,519	33,750	
1933	Home	77,479	126,173	
	Export	66,546	142,325	
1934	Home	62,833	147,853	
	Export	61,413	18,255	
1935	Home	62,173	159,412	35,747
	Export	51,245	21,432	19,832
1936	Home	62,752	187,630	50,335
	Export	48,477	25,985	23,783

Although firms like these were major entities in the toy world, Lines Brothers towered over them all, developing at a prodigious rate after its initial establishment early in the decade. By 1924/5 it employed 533 workers, almost twice as many as G. and J. Lines, and more than twice as many as Patterson Edwards, the other leading makers of wheeled toys. By 1931 the labour force had reached 1000, by which time Patterson Edwards still had only 300, while Tan-Sad, another important employer in this sector, had 200.[30] The three initiators of the famous Triang trade mark, Walter, Will and Arthur Lines, had a good appreciation of the importance of modern production techniques, since their early working experience had been gained in the family firm, G. and

J. Lines. That business had been organised on the most modern principles, its factory designed by an architect in consultation with the proprietors as a series of contiguous process workshops. These had been separated from the showrooms in order to keep insurance premiums to a minimum. Power was provided by electricity and internal communication facilitated by the provision of telephones in every department. All completed goods were subjected to a final inspection process before delivery, either in the firm's own transport, if the destination was within fifty miles of London, or via the railway sidings adjacent to the plant.[31]

Similar features were incorporated when the three Lines brothers opened their own factory just after the war, although the sub-division of processes and operations was carried much further. The plant had no fewer than thirty separate departments which permitted the specialised training of workers on single tasks. The benefits emerged very clearly when the Ministry of Labour set up an inquiry into the scope of the Toy Trade Board. This had been demanded by the pram makers, a number of whom also made dolls' prams and other large wheeled toys, in the belief that they were disadvantaged by the high wage rates prescribed by the Perambulator Trade Board. Lines Brothers, it was contended, gained an unfair advantage because they were required to pay only the lower rates laid down by the Toy Trade Board. The investigating civil servant would have none of this, though the sharpness of his judgement was somewhat blunted by his verbosity:

> the real issue is not so much between perambulator firms proper and toy firms in regard to the manufacture of toy perambulators etc., as between all firms making perambulators whether real perambulators or toy perambulators by old fashioned methods on the one hand and the one firm referred to above [Lines Bros] who make both types of article on the modern mass production and subdivision of process principle.[32]

The inquiry found that Lines Brothers minimised labour costs by maximising the deployment of juveniles. This was quite common in the toy trade generally, as was the practice of discharging such workers once the Christmas rush was over. Lines, however, retained a greater number of theirs. One investigation noted that at the end of the 1924 season the company laid off only seventy-six as opposed to the 112 who left Patterson Edwards and the 200 laid off by Peter Pan in Wolverhampton.[33] Labour productivity was raised by paying 95 per cent of the workforce on piece rates (which meant that many employees received well above the trade board rates), whereas firms like Patterson Edwards and the original Lines company paid time rates. Further efficiency gains were achieved by the extensive utilisation of specialist machinery, which enabled almost everything to be made on site rather than being bought in, as was still common practice among other manufacturers. All smithing work was mechanised and tin work was not put out to tender. Lines also invested heavily in capstan lathes, electric welders, specially-designed grooving machines, and electric leather cutters, providing their workers with far more heavy equipment than was customary in the contemporary toy trade. As a result, each employee produced 625 doll's prams in 1923 against 181 each at G. and J. Lines, and 458 at Patterson Edwards.[34] Greater efficiency and the economies of scale achieved by mass production brought prices down, even though the Lines Brothers also produced a lot of relatively expensive toys for the comparatively wealthy (Table 25).

Table 25
Dolls' Prams: Manufacturers' Prices, 1924[35]

	Quality Range		
Firm	*Cheap*	*Medium*	*Best*
Lines Brothers	8s.	30s.	70s.
G. & J. Lines	8s.	35s.	75s.
Patterson Edwards	8s.	29s.	54s.
Peter Pan	17s.	27s. 6d.	not made

In other wheeled toys, such as cars, Lines Brothers were by far the cheapest at the bottom end of the market. Their 25s. car body was considerably larger than the equivalent model offered by Patterson Edwards at 28s. 6d., for instance.[36]

The presiding genius at Merton was undoubtedly Walter Lines. Brother Will was a dynamic and extrovert salesman, while Arthur ran the factories efficiently and diplomatically. Walter, energetic and prickly, was the ideas man and represented the company's public face. He was an extremely talented toy designer with an instinctive eye for a novelty and he built up a very successful design department. The Triang organisation was not afraid to back its judgement with money either, whether for capital equipment or in buying up small firms with particular products in need of development capital. One important acquisition made during the 1920s was the Unique and Unity Cycle Company of Birmingham, for which Lines provided a modern factory.

Early in the 1930s a controlling share was purchased in International Model Aircraft, and at about the same time Hamleys was bought from the bank when it ran into financial difficulty.

The famous toy store's plight was but one symptom of the economic depression which ultimately enveloped the entire industrial world in the aftermath of the Wall Street Crash of 1929. Not only was it followed by general recession and a shrinking in the volume of international trade, it also resulted in the withdrawal of American investment from Europe. This helped to carry the symptoms of contraction across the Atlantic with particularly serious effects for central Europe. In May 1931 the Kredit Anstalt, the largest and most prestigious bank in Austria, failed. Its collapse threatened the solvency of numerous foreign and domestic institutions which depended on it. In order to stop the flight of money out of the country the Austrian Government froze all assets. As a large proportion of these were German, the liquidity crisis was simply extended. When the German Government also tried to protect its position by halting the outward movement of gold and foreign currency, the pressure was transferred to Britain, Germany's main creditor. Foreign investors soon began to withdraw substantial funds from London, their fears exacerbated by the publication of the May Report, an official examination of current public expenditure levels. Its forecast of a budget deficit of £120,000,000 threatened to turn the existing outflow of gold into a flood. Ramsay MacDonald's Labour Government first dithered and then divided before finally disappearing. MacDonald himself reemerged at the head of a National Government, pledged to a programme of stringent economy cuts designed to restore foreign confidence.

As far as the international toy trade was concerned the alarm bells had begun to ring as early as 1929, when one of the best-known American firms, Harry Ives, went bankrupt. Others soon followed, while those that survived generally experienced shrinking revenues. So great was the contraction in advertising that by 1931 the leading trade journal, *Playthings*, was down to a mere eighty pages, although in 1928 it had normally carried in excess of 400.[37] In Germany the Bing Brothers were also in serious difficulties. Although reporting gross profits in 1929 of slightly more than £250,000, a drastic reorganisation of capital involving the liquidation of several subsidiary companies had failed to reduce expenses, with the result that the net profit was a mere £10,000. The following year gross profit itself fell to £104,000 and heavy net losses of £124,000 were incurred. This experience of plunging profits was shared by a growing number of manufacturers and the *Toy Trader* took an almost perverse relish in reporting the mounting list of failures. In 1931 alone they included the exporters, Seeligman and Meyer of Furth, and Zimmer of Nuremberg, as well as the tin toy Oro works in Brandenberg. At the end of the year Leo Präger of Nuremberg and the associated firm of Richard Bayer failed, with liabilities of £50,000.

There were plenty of British casualties, too. Domestic demand fell off as the effects of deteriorating levels of international trade and rising unemployment were compounded by wage cuts in 1931. Manufacturers, retailers and wholesalers were all affected. Although the majority of British firms had not been responsive to the pleadings of the trade press to look to export markets, the bigger firms in particular were alarmed by the prospect of rising overseas tariffs. In May 1930 access to one of Britain's most lucrative export markets, Australia, was apparently threatened by the very sudden imposition of tariffs, the remedy adopted by a government seeking to reduce a current trade deficit of £5,000,000. Another blow was the withdrawal of the government subsidy for the British Industries Fair, the main domestic showcase for British toy manufacturers and one which they had supported well. The timing was particularly unfortunate since the fair had only just got a permanent site at Olympia, having been housed in five different venues since its inception in 1915.

The best known of the merchant houses to go under was Wisbeys, whose goodwill was taken over by Whyte, Ridsdale and Co. in 1932. Bedington Liddiatt went into receivership the following year, although both the Liddiatts had already severed their connection with the company. Importers Hollas, Gillet and Kew were also among the failures with accumulated debts of about £9550. Prominent metropolitan retail victims of the depression included Shoolbreds, which went into voluntary liquidation in the summer of 1930 after 113 years of existence and Gamages (West End) Ltd. This was a relatively recent experiment by the People's Emporium to develop into London's West End but it collapsed with the suicide of a director in July 1931. In this year, too, Hamleys went into liquidation with gross liabilities of £159,200. The depression was certainly the final straw although the company had been in difficulty for some time. Its net profits had been pitifully small for some years, only £302 in 1928 and £1081 the following year. In 1930 a net loss of £4641 did not prevent the company paying out dividends, but the next year losses reached more than £12,000 and the receivers were called in.[38]

In its current form Hamleys had existed since 1902. It had never really recovered after the cost of rebuilding its Regent Street premises exceeded the estimated £80,000 by £40,000. To this were added the losses incurred by an ill-fated development at Eastbourne (£6418 plus £3000 of capital) and declining revenue at Regent Street arising from falling sales. As the largest single individual creditor, Lines Brothers bought Hamleys and closed down all the subsidiary branches, keeping only Regent Street open. Lines' prominence in the toy trade had already aroused adverse comment among competitors. There was some fear among fellow manufacturers that this latest acquisition was merely a disguised form of vertical integration. Walter was astute enough, however, to let it be known that a totally separate company had been formed and the general manager instructed to buy in the best markets, not to give preference to the products of any single manufacturer.[39]

If the depression saw off some well-known wholesalers and retailers, there is no doubt that it was the manufacturers who were the worst affected. Even well-established and successful companies found the first two or three years of the 1930s difficult. The jigsaw makers R. H. Journet survived only by making puzzles as adverts for manufacturers such John West, Crosse and Blackwell and Steven's Ink. Bassett Lowke reduced wages by 10 per cent and turned to importing high-quality models for a select market. Their first venture in conjunction with the German firm of Marklin faltered when that company's Jewish founder fell foul of the Nazis. Similar threats hung over Franz Bing and S. Kahn, manufacturers of the Trix trains for whom Bassett Lowke became sole concessionaires; in 1935 these two fled to Britain and settled into the Bassett Lowke operation at Northampton. For Britains, the general economic gloom was deepened by contemporary efforts to reduce the likelihood of war. At the international disarmament conference in 1932 the Dominican Republic even proposed a ban on the manufacture of all war toys. The death of William Britain in 1933 was a further blow and Fred Britain claimed that in 1936 the firm's profits had fallen by 75 per cent.[40] Hilary Page of Kiddicraft was not discharged as a bankrupt until October 1937, after what he described as a 'most difficult period'.[41] Meccano sold off its American factory in 1929 to A. C. Gilbert, manufacturer of one of its most successful rivals in the construction kit field, Erector. Profits fell badly in 1930 (Table 24) and did not really pick up until 1934. The appearance of Trix, a low-cost construction toy sold by multiples such as Woolworths, led the company to experiment with a cheaper and smaller version of the Meccano set called the X series. It was not particularly successful and was withdrawn

in 1936, the year in which Frank Hornby died. It was unfortunate that
neither of his sons were particularly interested in the family business, showing a marked preference for the golf course. As for
Walter Lines, he was at one point so depressed by the economic
situation that he had considered asking Frank Hornby to buy him out,
because he did not think that Lines Brothers could survive alone for
much longer.[42]

His pessimism was misplaced as far as his own company was concerned but others were not so fortunate. In 1930 one of Liverpool's
major firms, Gray and Nicholls, finally gave up the unequal struggle
and closed down. A net profit in 1927 of £501 on a turnover of £28,000
had deteriorated into losses of £602 and £1300 in 1928 and 1929 on
respective turnovers of £25,000 and £25,800. By 1930 the accumulated
debt had reached £13,383. In general, however, it was the smaller
companies that were the most vulnerable, lacking the financial resources
to tide them over a period of prolonged slump. It was also impractical
for them to diversify as readily as retailers and merchants into non-toy
activities. Some of the fatalities occurred among relative newcomers.
The Multiple Utilities Company Ltd had prospered on one good idea,
the Kum Bak tennis trainer, and had been incorporated as recently as
1928. Unable to find another successful product, it went into voluntary
liquidation with liabilities of £13,626 against assets of £4704.[43] Other
casualties had longer pedigrees. In 1930 J. R. Smith, a wooden toy
maker of seventy years standing, went down owing almost £5000. The
following year Multum in Parvo was liquidated. Founded in 1896, it
had been in almost continuous difficulties throughout the 1920s and
ended its days with assets of a mere £86. Reka survived but principally
by abandoning its established toy making activities.

The attritional effects of the depression can be seen in Table 26
which plots the longevity of toy enterprises during the interwar years.
Of the 1340 manufacturers, wholesalers, importers and agents active
in the toy business in 1920 some 560 (41.8 per cent) survived until
1930. Half of these still existed in 1940, including of course most of
the major firms like Chad Valley, Meccano and Britains. Of those listed
in 1930 only 1330 lasted through the depression until 1940. Altogether,
46 percent of the toy enterprises extant in 1930 disappeared during
the ensuing decade.

Table 26
Survival Rates of Toy British Businesses, 1920–40[44]

Number of Firms Existing in		Number Still Extant in 1930	Number Still Extant in 1940
1920	1,340	560	280
1930	2,460		1,330
1940	2,800		

There is another equally important implication arising from these figures. Even though it had become much more capital intensive and industrialised since 1920, toy making by its very nature was always likely to attract the small entrepreneur. More than three-quarters of the agents, manufacturers, wholesalers and importers extant in 1930 entered the industry during the 1920s. Despite the economic problems of the following decade roughly another 1200 toy businesses were started up, presumably on the principle that the best time to invest was at the bottom of the depression. This infusion of new blood was evident from the commercial information provided by the trade press, the *Toy Trader* reporting the following numbers of new company registrations in the fifteen months from February 1932.

Table 27
New Company Registrations, February 1932 to June 1933[45]

1932		1933	
February	11	January	2
March	4	February	7
April	8	March	4
May	6	April	12
June	5	May	7
July	7	June	84
August	6		
September	3		
October	6		
November	6		
December	5		

Among the newcomers were a number of companies which proved to be purely transitory because they sought to take advantage of contemporary toy crazes such as the yo yo, introduced with great success in 1932. Even more sought to exploit the enthusiasm for miniature golf, which swept the country in 1930. Between them they exhausted just about every known synonym for miniature. Those listed in *Games and Toys*, between October and December of 1930 alone, included B. B. Miniature Golf Ltd, Small Golf Ltd, Lester's Midget Golf Ltd, Super Little Golf Ltd, Bijou Golf Games Ltd, Littlelinks Ltd, Pigmy Golf Ltd, and Gulliver Golf Ltd. Others new foundations, like K. B. Ltd. of Aylesbury or H. A. Moore and Company at Radlett, also made little lasting impression on the trade. Nor did Practical British Toys Ltd, despite increasing its labour force from two to sixty within eight months of beginning work in the middle of 1932. A few of the new manufacturers, however, did have more success. Although Hilary Page founded Kiddicraft in 1932 on a capital of only £100, which soon led him to the bankruptcy court, he was one of the pioneers in experimenting with plastic as a new manufacturing medium. Charbens, which started making toy soldiers in 1929, lasted for about half a century.[46] A new firm of jigsaw makers, Williams, Ellis and Co., turned out more than 1,000,000 puzzles in the first year of operations. G. J. Hayter, an employee of Lloyd's Bank who had been cutting out jigsaws for some years as a hobby, went into full time commercial production with his well-known Victory range. Paul Abbatt, a schoolmaster who visited Vienna in 1932 for his honeymoon, brought back some educational toys. A positive market response, and a recommendation from the educationist Susan Isaacs in her book *The Nursery Years*, gave his business a promising start. Merrythought, directed by A. C. Janisch and C. J. Rendle, both of whom had been in the toy business for some years with Farnell and Chad Valley respectively, started making high-class soft toys in 1930. By 1939 there were 200 employees.

A further impetus to toy manufacturing in the early 1930s came from firms outside the trade, seeking ways of employing productive resources left comparatively idle by the depression. With the price of rubber down to two pence a pound and too much capital tied up in shoe heels and soles, the Premo Rubber Company launched Minibrix, a studded rubber brick, in 1935. Waddingtons, which had begun life at the turn of century as printers of theatrical programmes and posters, put out cardboard jigsaws and its first game, Lexicon, in 1933. The following year it brought to Britain the American game of Monopoly, which was to become the best-selling board game of all time. A similar path of diversification was opened by British Xylonite for its new acquisition, Cascelloid. This company, founded by Alfred Pallett, had its major production concentrated in a wide range of celluloid fancy goods. It had had a marginal interest in toys since 1920, when Woolworths had placed a very large order for windmills. A few years later the firm had produced its first doll, based on Mabel Lucie Atwell's character, Diddums. When control passed to British Xylonite in 1931 the new owners created a toy division under the name Palitoy, and Cascelloid went into doll production in a major way. It was the first to use Plastex, a non-breakable plastic more durable than celluloid, then in 1935 Bexoid, a non-inflammable material. The moulds for the first range of dolls were acquired from Germany and it took a while to get the new production lines working efficiently.[47] By the autumn of 1935 the technical difficulties had been largely overcome, sales were rising and future prospects for the doll business adjudged to be much better than in the past.[48] This optimism was borne out by Cascelloid's trading profits through the 1930s (Table 28).

Table 28
Cascelloid Trading Profits, 1931–39[49]

		£
Year to 31 August	*1931*	4,176
	1932	3,589
	1933	7,482
	1934	10,611
	1935	11,551
	1936	15,022
	1937	14,700
	1938	18,323
	1939	49,300

It was still, however, the older and bigger companies that led the way in recovery, notwithstanding their own individual difficulties. They struck out in new directions, reorganised existing activities, diversified their outputs or invested in new acquisitions and plant. A British syndicate, headed by the importer Leon Rees, bought a controlling stake in Bing Brothers in 1931, with the intention of restoring profitability by terminating its loss-making activities. Roberts Brothers expanded output to the extent that its labour force grew to 340 by 1935. Crescent Toys, a firm dating from 1922, increased its toy soldier production by acquiring Reka's abandoned moulds. The metal toy maker A. J. Wells was incorporated in 1930 and two years later took over Brimtoy. Although new machinery was installed in both plants, production was eventually concentrated in a purpose-built factory at Walthamstow. J. K. Farnell and William Bailey merged their sales forces in 1932. The Tottenham plant of H. G. Stone, makers of Chiltern Toys, was extended in 1934, providing employment for 150 by the following year. Tan-Sad amalgamated with Allwin in 1934 and the following year Allwin started to manufacture soft toys. J. W. Spear opened a new factory at Enfield, while the American Louis Marx began operations at Dudley in the midlands. Chad Valley acquired larger premises extending to twenty acres in 1935. Britains launched miniature gardens in 1931 and opened a third factory at Colne to manufacture Cadbury's Cubs, anthropomorphic animal models which the chocolate company used as an advertising gimmick. So extensive was the diversification that two-thirds of the items listed in Britains' catalogues between 1936 and 1939 were non-military subjects. They also did consistently well in the export sector, especially in empire markets and the United States, where the quality and reputation of their figures was sufficient to surmount the prohibitive tariff. At the end of the decade, by which time the firm's labour force had reached 500 workers producing an annual output of some 20,000,000 figures, Britains raised their capitalisation to £40,000.

Meccano's progress was on a different scale altogether, Hornby's decision to turn his company into a public one in 1932 enabling him to raise £300,000 of fresh capital. Part of this was used to finance the acquisition of a further 6000 square feet of factory space in 1936, part to fund experiments with special Meccano sets, model boats and kits of self-assembly tinplate aeroplanes and cars. Table 24 suggests that Meccano as a concept was probably past its prime, sales having peaked in 1930. Production continued but various price alterations and an experiment with hire purchase failed to rejuvenate it. Nevertheless, it still exercised a very wide appeal right across the social spectrum. Ralph Finn was moved to tears by the incredulous response of the small urchin to whom he presented his own Meccano set.[50] At about the same time Louis Herren, the Shadwell-born son of a printer, was sufficiently well off to save up in order to buy a set for himself.[51] Even so, the company's profits were increasingly sustained by its other products. The domestic sales of train sets held up well, befitting perhaps from the interwar construction of 4,000,000 new houses, most of them wired for electricity. The new, smaller Dublo system was announced in 1938. Die-cast miniature vehicles were another promising development, not least because, like Britains' toy soldiers, they very quickly became collectables. First marketed under the famous Dinky trade name in 1934, their outstanding features were widely acknowledged to be realism, quality and finish.[52] Children of all classes could aspire to own Dinkies, although George MacBeth recalled enviously that the son of his father's boss could afford to buy the khaki-coloured military vehicles which were more expensive than the civilian models which he himself could afford.[53]

Despite Walter Lines' earlier fears, Lines Brothers also expanded their interests, turning themselves into a public company in June 1933 when 200,000 first preference shares were issued. Initially the ordinary shares remained in private hands but they also became publicly available in 1936. The main factory at Merton was extended, production systems were revamped and new machinery installed on an almost annual basis. As a result there were 1600 employees by 1935. The purchase of Hamleys was followed by the acquisition in 1934 of the exclusive rights to produce K-boats, formerly manufactured in Germany. Lines left production in the hands of the original firm, in this case the patentee, George Kellner, being content to invest in plant and factory space.

A similar policy was adopted when in 1932 they bought into International Model Aircraft. The British public had became very air-minded following Britain's Schneider Trophy successes in the late 1920s. Model aeroplanes had been made by firms such as Warneford since 1914 and by D. A. Pavely since 1908, but the model produced by IMA was the first to combine flight with realism. As Walter Lines himself later put it, he acquired an interest in 'the first flying model aeroplane which ever looked remotely like the real thing'.[54] Lines provided capital (the first model cost £17,000 to produce), space, marketing and sales skills in return for their stake. The new range, marketed under the trade name of Frog, was given a high profile send off between September and Christmas 1932, and a Frog club for model flying enthusiasts was established in June 1933. In 1934 Lines had a new production facility purpose-built at Merton, and the following year bought up the rest of the shares. One other important benefit derived from this acquisition was a facility for plastic injection moulding. At the end of 1935 International Model Aircraft started production of Penguins, the first plastic non-flying scale aircraft kits. They were expensive because all the parts were moulded on separate machines. Furthermore, the piece-work system tempted workers to take them from the moulds too quickly, encouraging the warping tendencies inherent in cellulose acetate. The injection moulding process was utilised for other Triang toys, including the very successful Minic clockwork vehicles produced from 1935. To this was added the highly successful range of Pedigree soft toys. The result was a steady rise in profitability which more than doubled between 1932 and 1937 (Table 29).

Table 29
Lines Brothers Ltd: Net Profits, 1931–37[55]

Year	Profit £	Year	Profit £
1931–32	37,367	1934–35	61,774
1932–33	40,826	1935–36	68,406
1933–34	61,689	1936–37	79,717

Located away from the traditional manufacturing heartlands and utilising new modern factories and electrical power in order to produce small consumer goods, these toy firms may be regarded as exemplars of the new light manufacturing enterprises that were developing in Britain between the wars. In the opinion of some economic historians these 'new' industries went some way towards mitigating the effects of the faltering staples, pulling the economy out of the interwar depression.[56] Although toy manufacturing was not a new activity in any sense, it is clear from Table 30 that between the wars it was characterised by both an increase in the number of firms making returns to the census of production and also by a distinct upward shift in their size. The number of firms employing between fifty and ninety-nine people almost tripled and there was also a significant increase in the proportion of firms with more than 200 workers.

Table 30
Size of Toy Making Firms, 1930–35[57]

No. of Employees	No. of Firms	
	1930	1935
11–24	28	34
25–49	15	31
50–99	7	20
100–199	8	9
200–299	4	6
300–1,499	4	6

Lancashire remained as an important manufacturing centre with both Meccano and Paton Calvert situated in Liverpool (Table 31). For the rest, however, the expansion of the industry, like that of the other fast growing interwar industries, was largely concentrated in the midlands and the south, particularly on the outskirts of London.

Table 31
The Distribution of Toy Manufacturing Firms[58]

Location	1930	1935
Greater London	37	65
Lancashire	4	11
Warwickshire; Worcestershire; Staffordshire	10	14
Rest of England	12	16
Ex-England	3	

Between them, the general economic depression following the crash of 1929 and the financial crisis of 1931 had a purgative effect on the British toy business. Despite high levels of company mortality the industry broke all records in 1932 by applying for 40,000 square feet at the British Industries Fair. By the end of the next year *The Times* was suggesting that the trade was enjoying its most successful season in living memory.[59] In 1937 the manufacturers' association claimed that 60 per cent of toys being sold in British stores were domestically produced.[60] The renewed optimism of Walter Lines was evident in his even larger estimate of about 75 per cent.[61] At the same time the number of workers in the industry had risen to almost 15,500. The aggregate recovery was substantial, even though individual firms may still have had problems, manifested perhaps in the fact that 12 per cent of the labour force was still on short-time working in 1935.[62]

It is generally agreed that the British economy recovered more quickly than most other major industrial nations from the worst effects of the depression, despite the persistence of long-term structural unemployment. There has been less unanimity about the underlying causes of recovery, although few now would give much of the credit to government policy.[63] Much more weight has been placed on the incremental increases to real incomes provided generally by the falling cost of foodstuffs and, to a lesser degree and only for some of those at the bottom of the social scale, by redistributive welfare measures. Between 1921 and 1938/9 real per capita consumer expenditure in Britain rose by some 30 per cent.

It is true that some personal recollections of the interwar years indicate real deprivation in which toys virtually disappeared. Nigel Gray's survey, for instance, cites the case of a skilled iron worker, unemployed for the first time, who was reduced to making dolls for his daughters out of packing and paper, adding the faces with indelible

pencil.[64] Another contemporary, Arthur Harding, believed that in his
deprived part of London parents spent less on children's toys after the
middle of the 1920s.[65] However, it is clear that interwar Britain was not
characterised by the same levels of poverty which had so alarmed the
late Victorians. Table 32 shows rising per capita toy consumption even
in the 1920s. Some confirmation of this is provided by the evidence of
Nancy Thompson. On her eighth birthday in 1923 she awoke to find
that 'the sofa was laden with parcels, more parcels and bulkier ones
than I had ever seen at Christmas time'.[66]

Table 32
Per Capita Toy Consumption by Children under Fourteen[67]

	1924	1930	1935
Retained Imports	£2,200,551	£2,594,919	£1,406,408
Home Output (Less Exports)	£924,410	£458,175	£2,733,829
Total Home Consumption	£3,124,961	£4,053,094	£4,140,237
Children	1,194,020	1,082,500	1,082,500
Per Capita Expenditure	£2.617	£3.744	£3.825

By the 1930s aggregate real wages were considerably higher than they
had been in the previous decade, while falling unemployment further
increased the level of the national income. The toy industry benefited
from increased consumer expenditure in the same way as did the press,
the cinema and other forms of recreational activity. Children under
fourteen years of age represented 23.8 per cent of the total population of
England and Wales in 1931, considerably less than the 32.4 per cent they
had made up in 1901.[68] This did not, however, reduce total toy consumption. Although the figures in Table 32 are only approximations, they
do suggest a slight increase in per capita expenditure on toys by 1935.
It must also be borne in mind that rising real incomes facilitated greater
adult expenditure on toys as well which, as *The Times* pointed out

> have no exclusive connection with childhood. They are not children
> who buy rattles for cup-tie matches, nor false noses and squeakers for
> gala nights; nor are they all little girls who hang beside their bed or
> prop upon their dressing tables very long legged floppy dolls with faces
> of an extravagantly wistful or knavish beauty.[69]

Britains' figures remained popular with adults as did the new smal-
ler-scale railway sets associated primarily with the name of Frank
Hornby. Dinky cars proved themselves to be eminently collectable by
adults as well. Walter Lines expressed a commonly-held view when he

claimed in 1936 that a large percentage of toys were purchased by adults for their own amusement.[70]

It would be misleading to suggest, however, that the recovery of toy manufacturing owed absolutely nothing to government action, although in some cases the beneficial effects of the various measures were relatively shortlived, while in others the theoretical benefits of particular policy decisions do not seem to have materialised in practice. Following the abandonment of the link between sterling and gold at the end of 1931, the bank rate fell to 2 per cent by June 1932. Cheap money ought to have acted as an incentive to entrepreneurial activity but, according to the August issue of the *Toy Trader*, toy manufacturers were still being charged between 5 and 6 per cent on their bank loans.[71] More important, perhaps, quitting the Gold Standard should have resulted in cheaper exports. It meant, for example, that a British toy which had previously cost £1 in France now cost only the equivalent of 15s. 9d. But the general contraction in international trade and a widespread resort to economic nationalism meant that British exports in the 1930s never attained the levels that had prevailed in the 1920s (Table 22). The hoped for advantages of leaving the gold standard soon evaporated as other countries followed suit and exchange rates adjusted accordingly.

Ultimately the same was true for import prices also although as expected they certainly rose in the short term, by as much as 20 per cent in the case of German goods. But the overall level of toy imports never recovered. Although they picked up gradually after 1933, the restrictive impact of the Import Duties Act of February 1932 is clear from the dramatic decline which occurred in 1932 and 1933 (Table 33). Amendment of the rates in April included a 15 per cent duty on some raw materials. This had few serious implications for toy manufacturers, most of whose basic materials were home produced. Nor did it do anything to offset the potential benefits they stood to gain from operating in a home market which was protected from April 1932 by a 25 per cent ad valorem duty on imported luxury goods such as toys.

Table 33
British Toy Imports, 1929–39[72]

Year	Total £	From Germany £	From Japan £
1929	2,512,791	2,160,996	145,227
1930	2,651,844	2,214,970	189,698
1931	2,308,674	1,918,134	121,403
1932	1,144,019	787,048	212,156

Year	Total £	From Germany £	From Japan £
1933	1,092,684	746,732	299,108
1934	1,264,787	716,930	392,474
1935	1,475,368	913,448	394,467
1936	1,605,753	969,665	444,114
1937	1,774,873	1,013,838	514,535
1938	1,719,333	965,842	432,022

The reduction of imports may also have owed something to a new Marking Order in October 1932 that required toys priced over two pence to be marked as foreign or to carry an indication of their country of origin. This was a matter which the manufacturers had been considering since 1929, although it was not until January 1931 that they finally submitted a formal application to have toys covered by the provisions of the Merchandise Marks Act of 1926. Customs House officials were not enthusiastic, mainly because the matter of defining toys precisely had still not been satisfactorily resolved. They expressed the hope that the relevant Board of Trade committee would not grant the application.[73] The Manufacturing Confectioners Alliance shared that wish, arguing that any confectionery which their members packed into marked toy containers would be made to appear foreign.[74] The Fancy Goods and Allied Trades Association drew attention to the potential for a similar misunderstanding if the foreign content of made-up items such as board games and Christmas stockings had to be marked. To this they added other practical objections: the expense of opening up such items to ensure that every item was properly labelled; most foreign toys were already marked; and many were too small to allow for the carrying of relevant marks. They also feared that such marking would affect the reexport trade. Although the alliance was careful to stress that its objections were pragmatic rather than matters of principle, J. D. Kiley, who appeared on its behalf at the committee hearing, repeated the old canard that 'it is recognised the toy industry is an imported industry. . . It is practically recognised the toy industry is not a national industry in this country'.[75] After considering the evidence, however, the committee was not minded to agree. Members like George Barnes, the former Labour MP, were convinced that a prime facie case had been made and that without marking the British public was in danger of being misled about the origin of the toys which it bought.[76] An order was duly made, therefore, covering toys 'of a kind which are ordinarily sold to be used by children as playthings, whether or not they many also be capable of other uses'. This phrasing, it was hoped, would circumvent the difficulties of definition which had been emphasised by the opponents of the application.[77]

Although modest, the upward trend of imports after 1933 was still sufficient to worry the domestic producers. The inflow was aided when the import duty was reduced by 10 per cent quite abruptly in the middle of 1933 without any prior consultation with the trade. One specific cause of concern was the signing of the Anglo-German pact which allowed German imports to pick up again after 1934. Another was the surge of toys from Japan, some of them pirated versions of British products (Table 33). Several protests and requests for meetings were lodged with the Board of Trade between 1933 and 1938 but fell on deaf ears. The official line was that it was not in the national interest to amend the Anglo-German pact, nor to end the most favoured nation clauses in the Anglo-Japanese treaty of 1911, clauses which had enabled the Japanese to benefit from Britain's economic treaties with third parties such as Germany. Although the manufacturers were invited to participate in a trade delegation to Germany in 1939, their requests for genuine negotiating autonomy was firmly rejected. In the end the manufacturers' association decided that rather than decrying foreign imports they should devote their resources to stressing the quality of British toys. This was perhaps just as well because, in March 1939, the Board of Trade announced that pressure of work precluded it from considering toys in the Import Duties Act Inquiry.

That the manufacturers' protests were somewhat muted was doubtless due to the fact that, despite their upward trend, the absolute level of imports was well down on the 1920s. At the same time the domestic producers were reaping the considerable benefits of a home market that was both protected and buoyant. Even so, the failure of their various representations to government was in marked contrast to their relative success in making themselves heard in 1921 and 1932. In turn this points up the weakness of the trade as an organised entity between the wars. Although J. D. Kiley had been more vocal in the House of Commons on behalf of the merchant rather than the manufacturing interest, he was at least a voice; his defeat in Whitechapel by a Labour candidate in 1922 was a loss. Frank Hornby, elected for Everton in 1931, was certainly no substitute, for he never displayed much interest in parliamentary affairs. Indeed when he introduced a Bill to extend the Christmas shopping hours in 1934, the response from one Member was to say that he hardly liked to oppose it because 'the Honourable Member for Everton intervenes so seldom in our debates'.[78]

Lacking any strong parliamentary presence after 1921 it was perhaps all the more urgent that the newly-organised Toy and Fancy Goods Federation prove itself effective. It did not and the fragmentary tendencies inherent in its structure emerged quite rapidly. A separate section for importers was established in 1923 as a sub-committee of the wholesalers' section. At the end of 1925 a special meeting of the federation decided that the various sections should each form their own separate associations, though all would remain affiliated to the federation, which would handle matters of general concern. This, however, served merely to give a sharper edge to the differences on policy issues which soon emerged.

Old wounds were reopened when in the mid 1920s the wholesalers tried to get the McKenna duties remitted because they affected goods designed for reexport. This did not go down well with the manufacturers, not all of whom had entirely abandoned their hope of protection and inclusion under the Safeguarding of Industries Act. The wholesalers and importers had opposed the introduction of the Merchandise Marks Act in 1926, and it was not surprising that tensions surfaced during the hearing of the manufacturers' marking order application. They were not handled with much delicacy either. Totally ignoring A. C. Janisch's long experience in the toy trade, counsel for the Fancy Goods Alliance tried to discredit his evidence on the grounds that his current firm, Merrythought, had been in existence for only sixteen months. Yet, he said sarcastically, 'because of its antiquity you are in a position to speak authoritatively'.[79] Counsel for the manufacturers hit back in kind, suggesting that his opposite number's summing up of the case 'would have done credit to the Irish Party in the House of Commons in its most virile days'.[80] Small wonder that by 1934 the *Toy Trader* was appealing for an effective organisation.[81]

The debilitating effects of such internal differences were compounded by the fact that by themselves all of the federation's constituent parts were fairly weak. The retailers had been difficult to organise right from the start and remained a broken reed. Large-scale specialist toy retailing was never likely to develop in a trade so heavily influenced by seasonality, fashion and whim, all of which contributed to a relatively low rate of retail stock turn. By 1938 there were only between 750 and 1000 specialist toy shops which together accounted for about £3,500,000 worth of toy sales out of a total consumer expenditure of some £8,500,000.[82] This represented some 41 per cent of total expenditure, the rest going to shops operated by the Co-Operative Wholesale Society (4.5 per cent), departmental stores (30 per cent) and the multiples (25 per cent).[83]

Even without the seasonal nature of demand, the sale of toys by such non-specialist outlets was almost bound to compel toy sellers to diversify their own stocks. This, combined with the fact that the specialists were in the main independent and far-flung in location, served to reduce their interest in the retail association. The interwar years were littered with missed opportunities. In the aftermath of the Great War street-selling had reemerged, George Orwell, for instance, noting one pavement artist selling toys from a tray when he was demobilised.[84] But the retailers failed to make any input into the government's Street Trading Bill with its proposals for local authority licensing. Nor did they take any effective collective action to halt the growing tendency for manufacturers and wholesalers to offload cut-price goods onto the street markets, which still constituted a major source of supply for the poor. The toy stalls at Hoxton Market were particularly notorious in this respect.[85] Similarly, at the Leather Lane Market off Holborn, it was possible for a father to 'get toys for his Santa Claus work on Christmas Eve far more cheaply than in the shops'.[86] The retailers' weakness prevented any positive response to the idea of group buying when it was first mooted by the *Toy Trader* in October 1930.[87] Again, although they had traditionally set their own prices, they were unable to resist the practice of price-fixing increasingly adopted by manufacturers during the depression on the grounds that it prevented undercutting and ensured quality.[88]

The wholesalers' association was perhaps more in evidence as a body than the retailers, and certainly secured some rate concessions from the transport utilities. But, as a relatively small group, it was generally on the defensive in the interwar years. Internally, it was criticised as being run solely by and in the interests of the London firms. Perhaps this was why in June 1929 the wholesalers sought to broaden the basis of their appeal by renaming themselves the Fancy Goods and Allied Trades Association. Externally, their position was increasingly undermined by the growing tendency among manufacturers to deal direct with the retailers. Firms like Lines Brothers and Meccano had always eschewed the middlemen and their success encouraged others to adopt similar strategies. Cascelloid decided to go direct to the retailers in 1933, for example. By 1938 only about a quarter of retail sales were of goods supplied by the producer via a wholesaler; three-quarters went direct to the shops from importers or manufacturers.

Although the manufacturers were thus able to bypass the wholesalers and increasingly able to impose their will on the retailers, their own association was not without its problems either. In part, these sprang from a fierce independence which militated against cooperation at anything other than the most general level, for example in the establishment of a press committee to handle publicity for the industry in 1937. It was perhaps natural that firms should wish to protect trade secrets. Britains eliminated a paragraph from a 1926 report on the trade because it revealed details of how they packaged their models. 'We particularly do not wish this to appear.' Another company removed information about its method of maximising the use of material in the cutting out of soft toy patterns.[89] This was in marked contrast to the American toy industry in which, it was observed by a British delegation, trade secrets had virtually disappeared.[90] The *Toy Trader* was sounding a forlorn note in urging British manufacturers to adopt the sort of cooperative approach that had allowed American manufacturers to undertake joint advertising schemes, and which later underpinned a national scheme to encourage toy buying throughout the year. People in the trade, argued the paper, should think imperially rather than personally.[91]

When scope for effective joint action did appear, the response was often lukewarm. Very few manufacturers supported the corporate approach made to the Australian Tariff Board to get the 1930 duties lowered. There was an equally lethargic response when the matter of the merchandise marks application was first mooted in 1929. The campaign may have been ultimately successful but it was widely remarked that neither Meccano nor Britains had actively supported it. As chairman, Walter Lines did his best, reviving the annual dinner in 1928, but by 1934 the *Toy Trader* was damning the manufacturers' association as 'practically moribund'.[92] A. J. Wells admitted as much when he was elected chairman in the same year. 'Frankly, I am not satisfied that the Association is anything like as strong and important as it ought to be.'[93] With attendance at meetings averaging about twenty, membership down to about a hundred by 1935 and even major companies like Chad Valley remaining aloof, his dissatisfaction was well founded.

Nor did things improve very much from the manufacturers' point of view as the 1930s drew to a close amidst growing portents of economic and international gloom. Labour costs were rising. The advent of paid holidays in 1939 was one cause of increased expenditure. With a relatively high proportion of juveniles in its labour force, the toy industry was also particularly vulnerable to new factory legislation reducing young peoples' working hours from forty-eight to forty-four a week. Adult wages were also going up. Although the trade board had been twice reconstituted in January 1931 and August 1933, the full board did not meet at all between April 1930 and May 1935. By 1937, however, the workers' side was pressing for increases. The employers pointed out that, unlike their counterparts on other boards, they had not asked for reductions during the slump. They also argued that the cost of living was now lower than when the current rates were fixed. But the workers' case was a strong one, for women were receiving virtually the same rate as they had when the board had first been established. More generally, all toy rates were low in comparison with those of other boards and the armaments boom was making it difficult to get labour. This was sufficient to win an increase, thereby raising the manufacturers' costs.[94]

The appeal to the impact of rearmament was timely, for it was creating difficulties of material supply as well. A special meeting of toy manufacturers was convened in 1937 to discuss the impact of rising steel prices. One manufacturer was justifiably annoyed at having placed an advanced bulk order, then having been told that he could not have it unless he paid the higher price which it had now reached. With rising labour costs, signs of a slow-down in the domestic recovery, the continued existence of tariff barriers in overseas markets, and the trade federation weak and disunited, the outlook for the manufacturers was not encouraging. The Manchester fortnight in the summer of 1938 was said to be the worst for thirty years. The *Toy Trader* was unsure whether this was due to the recent rise in income tax or to the deteriorating international situation.[95] Either way barely a year elapsed before Britain was once more at war with Germany.

By contrast with 1914, the declaration of hostilities in September 1939 came as no great surprise. It had been widely expected for some time and this, combined with a determination to learn from the earlier conflict, ensured that government was far better prepared for the economic exigencies of modern warfare. Intervention was both swift and wide-reaching as government sought to divert resources away from consumer industries towards the war effort. Toy imports were promptly banned and the disappearance of £3,000,000 worth of German goods from the domestic market appeared to provide a golden opportunity for British manufacturers. It was not one which they were able to exploit, although several received inquiries from importers formerly supplied by German producers. The production of playing cards and board games for the armed forces was encouraged but the Government initially limited the manufacturers' toy sales to two-thirds of their peace time levels. In June 1940 the Limitation of Supplies (Miscellaneous) Order was utilised in order to restrict retail sales. Shortly afterwards toys were subjected to Purchase Tax, and at the end of the year the sales quota was reduced again, this time to a quarter of the prewar level. This was a staggering blow, which, it was suggested, none but the biggest firms could survive.[96] Such constraints on home sales were designed to push the industry's output into the export market. By the spring of 1940 the Export Council had been charged with coordinating the national effort through the medium of trade associations; in recognition of the urgency of the task the *Toy Trader* extended its title to include the words *and Exporter*.

The toy export group consisted of three manufacturers, Walter Lines, Fred Britain and A. W. J. Wells, while J. D. Kiley and Leon Rees represented the merchants. Theirs was not an easy task. For one thing, the relative indifference which the majority of firms had exhibited towards exports in the 1920s had been reinforced by the advent of a protected and prosperous home market in the 1930s. Protection, the *Toy Trader* had warned in February 1933 was making British firms too complacent, causing them to devote too much effort to existing markets and neglecting opportunities to broaden the market or to increase the total amount of sales.[97] Although exports picked up after 1934, they never regained the heights of the 1920s (Table 22). The appeal of the domestic markets was further enhanced in the 1930s by the restrictive international trading climate which made exporting even more difficult. Voluminous correspondence was necessary to export to Denmark, Norwegian tariffs were levied by the kilo and included the weight of the packing cases; fluctuations in the value of the franc made exports to France uncertain and the American market remained heavily protected. It was hardly surprising, perhaps, that when Wells had tried to float a scheme for a Toy Export Association, at a meeting held to coincide with the 1932 British Industries Fair, it had been sparsely attended and the matter adjourned.

The emergency of war caused further dislocations in the normal workings of the economy. For a while, during the brief period of the so called Phoney War, the toy trade tried to carry on as normal, despite the closure of the European markets. As late as June 1940 new firms were still being registered while others held displays in Manchester, even though both the traditional show and the British Industries Fair were cancelled. But production, even for export, was not easy. Firms with their own transport had it requisitioned for national use once the

war broke out. Labour costs rose when toy workers' rates were brought
into line with those of other trade board industries, while overheads
were further increased by the high cost of war insurance. Above all,
there were problems with supplies of raw materials and packaging, a
major cause of price rises when the war began. Meccano's mechanised
army set, for example, had gone up from 10s. 6d. to 12s. 6d. by January
1940. The following November it cost 17s. 9d. in the shops. Such
increases naturally attracted adverse comment but Walter Lines spoke
out strongly in defence of the industry (and himself) at a meeting of
manufacturers in October 1939. It was unrealistic, he argued, to expect
his firm to honour price agreements with retailers when his own materials suppliers had halted deliveries. His firm's recent price increases,
he added, had been accepted by nearly all his customers. Initially, too,
the Board of Trade seemed more willing to listen to the manufacturers
than it had been in the course of the First World War. Certainly it
accepted the argument advanced by trade representatives that in 1914–
18 large numbers of firms had entered the manufacturing trade, greatly
adding to the problem of raw material shortages. Accordingly, the board
acceded to their request that available raw material should be released
only to existing firms. Certainly this policy was followed when in May
1940 Walter Lines pursuaded the board to increase the quantity of iron
and steel allocated to the industry. Despite all the difficulties, it was
claimed that by August 1941 more than 80 per cent of output was being
exported.[98]

As the prospects for national survival grew ever darker in the first
half of 1941, so toys appeared increasingly irrelevant and their production a waste of vital manufacturing potential. The industry was one
of fifteen scheduled by the Board of Trade for a scheme of concentration
under which companies could combine to rationalise productive capacity. The majority of businesses would close down, transferring production to one of about twenty nucleus firm while leaving their own plant
intact. The nucleus firms were then to receive preferential treatment
as regards labour supply, government orders, the supply of raw materials, if possible, and a guarantee against requisitioning. Walter Lines
did not like this proposal, arguing that toy production was too scattered
and also too diverse because it used at least twelve major materials. In
any case, he added, there would be no saving of labour since most of
those working in the industry currently were either too young or old
for war work. Indeed, many of the major firms had been progressively
switching to war work anyway. Cascelloid reported a record trading
profit in 1940 but 'the Board has had to revise the nature of the

products of the factories so as to make the fullest contribution to the country's needs in the present emergency'.[99] Bassett Lowke was quite quickly engaged in making training models for the Admiralty and scaled-down versions of war equipment such as Bailey Bridges and the Mulberry Harbour so crucial to the success of the Normandy invasions in 1944. Britains continued to make some toys until 1941 but staff and other shortages made it necessary to reduce both the range and variety of production. By 1942 the company's factories were retooled for munitions and being targeted by the Luftwaffe.

The process of running down the industry was hastened by successive restrictions on raw materials. Quite suddenly and with no prior consultation the supply of metal toys was banned at the beginning of 1942. Meccano, by now mainly engaged on war work, managed to produce a few construction sets by utilising old stock. This ban was followed in August by a further embargo on the production of toys containing more than 10 per cent weight of metal, and also on those made of cork, kapok, hemp, celluloid and other plastics. Rubber was added to the list at the end of the year by which time the industry's production quota was down to 7.5 per cent of the amount made in the year ending 31 May 1941. With the additional price controls imposed in January 1942, large-scale toy production had been reduced to a trickle by the middle of the year and exports fell away dramatically (Table 34).

Table 34
British Toy Exports, 1940–44[100]

	£		£
1940	441,235	1943	83,344
1941	653,889	1944	46,445
1942	199,250		

There were only about twenty exhibitors at Manchester in July 1942, which the *Toy Trader and Exporter* expected would be the last such exhibition while hostilities continued.[101] This was perhaps just as well, given that the distribution side of the trade had been caught in the Blitz. A raid in February 1941 devastated Houndsditch and Moorgate, the traditional London centre of the toy business, so thoroughly that thirty-five companies, mainly wholesalers, had to find new accommodation.

As far as the home market was concerned there was always a certain ambivalence in the government's position. In the eyes of those charged with manpower planning toys were clearly not strategic, diverting labour and material away from other more immediate purposes. As one MP put it rather sinisterly in 1942, when a colleague raised the matter of the current shortage of summer toys, it was surely to the national advantage that the only spades manufactured 'should be for agricultural purposes and grave diggers'.[102] On the other hand, the work of educationalists such as Susan Isaacs and the Abbatts in the 1930s had done much to convince others, especially those in the Ministries of Health and of Education, that toys were vital to the well-being of children. Furthermore, like the appearance of scarce foodstuffs, their availability had a certain value in sustaining civilian morale. As a result it was never really clear whether toys were to be regarded as essential or not.

In the interests of morale the Board of Trade adopted a policy of temporarily increasing the production quota in the run up to Christmas. The general public was thus encouraged to expect supplies in the shops. The manufacturers, however, were rarely given enough notice to allow them to make the necessary adjustments in their production schedules. An added twist was provided by the fact that some of the restrictions were not applied universally, leaving some latitude for small manufacturers to continue with production. For example, the production quota was not applied to small makers, who were allowed to turn out £100 worth of toys a month so long as their annual production did not exceed £500. Again, the implementation of the 1942 ban on certain raw materials was delayed by several months for firms with less than five employees. It became a matter of some concern to trade representatives that this sort of policy encouraged the back-street manufacture of toys by inexperienced individuals, often using waste or even purloined raw materials.[103] The shoddiness of the results rather unjustly generated considerable public discontent with the major manufacturers, who were already in bad odour for failing to supply the Christmas toys promised by the Board of Trade. Nor were the manufacturers universally popular for trying to stop these 'amateur toys' from reaching the shops. For retailers, the source of supply was less important than the fact of supply, several pointing out that the black market makers were satisfying a public need.[104] The *Daily Worker* was upset when the manufacturers succeeded in securing an official ban on the manufacture of toys by firemen and civil defence personnel, who had tried to sell them on a commercial basis. This, said the *Daily Worker*, was another example of monopolistic manufacturers trying to corner the market, although the paper's concern was probably prompted in the main by the strong influence of the Communist Party in the Fire Brigades Union.[105]

The black market in toys was never totally eradicated but became steadily less significant as the turning tide of battle facilitated a less parsimonious official attitude towards peripheral parts of the economy. In 1944 toy production quotas were raised and thoughts began to turn once more to the future. For the toy trade, one line of future development was already emerging with the establishment of a new manufacturers' organisation. As early as 1941 the old association had discussed such a move, influential figures like Walter Lines arguing that it was inequitable for the manufacturers to pay five-sixths of the subscriptions to the federation but to have only an equal say with the Fancy Goods and Allied Trades Association. In March Leon Rees, president of the federation, offered to change its constitution so that manufacturers got the bulk of places on the council. Lines' dominance was such that in his absence the manufacturers decided against making an immediate response. Subsequently he made it clear that he would accept only an arrangement that gave the manufacturers total control. Although the matter was then left in abeyance, it is clear that Lines had the bit between his teeth. In June 1944 the motion was put by the chairman, Alec Bangham, to launch a new association 'in no way connected with any Wholesale or Retail Toy Association', because, it was claimed, the connection with the Toy and Fancy Goods Federation had not been in the best interests of the manufacturers.[106] When federation secretary B. G. Arthur objected on procedural grounds he was overruled, as was another member who attempted to get the vote deferred. Support for the motion was unanimous. A month later the decision was confirmed at an extraordinary general meeting. Thus restructured, the toy men turned their thoughts to the imminent prospect of peace.

Chapter 6

Middle Age Spread and Hardening Arteries, 1945–1970

The restoration of peace, first in Europe and then in the Far East, left Britain unbowed and unbeaten. It also left her broke, saved in the short term only by the provision of an American loan. Financial constraints, therefore, made exports a priority. There was the added incentive, too, that as a victorious nation Britain was virtually the only non-dollar country with a significant manufacturing capacity in a world where dollars were at a premium. At home military victory combined with the government's own propaganda to create popular expectations that were unrealistic. A sellers' market thus beckoned for those industries whose products had been largely denied to the public during the six years of war. Sentiment, if nothing else, suggested that children should be among the first beneficiaries of greater consumer choice. The prospects for British toy manufacturers were further enhanced by the unparalleled degrees of physical destruction visited upon two major prewar rivals, Germany and Japan. The priorities of Nazi economic policy had adversely affected German toy production as early as 1933 but a small output had been maintained until 1944, after which deterioration was rapid. All told, about 40 per cent of the industry's factory buildings and 10 per cent of its plant were destroyed. Nuremberg, the traditional centre of the German industry, had suffered particularly badly from Allied bombing. Even two years after the war, a British Intelligence Service Sub-Committee found that only a third of the thirty toy firms in the city had resumed operations. Among the thirty-four companies visited in other locations was the Rheinische Gummi and Celluloid Fabrik, a large organisation formerly attached to I. G. Farben. Its workforce was less than a fifth of what it had been in 1939.[1]

It was only natural that such favourable auguries should entice into the British toy business many newcomers in a replay of the pattern that

The British Toy Business

had emerged after the First World War. Company formation was, of course, a continuous process and some new firms like Timpo turned to toy manufacture even before hostilities ended. The peak of postwar activity was reached in 1946 when 216 new companies were established (Table 35).

Table 35
New Toy Company Formation[2]

	1944	1945	1946	1947
January			16	35
February	9	8	14	17
March		10	9	
April	6	6	20	11
May		8	19	10
June		10	15	23
July		9	32	
August		6	32	16
September		9	18	12
October	10	13	19	11
November	5	8	22	13
December	9	16		
Total	39	103	216	148

Not all were strictly new ventures. Among those listed for October 1946, for example, was John Hill and Company (Metal Toys) Ltd, turning the long-established producer of Johillco metal figures into a limited liability company. The previous month's registrations included Lines Bros (Ireland) Ltd and Lines Brothers (South Wales) Ltd. Merit Toys, established in 1947 by J. and L. Randall, was a new entity but replaced their earlier company which had been bombed out during the war. Nor were all of those listed in Table 35 manufacturers, for they included a number of retail and distribution firms, often established by ex-servicemen. However, as the *Toy Trader and Exporter* observed, 'there is an ever growing army of people who are forming companies with the object of manufacturing various classes of toys'.[3]

Some, like Wendy Boston, were founding businesses that were to become highly successful. Her career began when her unemployed husband sold a selection of homemade soft toys to a Cardiff department store. Subsequently, the company was among the first to spot the potential of nylon plush and also went on to patent a screw-locking eye. Lesney, destined to achieve fame as the maker of the Matchbox range of miniature vehicles, was established in 1947 by John Odell and Leslie Smith with their demobilisation gratuities. Poplar Plastics began in 1945 as a one-man operation run by Major E. W. Jones, while Cherilea started production in 1948 at Blackpool. Dekker, another firm started on the strength of a demobilisation gratuity, began making play-suits and wendy houses in 1946.

Although the plant and capital requirements of such businesses were usually quite small, suitable accommodation was sometimes more of a problem, given the continued existence of building controls and a shortage of premises. Green Monk Products, for example, began life in an old church school at Monk Bretton in 1945. The experience of John Plummer's company was fairly typical of the shoestring operations that characterised many of the new postwar manufacturers. Following an initial success in selling some soft toys from premises in Worthing which cost £50 to convert, the Plummers launched Tinka-Bell toys in April 1946 on a capital of £200. With this they purchased twenty-five sheepskins, a hundredweight of flock filling, glass eyes at 12s. a gross, needles and thread, placed advertisements for outworkers, and paid their small workforce. The company soon reached its maximum per-mitted turnover of £3600 and by 1958 it employed sixteen factory staff and between thirty-five and seventy outworkers on twenty-four different lines.[4]

Tinka-Bell, Dekker, Lesney, Wendy Boston and a handful of other postwar companies all became success stories, but as small enterprises they could not hope to meet the high level of demand prevalent immediately after the war. That depended on the resumption of pro-duction by the major firms, most of whom had been diverted to war work. The situation, said the BTMA's first annual report in 1945,

> cannot be remedied until the prewar established manufacturers are able to change over from war work to normal production with facilities for materials and the employment of skilled labour and with freedom from such crippling restrictions as the low price ceiling and the purchase tax. Our paramount consideration is the winning of the war.[5]

The war over, however, the giants of the toy industry were able to begin the process of reverting to peace time production patterns, although this was not particularly straightforward. Some of them were hampered by an initial shortage of specialist machinery, Germany no longer being in a position to supply it. Plastics manufacturers like Airfix were able to obtain appropriate plant, however, as was Sebel and Co., based at Erith in Kent. For £100,000 the company bought the local Vickers

Armstrong factory to make pressed steel toys. When it opened at the end of 1947, it incorporated a bonderising plant, a 500 ton capacity steel press and the latest spray painting equipment. More common, however, was the contrasting experience of J. G. Thomas who joined Meccano in 1948 to discover that much of the equipment in use (and indeed the works manager) dated from before the First World War.[6]

Secondly, there was a scarcity of factory space which, combined with building controls and a general government desire to influence the distribution of employment, led many firms to relocate. In October 1947 Cascelloid opened a new factory at Coalville, formerly used for making aeroplane parts. By the end of 1949 it was providing doll making work for 300 employees, most of them women. Mettoy, which in 1939 had employed a similar number to make metal toys in Northampton, moved to Swansea during the war in order to produce ammunition. By the autumn of 1947 the Swansea plant was back in toy production, and two years later the company opened a new factory incorporating internal conveyors and new spray paint machines. Near neighbours included Louis Marx, the subsidiary of Marx Inc. of New York, which moved to Swansea from Dudley in 1946; Crescent Toys which followed Marx to Wales in 1949 and had 190 employees by November 1950; Poplar Plastics with 110 workers; and Chiltern Toys which opened a new factory in Wales at the end of 1947, providing work for another 300 people by the end of 1950. Lines Brothers, too, set up in Wales, at Merthyr Tydfil, when planning permission for expansion at Merton was turned down in 1946. The same company also opened a new manufacturing facility in Belfast.

The net result of these postwar developments was a dramatic increase in the size of Britain's toy making labour force, which more than quadrupled between 1945 and 1958 (Table 36).

Table 36

Employment in the British Toy Industry[7]

	Male	Female	Total
August 1945			7,100
July 1946			20,700
June 1948	11,270	15,680	26,950
May 1951	12,220	20,510	32,730
May 1952	10,160	16,860	27,020
May 1958	11,430	18,770	30,200

Total production also picked up quite rapidly and the 1951 Census of Production recorded a gross output worth more than £25,000,000 (Table 37).

Table 37
British Toys: Gross Output in Selected Years, 1924–68[8]

Year	Value £	Year	Value £
1924	1,500,000	1951	25,100,000
1930	2,000,000	1954	31,500,000
1935	3,100,000	1958	50,500,000
1937	3,600,000	1963	72,000,000
1948	19,200,000	1968	120,300,000

In money terms this was an increase of over 800 per cent on 1935, and rather more that 400 per cent in real terms. Company profits in the immediate postwar years appeared healthy. Between 1945 and 1946 Cascelloid's trade profit went up by almost 350 per cent, net profit by more than 500 per cent. Lines Brothers' 1945 net profit of £51,679 was up on its previous year. Tan-Sad's annual trading profits averaged £26,000 between 1937 and 1947, but reached £69,471 in 1950 before falling back in 1951 to £44,666 under the impact of material shortages caused by the Korean War.[9] Sebel's net profits rose from £64,179 in 1946 to £87,558 in 1947, and £107,849 in 1948. Chad Valley, which became a public company in 1950, reported a post-tax profit of £108,643 at its first annual general meeting in 1951, an improvement of about 10 per cent over the previous financial year.

These were creditable achievements, given the many difficulties under which the postwar industry laboured. For one thing, the manufacturers were correct in anticipating that they would face escalating wage demands. In submitting a claim even before the war ended the leader of the workers' side on the trade board, Dorothy Elliott, urged that

in view of the great importance attached by the Government to the development of the export trade in the post war period . . . in order to play its part the toy trade should offer wages comparable with those paid in other industries so as to attract the right type of worker.[10]

The demand for an extra twopence an hour was settled at three farthings but the following spring the BTMA decided unanimously that, whatever arguments were put forward for any further increase, 'there must be a firm stand to say NO'.[11] Their resolution was broken, however, when the trade board was restructured as a wages council. The new panel of independent members, which included an Oxford don as chairman and also the Principal of the Dundee School of Economics, proved to be persistently more favourable to the employees than their predecessors on the old trade board had been.[12] In September 1947 the wages council reduced the working week from 48 to 45 hours with no corresponding reduction in pay and also recommended the introduction of annual paid holidays.

Secondly, the new Labour Government was not minded to dispense too swiftly with the plethora of economic regulations inherited from the war years. In part this was a matter of ideology, for they apparently provided a means by which the party's collectivist vision might be realised. It also sprang from a determination not to repeat the mistakes of the 1920s, when disaster had followed the overhasty abandonment of wartime economic controls. Although the ceilings on both manufacturers' and retailers' prices were abolished early in 1946, other prices on toys and games were not decontrolled until July 1949. Toys' liability to purchase tax remained a more permanent problem. The tax was constantly subject to budgetary manipulation by government. It was increased in November 1947 from 33.3 to 50 per cent, then reduced again in the following year's budget. Such variations gave particular problems to the toy manufacturers, who needed to receive orders early if they were to meet agreed delivery dates in time for the following Christmas. Yet rumours of likely purchase tax reductions made buyers wary of placing orders before the annual budget statement was presented in March. The BTMA made a number of unsuccessful representations to government on this matter, asking for rate adjustments to be announced in January.

As first chairman of the new BTMA, Alec Bangham enunciated a six-point plan which included the abolition of all government controls but the process was a drawn out one, taking three years, for example, in the case of the quota on domestic production. This had been gradually eased as the war drew to a close. In the first half of 1944 the maximum toy output allowable was set at 12.5 per cent of the 1939–40 level. It was raised to 25 per cent in February 1945. The following August the annual limit was raised to 37.5 per cent, and a year later it went up again to 66.66 per cent. In July 1948 the Limitation of Supplies (Toy and Indoor Games) Order was ended, freeing registered persons from any home production quotas. Controls on materials remained in place, however, and A. J. Wells described the more generous production quotas as 'silly and meaningless . . . The Board of Trade says we can make more toys, but it does not say how we can get the materials'. The only people to benefit, he concluded, would be the amateurs, making 'shoddy toys from odd scraps of material and selling at ridiculous prices'.[13] In effect, all relaxations of the quota tended to be counterproductive for the trade, generating expectations on the part of the public that the manufacturers could not satisfy because of shortages in the supply of labour and raw materials.

Although some materials were being released before the war ended, Britain's position as a major military power and the uncertainties of the international situation, shown in the Berlin Airlift of 1947 and then the outbreak of hostilities in Korea in June 1950, ensured that strategic considerations would continue to govern their allocation. Low-grade rubber was made available for toy production late in 1944 and a few months later the ban on toys containing more than 10 per cent of metal was rescinded. In August 1945 plastics were released for toy manufacture but only within the limits of their availability. Therein was the problem, for the toy industry had to compete with every other in the scramble for materials. Thus lead, vital to makers of metal goods like Britains, was released in unrestricted quantities from August 1945 but the manufacturers still had to obtain raw material licences, and supplies were soon rationed again when the house building programme was given priority. Paper, board and hardboard were decontrolled by May 1949, but steel, softwood and plywood were still scarce, although timber supplies improved somewhat after the conclusion of a trade deal with the USSR. British involvement in Korea resulted in shortages of steel and new controls on brass and zinc. As a consequence, both Marx and Lines Brothers were driven to lay workers off from their south Wales factories in December 1950.

Raw material rationing also threatened the industry's ability to meet its export target, set in July 1945 at 20 per cent of total production. Having agreed this figure with the BTMA, the Board of Trade did do its best to facilitate it. Some vital commodities, particularly tin plate, were made available only to firms making for the overseas market, while export licences for toys made of wood, metal, paper, rubber and plastic were abandoned in November 1945, although they were still required for some categories of soft toys. To some extent it was possible to get round restrictions and shortages by the constructive deployment of substitute materials, aluminium for steel, cotton waste and leather instead of plush, for example. There was also a greater utilisation of plastic, although the latter was not particularly suitable for exports to the dollar area as both the United States and Canada already had large outputs of plastic toys themselves. Apart from raw material shortages and rising wages, shipping space was scarce, even if export licences could be obtained – and the *Toy Trader and Exporter* cynically suggested that the word 'licence' was Greek for unobtainable.[14] In any case former customers, often short of sterling, were either developing their own industries or protecting existing ones behind tariff and quota barriers.

These specific difficulties were compounded by general production problems arising from the hard winter of 1947–48 and the fuel shortage. These coincided with the financial crisis brought about when sterling was made freely convertible again in 1947, leading to a huge outflow of dollars from Britain. With a deteriorating economic situation, the industry's monthly export quota for the year from March 1948 was fixed at £420,000, well up on the average monthly figure actually achieved in 1947, when total exports were slightly more than £3,000,000. In response the BTMA set up an export group from representatives of the major companies, which accounted for the bulk of exports, although it was later expanded to include smaller producers and wholesalers whose assistance in meeting the export target was necessary. The Geneva Agreement in late 1947 entailed some small reductions of American tariffs and the cutting of some imperial preferences as part of the effort to increase Britain's dollar earnings through increased sales to the United States. As a result, British toy exports to America quadrupled in 1948, making her America's most important foreign toy supplier. This was no mean achievement in view of the fiercely nationalistic policies pursued by the American industry. Although tariffs had been reduced, no foreign advertisements were accepted by the main trade journal and overseas exhibitors were banned from the New York Toy Fair.

The monthly export goal of £420,00 was in fact reached only once. When the American economy went into recession in 1949, depressing British toy sales, the target figure was reduced to £350,000. This was slightly more realistic, given that between May 1946 and April 1948 total toy exports were worth £7,190,300, or just under £300,000 a month. Despite a total ban on imports imposed by South Africa, still a major British export market, and despite troubles in the Middle East, the Korean War, and strikes in USA and Australia, aggregate exports reached an all-time peak in 1951 of £6,850,000.[15] This represented a doubling since 1948, although Swinburne Johnson, chairman of the BTMA, blithely ignored the fact that much of this was due to a 30 per cent devaluation of sterling in September 1949. 'During the last five or six years', he trumpeted, 'British-made toys have established a name and position for themselves all over the world, and this reputation is going to help carry them forward to still greater things.'[16]

His hyperbole faithfully reflected the self-congratulatory mood in which the toy industry entered the new decade. By the early 1950s the general consensus was that the postwar era of poor but expensive toys was over. *The Times* reckoned that Christmas 1952 promised to be the best since the war.[17] After several years of austerity the big department stores at last assumed an air of relative opulence and at least one major London retailer had a Christmas Toy Fair that recovered some of its prewar zest, displaying a much wider range of goods than at any time since 1945.[18] Ninety per cent of the toys being sold were indigenous products and Britain, *The Times* averred, was 'entitled to regard herself as the world's foremost toy factory' because she currently exported more than anyone else.[19] A favourable budget in 1953 took sixpence off income tax, made a substantial reduction in the purchase tax on toys, and abolished excess profits duty. It was hailed by the trade as the best budget since 1934 and facilitated a second successive bumper Christmas for retailers.[20]

This sense of well-being persisted throughout the 1950s, disturbed only by the occasional hiccup. The 80 per cent reduction in toy imports imposed by the Australians in 1952 proved to be merely a temporary set-back. So, too, did the dock strike of 1954 which hit Christmas exports so badly that Lines Brothers closed down their export-packing department and Chad Valley claimed that 20 per cent of its business was in jeopardy.[21] For the most part, however, the industry benefited from the growing domestic prosperity associated with the long postwar boom. Personal disposable income was growing at about 2.2 per cent a year between 1948 and 1958.[22] At current manufacturers' prices the British toy market, worth £2,500,000 in 1938, had expanded to £21,000,000 by 1954 and £27,000,000 by 1957.[23] It was estimated that by 1956 £19 11s. 0d. was spent each year on entertaining the average child between the ages of two and fourteen. Of this £6 went on toys.[24] Although the proportion of the population under the age of fourteen was only 22.2 per cent by 1951 compared with 32.4 per cent fifty years before, virtually all of those in the twelve- to fourteen-year-old bracket were still at school in 1961, and thus perhaps legitimately regarded as children. This compared with only 41.5 per cent of that group who had stayed on at school in 1900.[25]

Mean family size was also falling, which implied less reliance on passed down toys. Marriages contracted between 1931 and 1935 produced an average of 2.56 children each. Those taking place between 1941 and 1944, and between 1951 and 1955, had 2.13 and 2.28 children respectively.[26] The only countervailing factor to these favourable market developments for toy manufacturers was the changing parameter of childhood, caused by the backward extension of adolescence. The BBC's decision to axe its long-established daily Children's Hour programme was one manifestation of this trend. Another was the ballot organised by the Boy Scout Association on whether it should abandon its traditional uniform shorts because they were too redolent of childhood. Similarly, there was a growing tendency for the foundation garment industry to target pre-pubescent girls.

Even these changes, however, acted as a positive stimulus to some toymakers, encouraging the production of toys that were more consciously educational, technical, collectable, or more readily identifiable with adolescence. In 1962 Lines Brothers' subsidiary, the Pedigree Doll Company, sought to link the child with the adolescent by means of a new teenage doll, Sindy. Her carefully moulded and obviously feminine figure represented an outstanding thrust against all previous conventions of British doll design, although the trail had been pioneered by Jack Ryan's Barbie, sold from the late 1950s by the American firm, Mattel. Lines also encouraged International Model Aircraft to experiment with radio-controlled aeroplanes, and took over Rovex in order to gain access to its promising slot car racing system, Scalextric, a toy designed to appeal to older boys by exploiting the contemporary success of British motor racing drivers.

Model vehicles were among the most sought after collectables during the 1950s. Lesney capitalised on the 1953 coronation by producing a miniature of the coronation coach, small enough to fit in a matchbox. It proved enormously popular, selling a million at a retail price of 2s. 11d. It provided the inspiration for the infinitely extendable Matchbox range of vehicles. Lesney grew so rapidly that when it became a public company in 1959, offering 400,000 five shilling shares at one pound each, the offer was oversubscribed fifteen times. Playcraft's Corgi vehicles were equally collectable, being the first to incorporate windscreens and windows, and then in 1959 fully-fitted interiors. Plastic construction kits of ships, aircraft, cars, fighting vehicles, soldiers and historical figures also had a wide appeal to both adults and children, especially boys, whether their interests were primarily in technology, history, or warfare.

In the course of the 1950s British firms also made great strides in the use of plastic as a manufacturing medium, often pushed to do so by the scarcity or cost of more traditional materials. When Die Casting Machine Tools of Palmers Green found metal supplies difficult to obtain for their well-known brand of Lone Star toy guns, for example, they turned instead to plastic. With very few exceptions no serious attempts had been made by toy firms to utilise plastics before the war, even though one expert had suggested that there was likely to be 'most promising future' for 'a carefully designed mouldable interlocking brick'.[27] In fact an interlocking rubber brick, made by the Premo Rubber Company, had been on the market since the early 1930s. Hilary Page of Kiddicraft patented a studded plastic version in 1947, and successfully defended his patent against a British infringement in 1950.[28] Initially, manufacturers tended to be suspicious of plastic because it was associated with cheap (and often inflammable) goods imported from the Far East, but the newer varieties of plastics that were developed after the war had many advantages. They held colour, were washable, hard-wearing, light, flexible and adaptable. Such characteristics, coupled with growing concerns about the potential health hazard of lead, initiated a slow shift to plastic among toy soldier manufacturers. Britains, for instance, bought control of one of the best of the plastic figure companies, Herald Miniatures, in 1955. The late 1950s also saw the widespread adoption of large injection-moulding machines able to produce toys capable of bearing a child's weight. This considerably reduced the cost of big plastic toys since they now needed neither tooling nor cement. This gave an added boost to the growing market for nursery toys. Model railways were also revolutionised because what had previously been hand-made in metal could now be accurately mass produced in new types of durable plastic. So rapid was the adoption of the new material that by 1960 plastic accounted for 33 per cent of all domestic toy sales.[29]

By 1960 Britain's 350 toy factories had an annual turnover of £36,000,000 while retail sales were worth £85,000,000. Three years later the Census of Production recorded a gross output of £72,000,000, produced by 38,400 employees. Exports showed a similar upward trend, reaching almost £7,500,000 by 1960 (Table 38). At the level of the individual firm some notable export successes were recorded. By the early 1950s Tan-Sad was selling to more than fifty countries. Rosebud's new doll factory was the largest in Europe, turning out 10,000,000 dolls a year which were exported to seventy-two countries. The soft toy makers Farnell opened new a factory in 1959, by which date it was sending 40 per cent of its output overseas. Britains' toy soldiers and die-cast vehicles also made an important contribution to exports, especially in the American market. So, too, did the Mobo toys made by Sebels, and Lesney's Matchbox vehicles, 4,000,000 of which were sold to America in 1959. All told, there was much to justify the self-congratulatory prognostications with which Swinburne Johnson had welcomed the end of postwar austerity.

Table 38
British Toy Exports, 1946–60[30]

	Total £	Destination		
		Commonwealth and Eire %	USA %	Europe %
1946	2,080,854	72.75	4.2	
1947	3,052,687	74.83	2.1	
1948	3,383,802	65.02	6.7	
1949	3,623,837	68.65	5.4	
1950	5,347,363	62.21	10.5	
1951	6,846,058	62.91	7.0	
1952	4,973,289	60.95	10.9	
1953	4,307,161	57.12	13.0	
1954	5,930,278	67.38	8.0	
1955	6,292,227	68.03	7.6	16.3
1956	6,312,288	59.79	10.2	21.2
1957	6,699,100	57.30	8.2	24.1
1958	6,957,090	57.50	9.3	24.7
1959	6,817,210	54.94	12.2	24.0
1960	7,419,099	55.14	9.9	28.9

By the end of the decade, however, it had also become apparent that the relative position of the British toy industry was slipping. By 1962 both Germany and Japan had joined America ahead of Britain in terms of total production, although in Germany's case this might simply be viewed as the restoration of the traditional prewar position. More significantly, despite the increased overseas sales of British toys prompted by the massive expansion in world trade, the industry's export performance had declined steadily since the postwar peak of 1951 (Table 39).

Table 39

GB Toy Exports as Percentage of Production, 1923–60[31]

	Of Gross Production	Of Net Production
1924	36.0	
1930	27.0	
1935	13.5	
1949	17.6	37.8
1951	27.1	58.6
1954	18.7	39.5
1958	13.7	29.5
1960		22.8

In 1960 exports represented about the same proportion of output as they had in the mid 1930s. Overseas sales of just under £5,000,000 had been enough to make Britain the world's leading toy exporter in 1952 but a decade later she had dropped to fourth place (Table 40).

Table 40

Toy Exports as Percentage of Net Production, 1962[32]

Country	%
Japan	62.7
Germany	35.5
Italy	34.6
GB	26.2
France	16.0
USA	2.2

This, of course, was part of a more general economic retardation that first began to attract the concern of commentators during the 1950s. Although the value of exports rose fairly steadily, especially in the second half of the decade, the toy industry appeared to be as unable to raise its export profile as most other sectors of British manufacturing industry. Why was this?

Issues of prices, costs and labour efficiency are relevant here, but the dearth of appropriate statistical information makes firm conclusions difficult. Taxation took £74,555 of Chad Valley's £117,793 trading profit in 1951, when the company chairman complained that such a large bill was 'too heavy a drain on the liquid resources of a manu-facturing company to provide new plant and machinery'.[33] This was a common theme among contemporary toy executives. Walter Lines used it to explain why his 1951 increase in trading profit had not been reflected in the net figure. The following year Sebel's managing director also argued that heavy taxation 'represents a severe drain on our cash resources'.[34] Such comments tended to become less frequent after 1952 and there is no real evidence to support the implication that the British industry became less competitive through any overall lack of capital investment.[35]

It is possible that persistent inflation in the 1950s caused British prices to get out of line with those of some of her competitors. Between 1947 and 1955 the cost of a box of tin plate rose 45 per cent, Thames board by 41 per cent, while lead increased from £68 17s. 6d. to £118 0s 0d. a ton: a rise of more than 70 per cent.[36] In so far as such rising costs were not experienced by other countries they obviously placed British manufacturers at a price disadvantage. Employers, however, were more inclined to link export difficulties with labour costs. Swinburne Johnson of Chad Valley took the view that the British would never be able to compete successfully in Europe because workers aspired to a higher standard of living than they actually worked for. Arthur Katz of Mettoy disagreed with this conclusion, though he did believe that the Germans could cut down on supervisory staff because their workers did what they were paid to do conscientiously and without supervision.[37] Toy chiefs complained frequently about labour shortages and the high wages expected even by junior workers for doing very little. Wages were thus very difficult to hold down, particularly as the independent members on the Wages Council were more influenced by the workers' rising cost of living than by manufacturers' costs.

In 1952 the workers' side put in a claim for a pay rise and increased holiday entitlement which, it was calculated, would cost the industry an extra £727,000 annually. Not surprisingly, some members of the BTMA council wanted to know how this sort of cost could be reconciled with the task of increasing exports.[38] The employers' side of the Wages Council was accordingly urged by the council to take a firm stand against a further wage increase.[39] In the event the firm stand once more evaporated and the claim was granted because, Dennis Britain claimed later, the chairman had a 'strong bias in favour of the workers'.[40] Another proposed increase in 1954 was damned by Britain as 'suicidal' but the independents once more accepted the workers' case, this time on the grounds of equality with other wage council industries. A further claim in 1956, the third submitted in two years, brought the cumulative increase since 1947 to 74.6 per cent for men and 89.3 per cent for women.[41] It is true that rising labour costs and scarcities were the fruit of a political commitment to full employment, sustained by the long boom and high demand. In fact while rising labour costs may have caused problems for small enterprises, most of the major companies paid over the minimum rates prescribed by the wages council.[42] Furthermore, labour input costs were substantially higher in both the American and the German toy industries than in the British.[43]

In studies of other sectors of British industry it has been commonly concluded that qualitative defects were major causes of failing export performances.[44] Such deficiencies were also to be found in toy manufacturing, a fact virtually admitted by one BTMA council member at a meeting held to discuss European free trade in 1956. It would, he remarked, be disastrous for the British toy trade. 'In many instances German toys were of better quality and finish and German salesman were more efficient.'[45] The *Toy Trader and Exporter* agreed. For the British industry, it warned, the coming of free trade would mean that 'marketing, merchandising, honoured delivery dates, advertising – even ordinary civility – will assume greater importance than has been accorded them in recent times. Almost certainly', it added grimly. 'there will be casualties.'[46] There was plenty of evidence to support the underlying contention that, in matters such as design, service, reliability, presentation and delivery, the British generally had an unenviable reputation. A major influence on this was the legacy of the industry's success in raising production and export levels so rapidly in the sellers' market of the immediate postwar years. Both the opportunity and the imperative to produce inevitably entailed some lowering of quality. Transport difficulties, along with shortages of material and skilled labour, caused even major manufacturers to miss delivery dates and to turn out sub-standard goods. International Model Aircraft, a Lines group subsidiary, sent out its Penguin aircraft kits with parts missing or duplicated. Initially this caused only minor irritation but, once the sellers' market was sated, it undermined the confidence of retailers and the range was abandoned.

In the longer term the price was even higher, for such occurrences caused the British industry to acquire a very negative image, which was very difficult to shed. A survey of the American market by the British Export Trades Research Organisation and Time Incorporated in the summer of 1948 pointed out that the most frequent complaints were about price and delivery. Some critics pointed to designs which were inappropriate for American children, while others referred to a lack of product promotion and inadequate company representation. Significantly, only ten out of sixty-two stores questioned thought that a tariff reduction would result in higher sales of British toys. Interviewed by a representative of the *Toy Trader and Exporter* early in 1949, the chief toy buyer of Macy's conceded that the British were good craftsmen but suggested that their designs had remained static, while their poor packaging was a major source of discontent among potential American purchasers.[47] The following year a report on the Belgian toy market, where imports accounted for 60 per cent of sales, stressed that, while British metal and plastic toys were doing quite well, the rejuvenated German industry was regarded as superior in mechanical and electrical toys. British dolls were unsuitably dressed for the European child while their dolls' prams were too high off the ground for local taste. British toy train manufacturers were criticised for failing to make models of continental trains and the report concluded that board games would sell better if their style and presentation were modernised.[48] At about the same time, an assessment by the commercial counsellor at the British Legation in Berne agreed that British model railways were outdated, adding that in Swiss experience the British industry was characterised by sloppy after sales service and poor delivery. This, he concluded, was allowing the Germans to regain much of the ground lost since 1930.[49] Contemporary foreign buyers attending the Harrogate Trade Fair were also contemptuous of British amateurism. Even big firms, it was complained, used paper without proper letter heads, suggesting 'that we are much more interested in saving coppers than giving a good impression of ourselves or trying to go out and get the business'. There were also unfavourable comments on the general reluctance of British firms to spend a few pounds on supplying samples quickly and on time.[50]

Nor did such complaints disappear once the postwar restocking boom was complete. An equally critical tone was apparent in a 1954 digest produced for British toy makers by the UK Trade Commissioner in Canada. It suggested that the growing market for toys would be tapped only if they were attractively packaged, if delivery dates were kept, regular visits paid to customers and thought given to ensure that designs appealed to foreign taste. Design, it appears, remained a particular deficiency, even though as early as 1947 the few British participants at the Leipzig fair had reported that 'a great variety of toys were exhibited and it was remarked that the dolls and wooden toys were of excellent quality and surpassed the British equivalents'.[51] Only a few German toy firms were eligible to exhibit at the Hanover export fair in the same year but one British trade representative, Fred Allen, noted many instances of new designs.[52]

The failure of the industry to pay much heed to these warnings was highlighted in 1957 when Children's Play Activities produced a comprehensive indictment of British toy design. It was not altogether a disinterested document since CPA Ltd was the brain child of Paul Abbatt. It had been established to act as a research forum and lobby for educational toys, although Abbatt's motives were perhaps not quite so altruistic as they appeared. At least, the objects to be pursued, in return for an annual subsidy of £2000 from P. and M. Abbatt Ltd, included pursuading interested parties to buy the firm's equipment, establishing contacts that were not available to the Abbatts as directors of a commercial enterprise and, more crudely, 'to increase the turnover of P. and M. A. Ltd'.[53] Nevertheless, the CPA did provide an effective forum for Abbatt, who stood in a long tradition stemming from John Locke and the Edgeworths. An extensive series of public lectures, broadcasts and publications running back to the 1930s all had as their constant target an industry which, in his opinion, was

> more interested in quick sellers than in how much play value a toy has, or how long it will last. . . The toy manufacturer vies with the patent medicine vendor in collecting your money for worthless articles.[54]

Biased or not, the CPA's design report was damning. An early version drafted for the Council of Industrial Design admitted that while there were exceptions there was

> altogether too high a proportion of those in which no serious effort of imagination has been spent at any stage . . . almost total ignorance even on the possibilities of design, relative to the invention, manufacture and packaging of toy of all kinds . . . manufacturers simply do not know how to command the services which design alone could give, within their own organisation or outside it.[55]

Even a milder version complained that the attitude of most makers to design was 'an entirely haphazard affair . . . a process of compromise, cost, plagiarism, or amateur suggestion'.[56] The report's trenchant tones stimulated a lot of adverse criticism of the contemporary industry. *Design* magazine commented that

> in practically all other spheres of design increasing attention is being paid to the real rather than the imagined needs of the consumer; it should not be too much to ask that a little more attention be paid by the larger manufacturers to what could be called infant ergonomics.[57]

The BTMA was greatly embarrassed by the whole affair. It offered luke-warm approval, conceding that while there was much to commend the report, most of its members already observed its various recommendations and also had special departments studying design matters. The association declined to lend official support to the CPA document.[58] A more positive response might have been preferable for, despite some notable successes, the British industry never managed to slough off its reputation for producing toys that were tired, out of date or imitative. While American manufacturers were exploiting the commercial potential of the space race, the British were increasing from one to four the number of major model car ranges available. Meccano's Dinky range was being challenged by Matchbox from 1953, Corgi (made by Playcraft, a Mettoy subsidiary) in 1956, and Triang's Spot On range in 1959, although all did incorporate rather better features than the Dinkies. Even Pedigree's Sindy Doll was an imitation of Mattel's Barbie. When the BTMA decided to exclude Japanese visitors from the Brighton Fair in 1959, lest they copy British-designed toys, *The Times* was incredulous, asserting that it was beyond imagination as to 'why anyone should wish to imitate some of the unoriginal baubles on show here'.[59] Although he was hardly an objective witness, one of the barred Japanese, Yoshihiro Kishi, added that if what he had seen was typical then the British industry was at such low ebb that no one would think of copying its products.[60]

Poor packaging was another constant source of complaint, on both aesthetic and economic grounds. One wholesaler suggested in 1952 that presentation could be improved by the use of brightly-coloured display boxes, carrying descriptions of the contents. He also asked for better external protection to avoid breakages.[61] But general indifference prevailed, even after the appearance of the CPA report which had also commented on this deficiency on the part of toy manufacturers. In 1958 it was reckoned that some British firms had 10 per cent of their exports to American damaged in transit because of poor packaging.[62] In the same year the Institute of Packaging organised a series of seminars for various industries. With only ten firms bothering to attend, the toy session was by far the worst supported, further evidence of a widespread indifference within the industry to a crucial aspect of commercial success.

To lack of price competitiveness, thoughtless design and inadequate packaging must be added poor salesmanship. In the course of the 1950s American firms such as Revell, Lindberg and Baby's Pal established manufacturing plants in Britain. This prompted the *Toy Trader and Exporter* to comment that while the advent of American marketing and merchanting techniques would boost retailers' profits it would also act as a spur to the British manufacturing industry which, it suggested, was singularly backward in promotional work.[63] The article did exempt some of the bigger firms from its indictment and it is true that companies like Waddingtons, Airfix and Lines had not been slow to exploit the possibilities of commercial television, Graeme Lines observing that this was the American way of doing things.[64] Others had responded well to the development of premium sales techniques, providing, for example, some of the small toys with which cereal makers sought to boost their own sales in the mid 1950s. Even more significant was the growing utilisation of character merchandising.[65] Most major companies had cashed in on the appeal of Snow White, Mickey Mouse and other Disney characters in the 1930s but growing television ownership opened up new avenues for exploitation, especially with the popularity of American cowboy and detective characters. In the course of the 1950s it came to be handled in a more organised and planned fashion, the standards being set by Walter Tuckwell and Associates.

Such positive features of toy promotion were more than offset by shortcomings in what should have been the industry's annual showcase, the toy fair. It was not just that foreign visitors repeatedly complained of inadequate facilities, sub-standard accommodation and a general lack of information. Rather, it was also the inability of the various trade interests to sink their sectional differences for the sake of the common good. Traditionally, the major exhibitors at the Manchester Fairs had been wholesalers, while since its inception the manufacturers had tended to favour the London-based British Industries Fair. In November 1944 the BTMA and the National Association of Toy and Fancy Goods Wholesalers met with the Toy and Fancy Goods Association to discuss future arrangements. Walter Lines was an ardent champion of the British Industries Fair, having served on the Ramsden Committee which had recommended its speedy resumption after the war. Under his influence, therefore, the BTMA decided not join Toy Fair (Manchester) Ltd, the company being established to promote the Manchester Fair. Thus when the British Industries Fair resumed in 1947 it was supported by 226 toy manufacturers, most of whom had never bothered with Manchester. Yet the BIF had a major drawback from the manufacturers' point of view in that it was held in May, too late in the year to take orders for the following Christmas.

Meanwhile, the inadequacies of postwar Manchester caused Toy Fair (Manchester) Ltd to hold its first fair at Leeds in 1948 and then to move to Harrogate in 1950. The unsuitable timing of the BIF, combined with the great success of the first Harrogate Fair, led to some rethinking within the ranks of the BTMA. Walter Lines put up any number of obstacles in the way of co-operating with Toy Fair (Manchester) Ltd. If the BTMA was to have any truck with the Harrogate venture, he insisted, then the chairman of the organising company must be a member of the association. His preference, shared by other influential council figures such as Dennis Britain, was to campaign for the date of the BIF to be brought forward, because London was a more popular venue. In the meantime, the BTMA decided to hold its own independent fair at Brighton, producing a new journal, *British Toys*, in order to publicise it. This was justified on the grounds that while Harrogate was primarily a fair to bring the world's toys to Britain's wholesalers and importers, Brighton was to be a shop window for British manufacturers to show to the world. Despite the enthusiastic tone of *British Toys*, however, the first Brighton Fair in 1954 not very successful. Furthermore, a ballot organised by a trade magazine in 1954 showed that 76 per cent of British buyers preferred a BIF in London compared with only 21 per cent who opted for the BTMA fair in Brighton.[66] For their part, members of the NATR also preferred a London venue, although the vote taken at the organisation's AGM in 1955 perhaps reflected the fact that most of those present were from the south east, where the bulk of the industry's retail sales were concentrated.[67]

With rumours circulating that the BIF was about to announce a new, earlier date, participants at a special meeting of the BTMA questioned the wisdom of holding a third Brighton Fair in 1956. Walter Lines interpreted this as a measure of no confidence and promptly resigned as president, a position he had held since 1944. Though he refused to reconsider, he had perhaps acted overhastily. Shortly, it was announced that the 1956 BIF would be spread over two different dates. Accordingly, the BTMA decided to merge its own fair with the BIF event being organised in February or March at Olympia. But when a year or two later the Board of Trade stopped funding the BIF, the BTMA decided to return to Brighton. Lines Brothers, meanwhile, had added a further convolution to this merry-go-round of fairs by holding their own London event which clashed with the BIF. Their first fair generated £1,000,000 of business, sufficient for it to become an annual event, and also to encourage a few other big firms to mount independent trade exhibitions. This plethora of fairs, moveable both in time and space, created a very bad impression among foreigners, who tended anyway not be seduced by the dubious attractions of any of the various settings.

There seems little doubt then that declining export performance owed much to these qualititative defects in marketing, design and packaging. That they persisted for so long was, in part at least, a function of the industry's markets. A second by-product of the war and its aftermath was to reinforce links with the old prewar trading partners in the empire countries. After 1945, protection and an aggressively anti-foreign attitude on the part of indigenous manufacturers made the largest market of all, the United States, very difficult to penetrate. Established and well-resourced firms like Lines Brothers were able to set up their own American organisations, and, by the late 1950s, the dollar market became their largest export earner. But for smaller companies such steps were virtually impossible. For example, the range of Bendy toys produced from 1948 by Charles Neufeld had a strong appeal to American customers but the high tariff meant that he could not keep the price low enough. An attempt to manufacture directly in the United States failed because, as a small producer, Neufeld lacked adequate resources to compete in a market where dealers expected far larger mark ups than those common in the British trade. Preferential tariffs and a general shortage of dollars reinforced the tendency for the bulk of British toy exports to go, as they always had done, to the old imperial countries associated with the sterling area. This was why the closure of the South African market in 1948, and the ban on imports to Australia in 1952, appeared to be such severe blows to the British industry. Of record exports worth £6,000,000 in 1951, a third had sold in Australia.

From the longer-term perspective this reliance on imperial markets had a number of drawbacks for the British industry. For one thing, most of them were a long way away, leading to high freight costs which only a few could circumvent by establishing manufacturing plants abroad. Lines again led the way in this regard, setting up in New Zealand in 1946 (New Zealand kept a total ban on imports well into the 1950s), Canada in 1947, Australia in 1951 and in South Africa in 1954. This was all very well but countries populated to varying but usually significant degrees by British immigrants for whom traditional British toys somehow acted as a sentimental link with home, did not provide much innovative stimulus, either to design or marketing.[68] In Australia considerable resentment was caused by the attitude of British manufacturers who 'expect to get the business on a platter simply because Britain is the Mother Country'.[69] Furthermore, the old imperial territories tended to be relatively sparsely populated while their economies were generally growing more slowly than those of western Europe.

The established pattern was hard to break. Hilary Page of Kiddicraft may have turned down a 1952 invitation to set up in Australia on the grounds that the market was not big enough, but the BTMA's attitude was driven by tradition and sentiment rather than economic logic. Asked in 1948 by the Board of Trade for an opinion about the European Customs Union, the secretary W. J. Hawker replied that 'we must not lose our Commonwealth connection for dubious new relationships'.[70] Even though the focus of Britain's trading activity was gradually being shifted during the 1950s towards the vast potential sitting, as it were, on the doorstep, it was only very slowly, as Table 38 indicates, that there was a shift of toy exports towards Europe.

To some extent this was the almost inevitable outcome of Britain's entry into the European Free Trade Area (EFTA), rather than of any positive action on the part of toy exporters. Like many other business-men, they generally remained unenthusiastic about Europe. The *Toy Trader and Exporter* pointed out that the creation of EFTA presented great opportunities but that no one had any statistical information on the continental market, the pattern of consumer spending or the nature of distribution. Here, said the paper, was a great opportunity for the trade yet 'there are no outward signs that anyone is doing anything really constructive in the matter'.[71] Indeed, so uncertain was the BTMA about EFTA that it turned down a request to discuss the matter with the retailers, doubting whether 'such an area with British involvement would ever materialise'.[72] The British toy makers' attitude was well illustrated when the First International Toy Congress was held in June 1959. It was attended by 1280 people from eighty organisations repre-senting nine European countries. The German manufacturers sent twenty-five delegates, the French seventeen. Britain managed only seven, and their conservatism soon became readily apparent. When the congress overwhelmingly accepted a motion calling for every toy to carry an indication of the age group for which it was intended, only the British dissented.[73] With EFTA membership a reality, a more posi-tive attitude did begin to develop. In 1958 only six of sixty-seven foreign firms attending the Nuremberg Toy Fair were British; the next year thirty went, with fifty-three going in 1962.

The other aspect of market structure which served to inhibit qualiti-tative progress was the long persistence of import control. Of itself this must have contributed to the deteriorating export performance, since it was always easier to sell at home where import controls ensured that 90 per cent of sales had to be British. Toy manufacturers always insisted that a protected home market was the necessary basis for exports. As the figures show, however, the argument was not proven by experience and there was a deserved rebuke implicit in a communication sent to the BTMA by the Board of Trade in 1959.

> Import licensing control is not designed for the protection of domestic industry, but we hope that during the time in which industries have been sheltered from free imports they will have had an opportunity to establish themselves and be better able to face competition.[74]

As early as the autumn of 1946 token imports (twenty per cent of the prewar level) were allowed into Britain from Canada, the United States, Belgium and Switzerland. Apart from the Americans, none was a major toy producer and import licences were still required. Nevertheless, the concessions led the BTMA to protest that the British manufacturers were being sacrificed in a bid to get world trade restored. By the end of 1947 similar import provisions had been extended to France, Denmark, Sweden, Norway, Luxembourg, Finland and Italy. Despite the BTMA's fears, import values remained relatively insignificant. Although twice as much was imported in 1947 as in 1946 the value was still only a trifling £202,678, as compared with about £1,720,000 in 1938.[75] Nor did the granting of an open import licence for West German imports in October 1950 have much impact since raw material shortages there meant that prices were high and delivery dates often missed. In any case, imports were still subject to a tariff. At the end of 1951 the Board of Trade, concerned by Britain's adverse balance of payments, imposed fresh import controls and continental toys were not allowed to be imported on open general licence. Gradually, however, the quotas restricting imports to 10 per cent of current British toy sales were reduced and then, except for those on Japan and the Sino-Soviet bloc, they were abolished entirely in 1960. This process was accompanied by a downward adjustment of the tariff.

Even before this, rising imports from Hong Kong had been causing concern, not least on grounds of safety and copyright infringement. The rapid growth of the Hong Kong plastics industry was already verging on the extraordinary. In 1948 the colony had possessed three plastics plants employing thirty-three people. By 1964 31,408 were engaged in 968 factories; of these 418 made toys. By 1958 Hong Kong's toy exports to the UK reached £1,000,000. Japanese imports grew even more spectacularly from £2,550,000 in 1958 to £5,230,000 in 1960. This prompted the BTMA to tell the Board of Trade that any continuance of such a trend could be only at the expense of British firms, who would be forced out of business. The quota on Japan was not abolished in 1960 but it was raised from £180,000 a month to £415,000. This, claimed the BTMA, was a sop to offset recent trade negotiations with Japan, which had resulted in a substantial upsurge of British goods going to Japan.[76] Once more, it was claimed, the interests of the toy manufacturers were being sacrificed in some broader interest and the BTMA warned that domestic manufacturers would be diverted from the export effort in order to secure the home market.

The relaxations of import quotas greatly pleased the importers and wholesalers, however, and their differences with the manufacturers boiled over at the time of Brighton Fair in 1959. The president of the Factors' Association first refuted the manufacturers' 'nasty and improper remarks' about toy imports from the British colony of Hong Kong. He then urged his members to get as large a slice as they could of the new Japanese quota.[77] The toy manufacturers promptly closed ranks, quite literally. When Japanese visitors tried to gain admission to Mettoy's showroom at Brighton they found the doorway blocked by company staff. The Airfix representatives simply shut their doors when they saw the Japanese approaching their display rooms. Both firms were implementing the BTMA's decision to exclude the Japanese from entry because, it was alleged, they merely copied British ideas.

Such conflicts of interest within the toy business had been apparent even during the First World War and the old toy federation had done no more than paper over the worst of the cracks. The establishment of the independent manufacturers' association in 1944 was itself acrimonious, with membership being barred to those who 'call themselves makers but who will revert to importing as soon as they can'. This, said one leading wholesaler and importer, was the 1918 complex all over again and the decision of the manufacturers to go it alone in the BTMA was a recipe for dictatorship by the big companies, 'which we shall all be glad to see abolished for ever'.[78] Although the Toy and Fancy Goods Alliance organised a wholesale section, catering for those no longer eligible for BTMA membership, only sixty had joined by June 1946.[79] Four years later this group, which was essentially London-based, merged with the larger National Association of Toy and Fancy Goods Wholesalers of Manchester into the 230 strong Association of Toy and Fancy Goods Wholesalers.[80] However, the number of wholesalers steadily declined as cost considerations led more manufacturers to go direct to retailers. Although by 1964 40 per cent of manufacturers sold 90 per cent of their output to wholesalers, and 50 per cent sold 70 per cent through wholesalers, virtually all of the major companies dealt only with retailers.[81] This tendency was fostered by the further development of. retail chains able to order in bulk and negotiate favourable terms for their members. When the wholesalers protested on this score in 1952 the manufacturers replied that the retail chains ordered twelve months ahead, took early delivery and paid within fourteen days. Wholesalers, they claimed, were generally too small to hold sufficient stocks, or to have adequate funds to settle their bills on time. If anything, the retailers were even more critical of the wholesalers. Edward Brady damned them as being inefficient, grossly overmanned, 'a mixture of sundriesmen and pedlars who find the easy going toy trade the answer to a simple and lazy life'.[82]

Brady was speaking in his capacity as current chairman of the National Association of Toy Retailers, which had been formally launched in 1950. That the retailers had at last been able to organise themselves successfully was a product of two developments. First, there were many more of them than there had been in earlier periods. According to the 1950 Census of Production Britain had 2385 shops dealing exclusively with toys. Manufacturers' lists, which included the non-specialists, contained about three times this number. The specialists sold £8,224,000 of toys in 1950, the general shops about £11,700,000. A second impetus to organisation was provided by the retailers' alarm at the growth of what they regarded as unfair business practices on the part of wholesalers and manufacturers alike. These included the preferential terms given to large customers, sudden price alterations and the supplying of toys to non-specialist outlets during the Christmas season.

As for the BTMA, its driving force had been provided in the main by Walter Lines, whose forceful personality would have ensured his prominence, even without the fact that his companies alone were responsible for 40 per cent of Britain's total toy output. His stature gave the BTMA great credibility. While the association's various representations to government were not always successful, they were treated far more seriously than those of the old federation had been. Lines resisted suggestions emanating from the wholesalers in 1953 to resurrect some sort of joint trade body. It was also Lines who stiffened the council's determination to press ahead with the publication of *British Toys*, even when H. Richard Simmons of the *Toy Trader* threatened that both he and the proprietors of the other leading trade journal would do everything they could to protect their livelihoods.[83]

The downside of Lines' forcefulness, however, was that he – and indeed the representatives of the other big companies – tended to regard the organisation as a vehicle for their own interests and attitudes.

On one occasion there was a highly revealing discussion when Norman Craig of Meccano asked if he could send a substitute to a meeting he could not himself attend. Constitutionally, the council had to reject the request because members were elected in their own right, not as company representatives. Nevertheless, the minutes noted that 'it was however obviously very desirable that that company should be regularly represented on the Council'.[84] Furthermore, the major producers were reluctant to entertain proposals that threatened their dominance of the council. Five members retired each year and it was common practice to reelect the entire group en bloc at the annual general meetings. When a vacancy occurred, the council usually selected a replacement and added the name to the panel put up for reelection. In 1950 it was suggested at a general meeting that at least one of the retiring members should automatically be replaced each year. Council rejected this. A year or two later Hilary Page of Kiddicraft resigned from the council, partly as a protest at its reluctance to adopt schemes to ensure a steady supply of new members. Why, John Blunt demanded to know in the *Toy Trader and Exporter*, did the association's officers continually complain about the amount of work entailed, yet they 'don't resign and give new blood a chance, but hang on to office like drowning men clutching straws'?[85] Interestingly, the secretary hid behind the cloak of confidentiality when he was asked in 1963 how many council members represented firms with less than 25 members, although such information must have been easily available.

In a way this conflict of interest between the major companies and the rest had been implicit in the débâcle over the toy fair, for, as one executive from Green Monk rightly complained, the Brighton venue suited the big producers who dealt mainly with retailers. For smaller ones like his it was inappropriate because few wholesalers bothered to attend.[86] Even after he resigned over the Brighton issue, Lines continued to regard the association with a sense of patronage. In 1957 he demanded that it cancel the membership of a firm which had distributed its own promotional leaflets at his company's fair.[87] A few years later he asked that action be taken against the *Observer* newspaper because it had accused his firm of copying.[88]

Walter Lines' resignation in 1955 was a major blow to the BTMA, the more so as it was followed by the decision to hold a separate Triang Fair in London. It was no great coincidence that shortly after he quit the wholesalers again to put out feelers for some closer organisation. The time was surely ripe, said the president of the Toy and Fancy Goods Factors in June 1956, to bring together all sections of the trade in one big association.[89] A month or two later 'John Blunt' was asking in the *Toy Trader and Exporter* why there were four separate trade associations.[90] No positive response emerged but the president of the Toy and Fancy Goods Wholesalers raised the matter again towards the end of 1958. Any prospect of reconciliation vanished when the two sides clashed over the issue of Japanese imports in 1959.

The progressive relaxation of import controls, commented *The Times* in 1960, left the British toy industry facing increasing competition and a testing time in the future.[91] It was an accurate assessment. Japanese imports alone were worth £700,000 in 1963 and £950,000 in 1964, while total imports rose by almost 350 per cent between 1960 and 1968 (Table 41).

Table 41
British Toy Production: Exports and Imports, 1960–68[92]

	Production £	Exports £	Exports %	Imports £
1960	40,560,000	9,250,000	22.8	5,230,000
1961	42,140,000	9,520,000	22.6	5,930,000
1962	42,240,000	10,730,000	25.4	7,280,000
1963	44,840,000	11,760,000	26.2	8,420,000
1964	49,150,000	13,250,000	26.9	10,940,000
1965	60,500,000	15,230,000	25.2	11,240,000
1966	66,400,000	16,480,000	24.8	13,850,000
1967	64,780,000	18,720,000	28.9	13,820,000
1968	93,790,000	24,440,000	33.1	18,130,000

Although it was still true that in 1961 90 per cent of toys being sold in Britain were indigenous products, in the bigger toys shops that proportion was much lower at about 60 per cent.[93] The temporary imposition of a 15 per cent import surcharge in 1965 did not stem the tide, while the anticipated benefits of sterling's devaluation in 1966 were shortlived.

It is true that over the same period the decline in the proportion of toys exported was halted and indeed some marginal improvement was recorded towards the end of the decade. There is no indication that this was due to any wholesale elimination of the qualitative defects so apparent in the 1950s, for they remained very much in evidence. A survey conducted by a Watford consumer group uncovered numerous instances of poor design and premature breakdown, especially among wheeled and mechanical toys. Its report concluded that many toys were designed casually, made contemptuously, sold irresponsibly and bought indiscriminately. *The Times* took the matter up, deducing that something was 'horribly wrong' with modern toys.[94] The paper's correspondent found little change by the end of the decade. The goods on offer at the 1968 Toy Fair were marked by a 'glaring lack of good quality and original toy designs'. The dolls were all identical 'like replicas of toys in American catalogues'. Educational and action toys were good value for money but were still unimaginatively presented. The whole event was characterised by 'dreary toys, dreary displays, and dreary salesmen who do little to boost the British image'.[95] A year or two later the American designer Marvin Gass addressed a meeting organised at the Brighton Fair. He pulled no punches in damning the majority of British toys as derivative and dated, or products which the manufacturers believed would sell on the old criteria of tradition, pride and quality. The British, he said, had been slow to utilise television advertising and to employ independent designers. Although he confessed to enjoying Brighton, its genial and relaxed atmosphere was in marked contrast with the American Toy Fair to which people went 'in a tank', so competitive and ruthless was it. The British industry, he concluded, lacked any sense of contemporary rhythm or tempo.[96] This was supported by a retail manager who suggested that the Americans were producing products of far greater interest to children than the British.[97] Nor had customer service improved. An export agent complained in 1967 of the slowness of British deliveries and the unwillingness to provide quotations in local currencies.[98] Australian buyers may have picked on smaller producers as being particularly lackadaisical in their attitudes, but they felt that the entire British industry was generally still too complacent about exports.[99] Certainly, the success of firms like Lesney and Britains in the American market showed that tariffs were not an insuperable barrier to success there, but the British industry could still manage to sell only $4,500,000 of toys in a US market worth $1,000,000,000 a year in 1965.

Despite the persistence of old faults, however, exports did show a rising trend in the 1960s. This was the outcome of four influences. First, and notwithstanding the strictures of Marvin Gass, British toy makers were still capable of coming up with innovative ideas, the most outstanding perhaps being Denys Fisher's Spirograph, designed in 1964, sold from 1966 and voted educational toy of the year in 1967 and 1968. Equally successful were the high-quality ranges of die-cast miniature vehicles being produced by Lesney, Mettoy, Lone Star, Meccano and others. In 1967 over 50 per cent of all exports were die-cast.

Secondly, the rapid growth of firms like Lesney, Mettoy, Airfix and Dunbee Combex meant that the share of total output provided by the older, more staid organisations, actually diminished. The younger companies all exported heavily, Lesney selling 80 per cent of its output abroad in 1968, the year in which it won the second of its three Queen's Exports Awards to industry. Mettoy received similar recognition in 1966, 1968 and 1969.

Thirdly, there were some amalgamations and plant expansions designed to improve productive efficiency and viability. In 1964 Sebel diversified into soft toys, Airfix bought Crayonne and Dunbee Combex acquired the House of Rees. Lines bought a number of new companies and undertook some restructuring in the middle years of the decade. Thomas Salter abandoned five cramped factories in London and moved to Glenrothes New Town in Fife; Denys Fisher purchased Wendy Boston in order to gain a wider product base; and Chad Valley took over the Chiltern soft toy business, making it the largest manufacturer of such goods in Britain. The underlying motive behind this surge of business reorganisation was well expressed by Britains' managing director when his company opened a new factory to run its die-cast metal moulding machines twenty-four hours a day. 'The whole idea behind the move', he said, 'is for more efficient production, greater competitiveness, and provision for further expansion.'[100]

Finally, and perhaps most importantly, the rise in exports was a product of government policy. Concerned by the impact on sterling of a deteriorating balance of payments, the new Labour Government introduced an export rebate scheme at the beginning of 1965. Reaction within the toy industry was mixed. Arthur Katz of Mettoy welcomed it because it meant his firm got an unexpected bonus on exports. Lesney was less enthusiastic, for the rebate did not compensate fully for the effects of the import surcharge, which pushed up the cost of the company's machinery and cartons, most of which were supplied from Germany. The rebate scheme was terminated in April 1968, by which time the government had tackled the trade problem by the much more radical expedient of devaluation. While this had the effect of raising the costs of some imported raw materials, there is no doubt that devaluation was the primary cause of the sudden surge of exports which occurred in 1967 and 1968. Lines Brothers anticipated that their overseas sales would rise by 25 per cent in 1968 solely because of the reduced value of sterling.[101]

In general, the British toy business in the 1950s and 1960s displayed some of the paradoxes of middle age – expansion and growth but

The British Toy Business

mainly within fixed dimensions and tempered by shrinkages and losses elsewhere; still capable of inspired ideas but with diminishing responsiveness to external stimuli and characterised by a growing conservatism. While not immediately serious, such indicators were portents of the future. Although the crude figures show steadily expanding toy production and a rising value of exports, the downward trend in the proportion of output exported was halted and reversed only very slowly and even then not primarily because of any fundamental improvement in performance. There were a number of very successful products and developments, but the competitive edge of some companies was dulled by inattention to design and by complacent, old-fashioned business methods. Despite attempts at rapprochement, sectional interests remained unresolved.

It is perhaps not surprising that most of the dynamism was being exhibited by relatively young companies. The sales manager of one such firm, Airfix, which turned its plastics expertise to toy making in 1947, certainly blamed the older manufacturers for shoddy goods, suggesting that they had been hypnotised by the experience of 1945 and 1946 when anything would sell.[102] It would be misleading of course to imply that all the newer companies were successful – the constant trickle of bankruptcies among postwar foundations puts the lie to that. Nor would it be accurate to infer that older enterprises were uniformly static or laggardly. Between 1947 and 1957 Harbutts increased the sales of its plasticine by 221 per cent and exported it to seventy countries. Other long-established firms which did well in the 1950s included the soft toy manufacturers Farnell and also Britains. The latter's quality hand-finished goods could always command attention, especially in an American market more accustomed to mass-produced goods. The CPA report also commented very favourably on the design work carried out by Britains, as well as by other older enterprises like Cascelloid. Nevertheless, its highest accolades were bestowed on newcomers. Summit Games was praised, for example, because it was 'something new in the toy trade to go to outside for really competent designers'.[103] Equally the report tended to single out relatively new firms like Kiddicraft as being generally more innovative in their use of materials, packaging and in the range of items produced. The packaging of Herald Miniatures was described as outstanding because the boxes acted as display units as well as containers.[104] Herald Miniatures had been produced from 1952 by Roy Selwyn-Smith working in partnership with a small-scale Polish diesinker, M. Zang. Britains' managers were astute enough to buy into the firm in order to bring the outstanding Herald range under their own umbrella.

Britains' success notwithstanding, it was also the newcomers who returned the most impressive performances during the 1950s, both in terms of exports and overall progress. By the standards of the major companies, Dekker Toys' £50,000 profit in 1964 was modest but it was sufficient to encourage the company to go public in the following year. In that year J. and L. Randall made £358,000, a 15 per cent improvement on 1964. Dunbee, a postwar plastics company that was moving into toy production in the late 1950s, bought Combex from Max Reich in 1960 and expanded so rapidly that it went public in 1962. Five years later it paid £1,000,000 for the British subsidiary of the famous American firm, Marx Inc. As Table 42 reveals, Sebel and Co., whose first toys appeared in 1947 and which accounted for a half of all British toy exports to America by the end of 1949, enjoyed steadily growing profits, apart from a downturn in 1957.

Table 42
Company Profits: i, 1953–66

Year	Mettoy £	Sebel £	Airfix £	Lesney £
1953	42,886	88,425		
1954	90,882	110,332		
1955	72,400	102,989		
1956	9,766	107,660	65,194	
1957	(22,346)	70,231		
1958	44,758	101,098	114,878	
1959	64,470	117,819	149,544	
1960	82,909		342,484	332,355
1961	110,105		534,438	384,694
1962	346,077		577,000	558,150
1963	426,000		426,525	
1964	516,000		516,096	
1965	699,000			771,053
1966	890,083			2,261,000

Most dynamic of all were Lesney, Mettoy and Airfix, which together with Lines, made up the industry's 'big four.' Between 1959 and 1963 Lesney doubled its capital and sales. Pre-tax profits, which averaged about £425,000 in the early 1960s, were over £750,000 in 1965 and

£2,260,000 in 1966. *Management Today* ranked Lesney at the top of the league of Britain's most successful companies in 1968.[105] Second in the same league table was Mettoy. It had experienced some difficulty arising from the introduction of new ranges in the middle of the decade, but by the early 1960s profits were rising substantially, carried along mainly in Corgi cars. When it followed Lesney's example by becoming a public company its record ensured that the share offer was oversubscribed ninety-one times. By 1965 Mettoy had 2250 employees at Swansea and a further 250 working on design and development at Northampton. So good was this team that Corgi's model of the Mini Cooper S was on the market ten days after the real version won the Monte Carlo Rally in 1965. Another runaway winner that year was the gadget-packed James Bond Aston Martin model.

Airfix was another 1950s success story. Originally founded in 1939 by Nicholas Kove to make air-filled rubber toys, it ran into difficulty almost immediately when Far Eastern rubber supplies were hit by the war. Kove turned to making plastic combs and by 1947 he had the largest output in the country. But the market was declining and he was faced with large tax bills for his past successes. Almost by accident, he found an alternative source of income when in 1948 he was commissioned to produce a promotional plastic replica of a Ferguson tractor. Because his budget was so limited he made it up in kit form, finding that some spare sets sold very well. In 1952 Airfix produced its first proper kit, a model of the ship *Golden Hind*, using polystyrene DS which included a rubber compound to give accurate detail. Marketed through Woolworths, which ensured volume sales, the kit was so successful that it was produced for twenty-four hours a day over a nine-month period. As with Lesney's miniature coronation coach, the concept was capable of indefinite extension and Airfix boomed, as its pretax profits showed. By the early 1960s it was making £500,000 a year, compared with the 1950 profit of slightly over £15,500. It established an American operation so that its products could compete on even price terms with indigenous makers.

Such undoubted successes tended to be overshadowed, however, by the less than spectacular performances of some of the prewar giants. These makers, suggested one journal, were still tarred with the old brush of tradition.[106] Chad Valley revealed alarming symptoms of distress in the 1950s. After reaching a record postwar figure of £117,793 in 1951, profits fell back badly. In the middle 1950s the company chairman, Kenneth Horne, had to unfold a plan for radical restructuring designed to update products, to modernise and improve equipment,

and to support products with a suitably trained salesforce. Plant consolidation followed, with the Gloucester manufacturing facility transferring to Birmingham. Prices were increased across the range by about
8 per cent at retail level, and at the end of 1957 Chad Valley contracted
to use its machines for the manufacture of the metal toys designed by
a German company.[107] Even so, recovery was slow. No ordinary or
preference dividends were paid in the trading year 1958. Costs were
evidently still not under control and by 1959 the overall debt stood at
£216,714. Restructuring finally began to pay off in 1961 when the first
overall profit for some years was registered, albeit only £33,561. In that
year shareholders received a dividend for the first time in five years.
Unfortunately, the pattern repeated itself in the 1960s, with a promising
start deteriorating into loss again by 1969. Lines Brothers enjoyed fairly
steady·profitability during the 1950s but that very stability was in marked
contrast to the huge growth shown by some of the newer companies.
In general, Lines' costs were outstripping price increases and this was
reflected in modest returns during most of the 1950s (Table 43).
Furthermore, the structure of the group was becoming rather distended,
running to thirty-nine separate manufacturing units at home and
abroad, as new acquisitions such as Rovex and Minimodels Ltd were
taken over, as well as the Youngsters retail chain. In part, too, expansion
reflected substantial activity in Europe, designed to give a manufacturing capacity inside the tariff barriers operated by the Common
Market. By 1961 there was a distinctively edgy tone creeping in to the
chairman's statements as he hammered home the message that trading
profits were the highest in the company's history, 'in case there are
any doubts in the minds of our shareholders'.[108] A large fall occurred
in 1962, despite an increase in total group sales which was insufficient
to offset higher overheads within the United Kingdom, a very bad result
in America and more substantial development costs in Europe. A
vigorous economy drive followed with active directors taking salary cuts,
uneconomic factories being closed down, capital expenditure capped,
stocks and tools written off or disposed of, unprofitable lines cut and
overheads in all component companies in the group carefully reviewed.
Walter Lines reacted with characteristic vigour when the *Observer*
suggested that his vast empire was shaky, but between 1962 and 1964
it was the recent acquisitions which did most to sustain the group's
profits.[109]

Table 43
Company Profits, ii, 1950–70

Year	Lines £	Meccano £	Chad Valley £
1950		91,121	108,643
1951		173,889	117,793
1952	271,342	120,289	
1953	248,211	206,405†	
1954	256,390	180,466†	
1955	263,051	297,327†	
1956	262,268	309,796†	
1957	261,440	177,511†	(103,104)
1958	290,396		(80,473)
1959	387,723	492,813†	(216,714)
1960	684,689	235,464†	33,561
1961	456,142	80,095†	
1962	283,005	88,813	82,724
1963	317,814	(164,534)	161,371
1964	536,300	(888,247)	
1965	497,979	(671,721)	
1966	1,604,455*	(311,000)	
1967	1,271,829*	1,068	4,000
1968	748,000*	150,000	56,000
1969	367,000*	(147,741)	(4,000)
1970	(779,000*)	(148,599)	(90,000)

* trading profits only which is what Lines reported from 1966 onwards
† post-tax profits

There was some truth, too, in the suggestion that the firm's toymaking was becoming more imitative than creative. Triang railways may have been cheaper but the basic concept had been pioneered long ago by Frank Hornby. So, too, had model vehicles, which Lines began to produce in its Spot On range. Sindy, produced from 1962 by Pedigree, a Lines subsidiary, was a fashion doll barely distinguishable from her equally shapely American cousin, Barbie. Pedigree was only one of a number of companies with good ideas and products in which Lines traditionally invested. Others included Frog model aircraft in the 1930s, Minimodels who made the electric slot car racing system, Scalextric, and a model railway network made by Rovex, both in the 1950s. During the 1960s, however, this reliance on the ideas of others appears to have become much more prevalent. Shuresta was bought in 1963, Meccano in 1964, a 29 per cent stake was purchased in Subbuteo, a table football game much boosted by the staging of the 1966 World Cup football competition in England, and a controlling interest was acquired in G. R. Wrenn, maker of 00 gauge railways and Formula 152 slot car racing. Lines also tried to get production rights in Action Man from Hasbro, the creators of its American version, GI Joe. They were beaten, however, by Palitoy. By 1967 the recovery of the previous three years had been halted, devaluation not proving a sufficient boost to offset declining home profits. The result was another major reorganisation of production facilities. Regional distribution depots were closed down, as were factories at Hayes and Canterbury. The entire product range was also scrutinised, but the losses incurred from stock disposal combined with the costs of restructuring to lower profits yet again in 1968.

There is little doubt that Lines' position had not been helped by the acquisition of Meccano in 1964. After peaking in 1956 the Liverpool firm's profits fell away rapidly, turning in substantial deficits after 1963. Of all the older British toy companies Meccano was perhaps the most complacent. The long success of the construction set, the railway system and the Dinky cars had engendered a fatal lethargy in a firm which prided itself on high-quality workmanship, irrespective of costs, and whose managers were largely recruited from within. By 1963 *British Toys* could comment that 'Meccano has been made for over thirty-five years without any major change in its design or finish'.[110] In a survey conducted by *Which?* magazine neither it, nor the company's other construction set, Bayko, acquired from Plimpton Engineering in 1949, did at all well. They were judged to be complicated, not very versatile and inadequately packed.[111] Dinky cars lost their market edge as more finely detailed and finished rivals appeared from Lesney and Mettoy. Although the Hornby railway system remained technically of a very high standard, it was relatively expensive and further handicapped by Meccano's old-fashioned selling policy. When Lines Brothers bought Rovex in 1951, its salesmen were instructed to place that company's low-cost railway system in every available outlet. By contrast, Meccano's loyalty to long-standing franchised dealers restricted its products to one shop per area; by the 1950s the spread of the franchises reflected a much earlier pattern of population distribution. As a result it was Triang Railways that became, in the words of one enthusiast, 'the most successful British model railway system in the history of toy making'.[112]

Meccano chairman Roland Hornby appeared totally out of touch, permanently optimistic but unable to appreciate that times had moved on. He could not believe, he told shareholders in 1963, that Meccano was out of date. 'I cannot think that the boy growing up in the space age is any less imaginative than those in the days of Jules Verne and H. G. Wells.'[113] Small wonder, in the light of the figures which accompanied this statement, that one contemporary suggested that compared to Hornby's forecasts 'the Meteorological Office men are paragons'.[114] Hornby was eventually forced out and in 1964 Meccano was subject to a cut price take-over bid from Lines. The Lines offer valued Meccano's shares at less than half the current market price. It was accepted with alacrity by the majority shareholders, who alone knew that losses to January 1964 were running at £250,000 and that a further £600,000 of stocks and tools was to be written off.

A rapid revamping of products, the installation of new machinery and the sacking of the managing director enabled Lines to restore Meccano's profitability as early as 1965, but the accumulated losses of the previous years were not wiped out until 1967 when the overall net surplus was slightly more than £1000. Not until 1968 did Meccano earn any real money, returning a total pretax profit of about £150,000. Even so, Graeme Lines, installed as managing director in 1964, found it difficult to undermine the complacent conviction among Meccano managers that its products and systems were the best. Meccano, he recalled later, resembled an old auntie – friendly but believing that things should still be done as they had been when she was a girl.[115] His frustration was evident in a letter of August 1969 written to one senior Meccano manager:

> I hardly know how to answer your reaction to my memorandum . . . since it appears to indicate a reluctance on your part to even try to introduce the economies which are vitally and urgently necessary to Meccano. Accordingly, I do not propose to accept your answer as being in any way valid since the efficiency of the Company is impaired by your department already in view of its high cost.
>
> Believe me . . . I am not playing a game. I want a wholehearted, constructive and enthusiastic effort to implement the economies I am asking for, and the loyal support of senior members of the Company in endeavouring to achieve the position the Company must have.[116]

The original memorandum to which the hapless Meccano executive had apparently reacted with such indifference had been prompted by the growing difficulties of the parent company. In the wake of deteriorating overseas sales, uncertain home demand and the high costs of product rationalisation in England, Lines' net profits crashed disastrously in 1968. Things got even worse the following year. The group's component companies were instructed to cut back on buying, reduce stocks, secure as much credit as possible, offer customer discounts to secure early payments, and to hold back on capital expenditures. Meccano's contribution to the anticipated savings was £150,000, small beer compared with the £444,000 expected of Rovex and the £245,000 required of Minimodels.[117] First half losses of £118,000 were exacerbated when final quarter sales were some £2,000,000 off target. With the cost of borrowing soaring, and unexpected extra expenditures, share prices plummeted. In the summer of 1970 all but one member of the family resigned from the board. Neither further factory closures nor the recruitment of new board members and senior executives could halt the downward slide. Briefly, there were hopes that General Foods or Gallahers would come to the rescue but the situation was beyond help. In August 1971 Lines Brothers, at one time the largest toy company in the world, went into liquidation. The chairman explained the problems in terms of external pressures, although some of his relatives were critical of the advice received from management consultants.[118]

Others pointed to the sort of deficiencies which had characterised the postwar British toy industry. *Toys International* accepted that it was only natural for a company's founders to want to preserve family control but suggested that it had been unwise for such a large enterprise not to have made proper use of appropriate professional experts in management, marketing and finance. 'Until their very fall there was always something unrealistically family, paternal about the company.'[119] Certainly the directors appeared not to appreciate that their products were losing their innovatory edge. Not long after Marvin Gass had criticised the British industry for its amateur and outdated attitudes, Graeme Lines was claiming that 'all the bright ideas in the toy world today are British. Most of the good toys are based on British ideas'.[120] Company chairman, Moray Lines, was no less ebullient. Asked why only four British toys got into the top selling twenty at Christmas he replied that 'anyone can make a Toy of the Year Award toy – give it heavy advertising, do not deliver it, and say it is so popular it's in short supply'.[121] At a sales seminar earlier in the same year the Lines marketing director had been equally dubious about the effectiveness of television advertising. Gerald Lucas of the NATR was also critical of the firm's old-fashioned approach:

If you had to pin it down to one particular reason I would say – it was obviously bad management . . . there was a lack of understanding of the retail and distributive and promotional aspects of running a business today.

The accounts department, he added, never seemed to know what the sales departments were doing.[122] There is no doubt either that the rather haphazard growth of the group left it heavily overextended both in terms of manufacturing facilities and product ranges, problems which were not addressed until it was far too late. Even then, in the opinion of Basil Feldman, the joint managing director of Dunbee Combex, the correctness of the rationalisation strategy was nullified because 'the management simply wasn't up to it'.[123] Similarly, there were some glaring production inefficiencies. Despite growing pressures on costs in the 1960s the group was using 137 different types of rivet and 147 different formers for bending metal tubes. Nor was marketing always shrewd, Lines failing to exploit the growing potential of the mail order catalogue. That market was commandeered from 1960 onwards by other firms. In wheeled toys, for example, Sharna Ware's success through mail order catalogues bit deeply into a market of which Lines had once had 75 per cent. But as Sharna Ware's founder rather cruelly remarked, 'It's history now what happened to them'.[124]

Chapter 7

Heart Failure, 1971–1985

The failing performance of Lines Brothers, once described as being in the blue chip class of British companies, was a major worry in the toy trade at the end of the 1960s. It was not, however, the only cause of alarm. For some time, manufacturers had been disturbed by the way in which they were increasingly being subjected to outside scrutiny and pressures. The industry, commented the BTMA chairman in 1965, had been troubled by various organisations which seemed to think that they knew more about making toys than the manufacturers themselves.[1] He had three particular pressure groups in mind. First, there was a relatively unimportant, though persistent, propaganda from pacifist bodies. This of course was nothing new. It had surfaced strongly in the aftermath of the First World War and never entirely died away. In March 1953 a Private Member's Bill calling for a ban on the sale of toy weapons got as far as a Second Reading in the House of Commons before being talked out. The sentiments behind it, however, derived fresh impetus from the anti-war radicalism of the 1960s. Anne Kerr, Labour MP for Rochester, brought the issue back to Parliament in 1967. About a year later the Brighton Toy Fair was picketed by the Women's International League for Peace and Freedom as a protest against the manufacture of war toys. This demonstration was dismissed by a BTMA spokesman as yet another of 'these ladies' . . . pathetic attempts'.[2]

More influential, in that ultimately it forced a practical and allegedly costly response from the manufacturers, was the growing interest in toy safety. This also had a long pedigree but again the tempo quickened in the 1950s and 1960s. Previously, government intervention had not been particuarly prescriptive. In 1926, for example, the Home Office had merely warned the public against the danger of shocks if electrical toys designed to work off the domestic mains were placed on bare ground or near earthed metal. In addition, there had been two inquiries into the use of celluloid, one in 1914 and another in 1938, but neither had produced any important recommendations. Nevertheless, the conference of the Association of British Fire Services was touching upon a well-worn theme when it called for the abolition of celluloid toys in 1949. The BTMA countered by citing the conclusion of the 1938 committee that 'there does not seem a sufficient reason to make any further recommendation either restricting or prohibiting the uses to which celluloid is put'.[3] Since that inquiry's sole remit had been to ascertain if there was any effective substitute in the event of a ban on celluloid, this was somewhat disingenuous, though the BTMA got away with it.

It was indicative of the public concern with safety issues which developed over the course of the next ten years or so, however, that the association had to present a more thoughtful defence in 1959 when the Portsmouth Junior Chamber of Commerce published *Danger at Play*, a survey of toy-related accidents. Walter Lines wondered somewhat acidly if a document produced by a *junior* chamber of commerce was worth worrying about. It was certainly unsound statistically; drawn from an unspecified time period, the 'random sample' of 336 children on which it was based was nothing of the kind, although the compilers regarded that as an unimportant technical detail, not accepting that statistical proof of an accident rate was necessary to demonstrate the existence of a danger.[4] Yet despite its obvious defects, the report evoked a ready public response and prompted a leader in *The Times*.[5] By 1961 the British Standards Institute had moved to issue new toy safety regulations.

The manufacturers resented this type of external intervention, for it seemed somehow to imply that they were culpable even though, as the BTMA pointed out, most of them already observed the standards imposed by the new code: restrictions on celluloid; no sharp edges or toxic dyes; detachable keys for wind-up toys; and secure eye fastenings in soft toys. When the government introduced further controls on celluloid and lead levels in paint in 1966, the BTMA protested that this was going too far, interfering with the voluntary practices of the industry.[6] Dennis Britain made his resentment very clear when he attended a meeting organised by the Consumer Council on the subject of toy safety. In expounding the BTMA's opposition to statutory controls he complained that 'one of the basic problems of this country today is the number of committees founded by Do-Gooders to tell other people how to run their business, instead of doing an honest job themselves'.[7]

Undeterred by his rebuke, the meeting decided to reconvene at a later date to consider the establishment of a Toy Council. Against the wishes of both Britain and the current chairman, David Day, the BTMA decided to send representatives to this meeting. Thereafter it completely outmanoeuvred the 'do-gooders' by setting up a Toy Council as a subsidiary company and restricting membership to manufacturers. This was a clever pre-emptive initiative as the new body did virtually nothing other than hold an annual meeting. When the retailers asked for representation, the chairman replied that it had been set up to deal only with design, quality and safety. Faced with criticism from the Consumer Council, which was clearly annoyed that its intentions had been so neatly hi-jacked, Moray Lines told his sole fellow director on the Toy Council, Dennis Britain, that they had two possible responses. One was to set up a sub-committee to deal with the wider issues. This, he suggested, would 'temporarily take the wind out of the sails of the critics, but will inevitably lead to a lot of involvement which could easily cause both embarrassment and the loss of a great deal of time and money'. Alternatively, the Toy Council could simply be sold or given by the BTMA to its critics. This would silence the current complaints and put the ball firmly back in court of those who wanted it to have a wider mandate. If the offer was accepted, concluded Lines, the council would founder for want of money, even if it got off the ground, which he doubted.[8] In the event, the Toy Council remained a dead duck in the hand of the BTMA.

It was not so easy, however, to divert the educational lobby. Changing philosophies of child rearing were putting increasing emphasis on free expression and the role of play in the educational process. Such ideas were taken up by a growing number of articulate, educated, mainly middle-class parents who were becoming increasingly vocal through an expanding network of playgroups, parent-teacher associations and the toy library movement started by Jill Norris and responsible for the publication of *What Toy?* These were the sort of individuals and groups to whom the Abbatts had hoped to appeal in setting up CPA Ltd, whose critical report on toy design had so embarrassed the manufacturers. The advocates of educationally acceptable toys got a further boost in 1963 when the first Galt toyshops opened in London, Nottingham and Birmingham. Originally an educational bookseller dating from the 1830s, Galt had organised an educational section in 1949 to cope with the growing demand for instructional toys and teaching aids. This did so well that in 1961 a toys division was created, whose underlying philosophy was well summed up by Galt executive, Edward Newmark. Commercial manufacturers, he argued in words that might have been penned by Paul Abbatt, provided toys which 'hamper rather than encourage children's imagination'. They were made by adults for adults and probably enjoyed by adults – hence the manufacturers' equation of play value with realism.[9]

The trade was highly suspicious of such talk and of those who produced it. The BTMA delegates at the 1971 meeting of the European Federation of Toy Industries noted with some concern that the president's opening address had appealed for toys to be designed on educational criteria. They were equally alarmed to observe that the sessions were coming under the influence of pedagogues. The association council promptly declined to assist in the matter of pedagogues and declared itself unwilling to nominate representatives to attend meetings of the federation's newly-established pedagogues' group.[10] Small wonder that the industry stood accused of failing to grasp that the nature of its activities conferred upon it a social responsibility that it appeared unwilling to acknowledge.[11]

Public interest in the suitability, safety and educational value of toys was by no means confined to Britain, however. Similar forces were at work in all advanced societies. Germany's recent history, for example, made the trade there very sensitive about the production of war toys; indeed the use of any symbols associated with the Nazi regime was specifically banned. In Switzerland it was reported that there was a similar prejudice against toy soldiers, fostered in the main by evangelicals and women's groups.[12] In America several hundred toys fell foul of the Consumer Products Safety Commission and at least one firm, Remco, was eventually forced out of business after its Tru-Smok range was banned on the grounds that it encouraged the acceptance of pollution. So universal was the educationalists' influence that in 1959 an International Council for Children's Play was set up. Significantly, the leader of the German delegation pointed out that while they wanted good relations with the manufacturers this could not extend to active collaboration because economic interests should not be allowed to influence the criteria for good toys.[13] The activities of such interest groups were not unique to Britain and, whatever the BTMA chairman may have tried to imply in 1965, they could not be blamed for the more fundamental problems of which the Lines saga was the most obvious manifestation.

Although the collapse of biggest toy manufacturer in the country sent shock waves reverberating throughout the industry, the corpse was dismembered with almost indecent haste. Airfix bought Meccano while Dunbee Combex Marx acquired the Rovex Triang complex, paying £2,259,000 for the business and £741,000 for the factory sites. The

heart of the original business, Triang-Pedigree, went to Barclay Securities for £3,600,000 plus £1,678,000 for the freehold of the Merton
and Birmingham factories. Barclay was one of a number of finance and
investment trusts attracted into the toy industry at this time by the
profit potential revealed in the rapid growth of companies like Airfix
and Lesney. Courtaulds, Tube Investments, Phillips, Norcross and Wiggins Teape all bought into the industry in 1970–71. Thomas Salter
joined forces with a London investment company associated with Morgan Grenfell in 1971 in a bid to get finance for further expansion. A
similar motivation lay behind Mettoy's links with the Triumph Investment Trust. Another finance company, Heenan Beddow, bought Rosedale which had lost £186,000 in 1970, despite doing £1,000,000 worth
of business with Woolworths. Heenan Beddow managers reckoned that
rationalisation and modernisation could turn the company round.
Under new ownership Rosedale advertising even tried to make a virtue
out of its past weaknesses: 'We admit it. Nine months ago our production, delivery, packaging and marketing just weren't up to scratch. In
fact, we know we had a pretty bad name in the business.'[14]

Barclay Securities, by far the most voracious of the speculators,
swallowed up Sebel, Chad Valley, Chiltern Toys and Charles Methven
in rapid succession. All were subjected to ruthless reviews of management systems and performance – only two of Sebel's top seven executives
survived the take-over – and of product ranges, promotion and pricing.
Barclay's chief man at Sebel, Robert Upsdell, had a dim view of managerial quality in the toy business. 'In the past, with few exceptions, the
toy industry has rarely placed emphasis on management, and companies
have prospered in spite of themselves rather than as a result of having
strong management. They were in a bull market with little competition.'[15] He was particularly critical of financial management. 'I feel that
many toy manufacturers produce a toy, take a look at the prices competitors are charging for similar items, and then fall into line. This is
the sort of thinking which has produced troubles for many toy
firms.'[16] Barclay's chief executive, John Bentley, was equally contemptuous, telling Graeme Lines that 'any bloody fool could make money in
the toy industry'.[17] Certainly his methods appeared to pay off. In 1969
Sebel, Chad Valley, Chiltern and Methven had combined sales of
£3,000,000 but net profits of only £10,000. Within a year of the Barclay
intervention their sales had risen to £6,400,000 and net profits to
£180,000. 'The right management', commented Upsdell, 'working hard,
with no time off mid-week for golf, had achieved the results of which
they were proud'.[18] Spurred on perhaps by the anticipation of further

easy pickings in the industry, Bentley formed the Barclay Toy group in December 1971. The acquisition of Triang-Pedigree made it the largest organisation of its kind in the European toy industry.

There was no doubt that in many cases the activities of the financial entrepreneurs were directed chiefly to quick profits and asset-stripping. In part at least, Heenan Beddow had been drawn to Rosedale by the prospect of selling off £200,000 of its property. Barclay disposed of Triang-Pedigree's component parts within six months of their acquisition, hardly time enough to test their commercial viability. The adult cycle business went to Raleigh for £800,000 and the wooden toy business was purchased for £225,000 by Good Wood Playthings, an enterprise which been started in retirement by the irrepressible Walter Lines. The Merton factory site was sold off as prime building land for £3,300,000. Only another six months passed before John Bentley announced that he was quitting the toy business. It was no great surprise, for, as the BTMA's journal remarked, few people in the toy industry had believed that his interest in toys was anything more than a passing one.[19] He had done well out of his toy venture. Apart from the gains made in the various Triang transactions, he made £900,000 from other property disposals, and sold Chad Valley, purchased initially for £622,000, to British Northrop for £1,800,000. Even so, his success had been achieved by the exploitation of opportunities missed by the toy companies themselves. Speculating about the future of Triang when it passed into Barclay's hands the editor of *Toys International* wrote that

> At the moment, I would suggest, their profits have come from the reduction of overheads and galloping losses rather than from increased sales of any particular line . . . if the profits of Chad and Sebel [and Lines Brothers] were there all the time but hidden under a mass of unprofitable practice then their profits too can be dug out.[20]

This was perhaps borne out by the success of Dunbee Combex in turning Rovex's 1971 losses of £1,000,000 on a £4,000,000 turnover into a profit of £2,000,000 on £14,000,000 turnover by 1975.

It was not only British asset-strippers who were attracted by the potential of the domestic toy business, however. When Lines was liquidated, 74 per cent of the equity in Arrow Games was purchased by Milton Bradley Inc. This was the latest in a succession of major American ventures into the British market, for the high profits generated by some companies in the late 1960s had also caught the eyes of American toymen. Traditionally, the Americans had not exported much of their output and it was 1962 before the first American Toy Show was organised in London. However, internal competition was intensifying. A 1961 book on the industry in the United States forecast that manufacturing methods, market research and even educational change would spell the end of small and inefficient companies still content to conduct their affairs in old-fashioned ways.[21] This seemed to be confirmed when the failure of a major firm, A. C. Gilbert Inc., in 1966 was followed by a spate of take-overs and mergers, often involving multinational corporations with little or no previous interest in toy making.[22] Creative Playthings went to CBS and General Mills bought Play Doh and Kenner, while Milton Bradley's acquisition of Playskool moved it from sixth to second largest producer in the United States.

Not surprisingly, these larger firms began to seek wider markets, hence their interest in Britain. In 1967 one of the oldest American firms, the Ideal Toy Corporation, announced that it was setting up a manufacturing subsidiary in the United Kingdom. In the same year the Aurora Plastics Corporation established Aurora Plastics (UK) Ltd to sell its construction kits in Britain, recruiting the general sales manager of Airfix as managing director. Although the new firm was initially confined to boxing imported Aurora kits and distributing them through the wholesale trade, the eventual intention was to establish a manufacturing capability as well. In 1968 Tonka, the largest American maker of toy commercial vehicles, launched itself onto both the Australian and British markets through the medium of an intensive television advertising campaign. Fisher Price toys were marketed in Britain from 1972 by Mettoy-Playcraft. Other American companies simply bought up British firms. In 1967 Mattel acquired Rosebud, which then had annual sales in excess of £1,000,000. General Mills bought Palitoy from British Xylonite and followed this with the purchase of the Denys Fisher Group in 1970. The Ohio Art Corporation was prevented from getting Chad Valley only by a higher bid from Barclay Securities.

Because their internal market was large and highly competitive it was generally the case that American companies presented products in a much more professional manner than their British counterparts. They also spent far more on promotion, about 6 per cent of revenue as opposed to an average of 1 per cent spent by British firms.[23] This gave them an undoubted advantage in a British market, which until 1960 had been largely protected against such sharp competition. As one London retailer pointed out, even if the American invasion of Britain was short-lived, it would leave behind it a legacy of professionalism that would never be lost.[24] Mattel, for example, was prepared, at least in the short term, to lose heavily in the quest for market share. In 1968

alone the company's deficit on sales of just under £2,000,000 was
£324,000. Mattel also bought a new dimension to advertising. In the
United States the company had revolutionised toy marketing in the
1950s by its decision to advertise on national television throughout the
year.[25] In Britain it adopted a variant of this strategy of saturation,
devoting its entire 1968 advertising budget to one product and to
television. Lines Brothers spent more on advertising but the investment
was thinly spread over all its products and shared between several
different media. By 1970 Mattel's expenditure on televised advertising
was equal to that of the next eighteen highest spenders. It was also
distributed over the whole year in an effort to get away from the
Christmas peak. One toy retailer later commented that from then on,
'it was quite uncanny, however poor the toy or amateurish the advertisement, advertised products always sold much better than the rest of the
toys'.[26] While the American invasion did not cause, it certainly encouraged the subsequent increase in the amount devoted to televised toy
advertisements by British companies.[27]

Such expensive and aggressive tactics caused toy promotion in Britain
to lose something of its hitherto rather gentlemanly overtones and
initially at least provoked some rather ill-considered responses.[28] In
view of subsequent events, sheepishness might have been more appropriate than the bullishness displayed by the Lines Brothers in face of
the transatlantic threat. Shortly before his company went into liquidation, chairman Moray Lines rejected any possibility of agreements with
the American invaders, declaring that 'we are going to stay British'.
Graeme was equally resolute. 'We are going to harness every resource
to combat the Americans . . . Certain companies have looked across
the Atlantic for toy ideas. We shall not.' He added that Lines Brothers
had been advertising before Mattel was ever heard of, and that they
had no intention of trying to match Mattel in this respect. 'Lines
Brothers', he concluded, 'was established as a power when a fight was
needed during the slump. We won that battle. We are used to fighting.'[29]
The words were brave but the eventual outcome bathetic. Meccano's
more tangible reaction was no more successful. The company's Mogul
range of heavy steel toys was designed to compete with Tonka. Too
similar and too expensive to represent a serious challenge to the
American toy, it lost heavily.[30]

Mogul was commissioned from an outside designer because Meccano
did not have a department charged with long-term product development. Had it done so, it might not have turned down a suggestion that
was put to it for improving Dinky cars.[31] As it was, Mattel developed

the idea of providing model vehicles with modified axle systems in order to increase their speed. The resulting product, marketed under the brand name of Hot Wheels, devastated Lesney, hitherto the runaway market leader in die-cast vehicles. The impact was maximised because Mattel kept the innovation back from the American Toy Fair, unveiling it for the first time at Brighton in 1968. It was an immediate sensation and did much to save retailers from what would otherwise have been a bad trading year. Along with the rest of the British industry, Lesney was taken completely by surprise, for it had been widely thought that the United States' manufacturers were two years away from challenging British supremacy in die-casting because of high labour costs and a lack of requisite skills in tool making.[32] Mattel then added insult to injury and carried promotion to even higher levels by making Hot Wheels available as a premium offer with labels from Heinz Spaghetti.

Lesney had enjoyed virtually uninterrupted success in the 1960s, defying business gravity by doubling in size every two and a half years on a single product line. In 1969 it won its fourth Queen's Export Award and sales rose from £19,300,000 to £21,200,000. Hot Wheels appeared just as some £3,000,000 had been committed to new factories as part of a two-year forward plan designed to increase sales in the American market, which then took 40 per cent of the company's output. Mattel's innovation played havoc with Lesney's projected sales increase. Half-year profits in 1969 fell by 29 per cent and the profit/earning ratio went down to less than ten. Shares, which had once been worth 95s. 6d. were down to 7s. 3d. by the end of 1970, a collapse which was said to have cost Jack Odell, one of the firm's co-founders, £17,000,000. In the summer of 1970 the 6000 strong workforce was reduced by 900. Caught in the process of planning increased production of its existing line, Lesney had to retool in order to bring Matchbox cars up to the higher standard of specification set by Mattel. Die-cast tooling was very expensive, with each new set costing some £13,000, while a feature model, such as Corgi's Chitty Chitty Bang Bang car, could cost as much as £100,000.[33] The urgency with which the task had to be undertaken also led to production problems, further delaying Lesney's reply, the Super Fast range.

It was also necessary to promote the new product very intensively: this was virtually a new departure for a company in which success had induced the sort of managerial complacency evident elsewhere in the toy industry. In 1968, when Mattel spent almost £240,000 on advertising, Lesney's promotional expenditure had been a miserly £10,000, largely because the company believed its products were in such demand that they did not need to be extensively advertised.[34] By 1970 Lesney had been compelled to commit itself to extensive, worldwide promotional expenditure, with the UK advertising budget alone set at £200,000. In addition to retooling, Lesney reviewed strategy and decided to diversify, adding construction kits, dolls and preschool toys to its product lines. Arguably, this should have been undertaken much earlier, but in the short term at least, the existing product had proved so profitable that anything else would have lowered the return on investment. Here again there were suggestions of lethargy induced by unchallenged success. 'When a company is a genius it tends to get complacent, and doesn't work so hard on diversification and updating of the product line.'[35] On the other hand, Lesney did react positively and quickly to the Mattel challenge, once it appeared. Nor was its response unsuccessful. Lesney profits soon picked up again and by 1973 Mattel had been forced to retreat, selling its entire UK interests to Dunbee Combex Marx, which set up Burbank Toys to run the operation.

The impact of the American invasion, particularly on Lesney, Lines's difficulties, and serious fires at both Mettoy and Dunbee Combex, coincided with rising production and distribution costs. All helped to account for the generally depressed state of the toy trade by the end of the 1960s (Table 44).

Table 44

Toy Production, Exports and Imports, 1968–80[36]

	Production £	Exports £	Exports %	Imports £
1968	73,790,000	24,440,000	33.1	18,130,000
1969	81,000,000	28,920,000	35.7	14,930,000
1970	83,760,000	28,850,000	34.4	14,820,000
1971	101,910,000	32,260,000	31.7	19,730,000
1972	106,850,000	31,690,000	29.6	26,210,000
1973	128,450,000	36,760,000	28.6	44,810,000
1974	166,980,000	60,210,000	36.1	52,450,000
1975	214,000,000	64,910,000	30.3	45,670,000
1976	247,920,000	80,890,000	32.6	65,660,000
1977	285,380,000	116,580,000	40.8	99,470,000
1978	334,480,000	113,830,000	34.0	93,290,000
1979	360,770,000	128,910,000	35.7	125,060,000
1980	304,300,000	117,920,000	38.8	190,150,000

Labour costs had been creeping up throughout the decade. When the Wages Council made an award in 1964, the BTMA council had expressed its concern that in little more than a year male wage rates had gone up by 13.5 per cent and female rates by 17.5 per cent, despite the government's attempt to establish norms of between 3 and 3.5 per cent. In December 1969 the Wages Council granted its highest ever single increase of 5d. an hour, further driving up manufacturing costs. In the face of rising costs and stagnating American sales caused by recession and competition from Mattel, Mettoy Playcraft sacked a thousand workers in the spring of 1971. At about the same time the House of Commons was asked to approve an anti-dumping order against two American firms which had been selling dolls' eyes in Britain cheaper than in the United States. As a result, the main British makers, Myers and Parson, had been forced to lower prices rather than increasing them to meet rising costs.[37]

The depressed state of the trade also resulted in declining advertising revenue for *British Toys*. At £2771, the journal's monthly income in August 1970 was well down on the £3100 achieved for the equivalent month in 1969. This was particularly serious for the BTMA, whose financial health depended very substantially on the revenue generated by the Toy Fair and *British Toys*.

Table 45

Percentage Change in Price of Leading Toy Shares,
February to April, 1971[38]

Company	Price Change	
	+	−
Airfix		3.2
Cowan de Groot	11.1	
Dunbee Combex		31.3
Lesney	15.0	
Lines		21.4
M. Y. Dart		1.3
Mettoy		37.9
J. and L. Randall	15.2	
J. W. Spear		5.8
Waddington		1.5

The demise of Lines added further to the association's problems, depriving it of £500 in lost subscriptions and £5900 a year in lost advertising, as well as leaving a major gap at Brighton. Small wonder that the BTMA's annual report for 1971 should have dwelt on the current trade depression and the fact that a greater number of firms than usual had ceased to manufacture toys. Among leading companies there was a general tendency for share prices to fall as well (Table 45).

By 1972 the tide appeared to have turned once more, stimulated by an expansionary budget (Table 46). Profits taken by Dunbee Combex were twice the 1971 figure. Berwick Timpo's rose 38 per cent to £562,000. Airfix profits also rose, boosted by some improvement in Meccano's performance. In 1973, attendance at Brighton was well up on the previous year while the Harrogate Fair was the most successful ever for a number of firms. Waddingtons reported that 'all our new projects have had a wonderful launching and business is well up on 1972'.[39] Berwick Timpo recorded a 50 per cent increase in orders and this was reflected in profits for the year which were three times the 1970 level. At the end of the year the firm's prospects were further enhanced by the acquisition of Peter Pan Playthings, a private company with profits of £80,000 in 1972. Berwick's subsidiary, Model Toys, bought the tools, goodwill and sales rights of a major German maker of dolls' furniture. Dunbee Combex also did well and its profits for 1973 topped the £2,000,000 mark. Over the next year or so it acquired substantial overseas interests in Holland, Australia and South Africa.

Table 46
Leading Firms' Profits, 1970–82

	Berwick Timpo	Mettoy	DCM	*Lesney*	Airfix
	£m	£m	£m	£m	£m
1970	.260	(.599)	1.366	2.960	.807
1971	.407	(.439)	2.059	(1.23)	.812
1972	.562	.202	1.032	.839	1.420
1973	.808	1.013	2.550	1.930	1.936
1974	1.032	1.366	2.810	2.550	2.059
1975	1.035	1.662	3.509	6.851	2.603
1976	.995	2.632	5.917	10.191	3.440
1977	.880	2.778	6.433	8.015	4.034
1978	1.061	3.685	1.250	5.190	2.688
1979	1.565	.652	0.895	(3.609)	1.520
1980	1.780	(2.798)		(10.959)	(2.164)
1981	(.467)	(2.390)			(2.300)†
1982	(2.300)	(3.512)*			

* six months only

† six months to September 1980

In commenting that there was no shortage of orders for 1973, however, the BTMA report added that the manufacturers had run into severe problems in meeting demand. Raw materials and labour were becoming scarce while industrial unrest was increasingly depriving factories of fuel and power. These were to become recurrent themes of British life in the course of the 1970s, as the economy sank under the influence of a debilitating cocktail of inflation, industrial militancy, flat consumer demand and ineffectual government. In 1972 sterling was allowed to float in the belief that its fixed exchange rate had been a major brake on economic growth. At about the same time the government introduced an unnecessarily inflationary budget, the effects of which were further stoked up by the renewal of hostilities in the Middle East and the ensuing international oil crisis. By 1975 the annual rate of inflation in Britain had reached unprecedented levels at 25 per cent, and it is against this background that the upward surge in the level of the toy manufacturers' profits in the 1970s must be set. The pound of 1975 was worth only about 43p. in 1965 terms.

Between 1972 and 1973 the price of wood doubled and the scarcity of beech, the most popular toy wood, led to the utilisation of inferior substitutes. Fears of shortages led to panic buying which further pushed up prices. More serious still was the impact of oil shortages. Oil provided the feedstock for the plastics industry and its rocketing price carried plastics in its wake. The managing director of Louis Marx Ltd said in January 1974 that he was paying £400 a ton for plastics which twelve months previously had cost £130. As a result toy manufacturers were forced to break with convention by raising their own prices several times in the course of a single year. By January 1974 the trade was anticipating a further 50 per cent increase over the following twelve months because of rising costs.[40] This proved to be unduly pessimistic, but in the year to October 1974 prices rose 33.3 per cent and the overall increase for 1974 was between 20 and 25 per cent.

The other upward pressure on costs came from labour. Trade union power had grown in the 1960s during the regime of a Labour Government as unable or as unwilling as the TUC to resist the demands of its union paymasters. Between 1967 and 1969 the number of days lost through industrial inaction almost tripled to 6,800,000. In 1972 the figure stood at 23,900,000.[41] The strikes forced up wages to the extent that by 1972 inflation was out of hand with annual pay settlements reaching 20 per cent. A new Conservative Government attempted to return to a direct incomes policy but its efforts were effectively scuppered by the miners' strike which brought it down. The succeeding

Labour Government was totally unable to hold the line on pay and went down to defeat at the end of the Winter of Discontent in 1979.

While the major unions had been able to treat all attempts at pay restraint with virtual contempt, employees in the toy industry were still dependent upon the Wages Council, although it did respond sympathetically to their demands. The 1969 award had been the biggest single increase ever granted in the industry, but the rate of general wage escalation was such that by 1972 male and female toy workers' rates of 32p. and 27p. an hour put them respectively in twenty-first and nineteenth places out the twenty-nine Wage Council industries. In June 1972 the workers' side asked for a £20 a week minimum male wage and progress towards equal pay. The latter, it was reckoned, would add between £10,000,000 and £15,000,000 to the existing £60,000,000 wage bill. This prospect perhaps ought to have encouraged more manufacturers to look at ways of containing labour costs, perhaps by transferring manufacture to low-cost labour economies overseas, or by the further automation of production and packaging. Yet such systems were most efficient when utilised on long production runs and few British firms had sufficiently large markets to make such investments attractive to shareholders.

Another inherently inflationary ratchet on wages in the form of threshold payments was introduced by the Heath Government in 1974. As a result, toy workers were granted an automatic increase of 30p. for every percentage point rise in the retail price index. Almost inevitably these were consolidated in 1975, along with further increases which lifted the male and female hourly rates respectively to 57p. and 55p. In January 1976 the workers sought and were granted – again over the heads of the employers – an earnings supplement of £6 a week. Almost at the same time the BTMA council acceded to a request from the Department of Industry that toy manufacturers should adopt voluntary price restraint.

Rising material and labour costs, and downward pressures on prices, might have been absorbed had the home market been at all buoyant but rising unemployment and the general economic gloom kept it flat. In real terms toy sales fell by some 10 per cent between 1974 and 1976, recovering only slightly in 1977. To some extent compensatory markets could be found abroad although gains there were also more apparent than real, owing as much to the shifting value of the floating pound as to any great improvement in the efficiency of manufacture. Most of the doubling of exports which occurred between 1971 and 1976 was explicable in terms of inflation. Lesney profits in 1976 were £10,910,000 as against £7,964,000 in 1975 but almost £750,000 of this was the product of fluctuations in currency values. 'The toy trade according to most people', commented *Toys International* in October 1977, 'is really feeling the pinch now of the economic depression. The majority of people are very pessimistic about the future . . .'[42] By the end of the year further increases raised the toy price index to 277, an increase of 39 points since December 1976. Consumer spending was still subdued and there had been a big drop in the value of confirmed orders placed at the trade fairs. In the opinion of some experts it was the worst year ever experienced in the trade.[43]

Between 1974 and 1978 manufacturers' sales increased by 82 per cent, exports by 92 per cent. The twelve largest manufacturers increased their sales from £175,000,000 in 1976–77 to £220,000,000 in 1978–89, and a number of them added substantially to their assets. Berwick Timpo bought up Harbutts, the family-owned plasticine maker, whose 1973 profits of £107,303 disappeared into losses of £14,744 in 1974 and £30,546 in 1975. Berwick Timpo also purchased Aurora UK, Peter Pan and the toy interests of Wiggins Teape. Morris Vulcan acquired the Derby firm of BCM Ltd, the leading maker of die-cast toy guns, while Lettraset added Thomas Salter to its existing empire, which already included J. and L. Randall. However, only seven of the twelve actually increased their profits. Even their combined net pretax profit fell substantially while the historic cost basis return on capital employed declined from 26.2 per cent to 12.0 per cent. The average return on employed capital made by the twelve leading companies fell progressively, from 26.2 per cent in 1976–77, to 17.6 per cent in 1977–78 and 12 per cent in 1978–79. At the same time, they had increased their liabilities and three-quarters of them had paid more to their directors.[44]

The distributive side of the trade was also distressed by the problems of the 1970s. The abolition of resale price maintenance in the previous decade had radically changed the nature of retailing. Under a regime of fixed prices sellers had competed with each other in terms of service, advice and stock availability. This gave an inbuilt competitive advantage to specialists who not only carried stock all the year round but also acquired a level of expertise.not generally found in other types of outlet. Predictably, the NATR had opposed the abolition of resale price maintenance largely on the grounds that it would squeeze the already slender profit margins of small independent specialist retailers.[45] The BTMA had shared this view, further arguing that abolition would actually raise shop prices because it would increase manufacturers' and wholesalers' risks.[46]

The industry's four biggest current manufacturers, Airfix, Lines, Lesney and Mettoy, initially announced that they would fight for the preservation of fixed pricing, but they backed down when the confectionery manufacturers lost a similar case after a forty-three day legal battle in the Restrictive Practices Court. The way was thus open for price competition in which the small retailers were always going to be at a disadvantage compared with the bulk buyers. Their relative weaknesses were exacerbated in the 1970s by the rapid rise in the wholesale toy price index, which more than doubled between 1973 and 1978. One partial defence against this was the development of retail buying consortia, such as the Wessex buying group established in 1973 with thirty-four shops, but the general impact of abolishing maintained prices was as expected. Chain stores, supermarkets and mail order organisations all stepped up their purchases of toys, buying in bulk and discounting substantially. Between 1968 and 1973 the specialist retailers' share of the market fell from 40 to 29 per cent. Over the same period the mail order firms' portion rose from 12 to 15 per cent, the chain stores' from 10 to 14 per cent, and 'supermarkets' from almost nothing to 5 per cent.

With the general economic problems of the 1970s depressing the home market and making the future uncertain, retailers and wholesalers became increasingly reluctant either to place orders or to pay for them until the last possible moment. This caused liquidity problems for manufacturers who had to pay for their raw materials and other production costs. It also led to stock accumulation, a very expensive practice at a time of rising interest rates. Leslie Smith of Lesney was gloomy. 'All you can do is build stocks until the cash runs out.'[47] The pressure to sell to bulk buyers and to discount prices was thus enormous. At Christmas 1976, it was estimated that price discounting was running at between 20 and 40 per cent. Given that the usual trade mark up was about 50 per cent, smaller retailers struggled. Wholesalers were similarly caught as extended credit lines running from raw material suppliers via manufacturers to retailers were progressively tightened.

By 1979 the trade's position appeared to be deteriorating still further. In that year a lorry drivers' strike disrupted deliveries of raw materials and finished goods. Technicians at ITV also stopped work, blacking out television screens in the run up to Christmas, thereby depriving the manufacturers of what had now become their major advertising outlet. Raw material costs were still rising, by as much as 30 per cent; more in case of plastic. Wage increases, too, showed little sign of abating. In March 1979 demands were lodged with the Wages Council for a standard weekly wage of £44.50, with larger increases for higher paid workers, two more days paid holiday and a move towards a thirty-five hour week. The pay claim was way above current government guidelines: it was calculated that it would raise costs by 50 per cent. When the workers settled for two extra holiday days and a standard wage of £1 an hour, they were still left at the bottom of the Wages Council pay league, a fact which so impressed the chairman that in May 1980 he responded to another pay demand with an award raising rates to 122.5p. an hour. In addition, there was a widespread expectation in the industry that the newly formed Homeworkers Association, set up by the Low Pay Unit with help from the Nuffield Foundation, would bring pressure to bear on employers to raise pay for outworkers.

By this time, too, the industry's export performance had been hit by the rising value of sterling, while the high interest rates on which that depended further exacerbated the liquidity problems of an industry accustomed to heavy and extended borrowing against a short peak-time income. With no sign of any recovery in consumer expenditure, despite the change of government in 1979, a general move to reduce stocks developed in order to improve cash flow and reduce debt burdens. The resulting pressure on margins led to further cut backs in investment and employment. Between 1979 and 1980 the labour force was reduced by about a quarter. The volume of advertising in *British Toys* in 1980 was well down on its 1979 level and the BTHA took on a public relations consultant in order to improve the industry's rather battered image. However, the pessimism of the trade press was unrelenting. The Christmases of 1979 and 1980 were judged to be the unhappiest ever experienced by the industry. By June 1981 the situation still looked very bad with a reported drop in market sales at manufacturers' prices of 14 per cent.[48]

The immediate cause of the gloom was the mounting level of attrition. Casualties among both distributors and manufacturers had been occurring since the early 1970s. Tan-Sad-Allwin and Rosedale Industries had both gone to the wall in 1975, while Triang-Pedigree was rescued from receivership by a package worked out between the Department of Industry and Airfix. The government took a one-third equity stake, gave Airfix a loan worth £2,250,000 and provided cash guarantees, agreeing to grant up to £1,000,000 to cover 90 per cent of any losses. This, suggested *The Times*, was 'the last rattle from the old Lines Brothers' skeleton'.[49] But it was not, because shortly Airfix decided not to take up its option and Triang-Pedigree was again in liquidation. The rattle became a roar as British toy businesses collapsed in a domino-like sequence of failures. The BTMA Council meeting in June 1980 noted that the membership of fourteen firms had been terminated while another nineteen had lapsed. Twelve months later council was told of a further sixteen companies in liquidation, ten which had resigned following receipt of the final demand for subscriptions, and no fewer than thirty-five which had not replied to renewal requests.

The roll call of fatalities was fearsome and included some of the most famous names in the industry. Model Toys at Shotts closed in October 1979, having taken two years of losses. In April 1980 Malins, maker of the famous Mamod steam engines, went into receivership, to be followed by Joshua Harris, a well-known Liverpool wholesaler. In 1981 Toys Galore, a small retail chain run by an erstwhile president of the NATR, collapsed with debts of some £215,000. In 1982 receivers were called in by both Lundby, the Scandinavian-owned maker of dolls' houses, and the importers Einco, although the latter had been cited in a recent market survey as an example of a well-managed company.[50] The following year it was the turn of Morris Vulcan and Lone Star. The latter's exports had dropped by 50 per cent in just three years. Although the sale of assets worth £1,000,000 had brought down bank borrowings from £1,500,000 to £750,000, a fourth consecutive annual loss in 1982 (of £300,000) proved too much to sustain. Such a steady stream of losses was bad enough. The whole situation assumed catastrophic proportions when Meccano, probably the most famous surviving British toy maker, was added to the casualty list, to be joined in quick succession by five of 1979's top eight companies by turnover. In the space of just over three years the heart had been torn out of British toy manufacturing.

Meccano's doors were closed at Binns Road for the last time in November 1979. Neither Lines Brothers nor Airfix had been able to disabuse the Liverpool firm of its misconceived and complacent conviction that its products and systems remained superior to all others.[51] Management consultants Peat, Marwick and Mitchell had prepared a devastatingly critical assessment of management in 1964, but eleven years later Airfix was still frustrated by the absence of basic data necessary to plug the huge operational gaps which still existed.[52] Yet an Airfix memorandum concerning defective cash, purchasing and payroll procedures provoked an angry response from Meccano's managing director, who pencilled over it with comments such as 'displays lack of knowledge of our systems', 'criticism without knowledge', 'the present system does that and always has'.[53]

The company's inability to monitor overheads accurately was

compounded by the fact that management had largely forfeited control to the unions. George Perry, employed in the 1970s as a production chaser, recalled that labour discipline was so slack that the atmosphere was more akin to that of a holiday camp than a commercial manufacturing enterprise.[54] On his first day in 1975 Meccano's first formally qualified personnel director was told that the unions controlled the plant.[55] Certainly the GMWU convener at Binns Road, Frank Bloor, appeared just as unable as management to grasp the seriousness of Meccano's plight. Told that there was a liquidity crisis and that the company was losing money, he responded by claiming that 'none of this is true. We feel there is a future. Meccano will never die'.[56] Although belated attempts were made in the 1970s to update and widen the company's product range, the results were bound to be uncompetitive because the effort took place against an unfavourable backcloth of rising prices for raw materials and labour. In 1976 Meccano's production costs were about 20 per cent higher than those of other leading die-cast companies like Britains, Mettoy and Lesney.[57] Not surprisingly, perhaps, the post-tax loss in that year was £544,970.

Between 1976 and 1979 Meccano's cumulative losses came to about £4,000,000. Their burden not only destroyed Frank Hornby's empire but also dragged down the parent company, Airfix. Despite the existence of the government's guarantees, Triang-Pedigree had proved a major drain on resources. It had made some progress towards breaking even when in 1977 the demand for large, wheeled toys was adversely affected by the skateboard craze. With sales reaching only 50 per cent of budgeted levels, Triang-Pedigree sustained heavy losses. Airfix decided not to maintain its stake and in 1978 Triang-Pedigree was placed in receivership for the third time in less than ten years. The ongoing problems with Meccano, however, adversely affected Airfix's results and served to dissipate the management effort.[58] As a result, the return on assets employed fell steadily. From a peak of 24.5 per cent in 1975–77, it stood at only 9.6 per cent by 1978–79. In that year the Airfix group profit was virtually halved by the losses sustained at Meccano, with the return on the toy business was well down on previous years. As recently as 1976–77, 72.5 per cent of turnover and 88 per cent of profits had been generated by the toy divisions. By 1978–79 those figures had fallen respectively to 35.5 and 35.3 per cent.

With group profits for the year to March 1980 facing a 55 per cent fall, Ralph Ehrmann, the managing director of Airfix, hoped to sell Meccano as a going concern for £2,000,000. At an emergency meeting with the institutional shareholders, who held 60 per cent of his firm's equity, he unveiled plans in January 1980 to improve management performance and head office control over the group's various divisions. By dint of closing Meccano and disposing of two other profitable subsidiaries, Crayonne and Declon, Airfix brought its debt down from £23,300,000 in 1980 to £15,000,000 by 1981. But it was too late. An interim report in September 1980 pointed to impending half year losses of £2,300,000. The following January the banks rejected a reconstruction plan. Receivers were called in at the end of the month.

The immediate cause of Airfix's downfall was the refusal of the banks, mainly the National Westminster which was owed £8,000,000, to extend the overdraft. Almost exactly a year earlier the Midland Bank, owed £15,000,000, had similarly pulled the rug from under the feet of Dunbee Combex Marx. As recently as 1976 DCM had been the fourth most profitable company in the UK, with post-tax profits in 1975 of £2,930,000 representing a return on capital of 21.8 per cent. It had followed an ambitious programme of overseas expansion. An agreement had been negotiated with the Soviet Government whereby the Russians acquired old DCM tools and paid for them with part of the toys produced. These were then sold onto export markets by DCM. No fewer than eight Soviet factories were involved in this arrangement by 1978, the year in which a similar arrangement was made with China. In America, DCM had taken over the toy interests of Louis Marx in 1976 and followed this with the purchase of Aurora. The latter appeared to be a particularly good proposition. Its assets, valued at $19,000,000, were written down and purchased for $10,000,000. A down payment of $1,400,000 was to be completed by instalments staggered over four years. But the American market was in depression and neither investment proved profitable, although Marx did initially make a little money. In 1978 Dunbee's toy business in Britain made a profit of £1,250,000 but this was offset by losses of over £4,000,000 incurred by the firm's overseas operations, mainly in America.

By November 1979, Dunbee's liabilities in the United States exceeded its assets there by some $12,000,000, a deficit which, under American law, prevented the company from obtaining or providing credit. This added significantly to the burden of five years of recurrent annual losses of between £500,000 and £1,000,000 incurred by a French subsidiary. At the same time the rise of the minimum lending rate to 17 per cent placed a crippling interest burden on a company whose borrowing at one time stood at £50,000,000. As with Airfix, Dunbee sold off profitable assets in the form of its DIY interests in an attempt to bring down the borrowing requirement. Turnover in 1979 was £150,000,000 but domestic profit was under £1,000,000, insufficient to support the ailing American enterprises. By the time dealing was suspended altogether in February 1980 the share price (which had once stood at 200p.) was down to 22p., trading debts stood at £16,400,000 and a further £2,400,000 was owed to shareholders. Chairman Richard Beecham felt that the company's American creditors had been too precipitate and that if he had been given more time everything would have been all right.[59] He claimed that the ill-starred American venture had caused his downfall, thereby implying perhaps that Dunbee was a victim not of the general malaise but of its own unwieldy growth. In retrospect he admitted that buying Aurora was a mistake because, while its kits were good, the company was characterised by inefficient manufacturing, administrative and distributive practices. It was also the case that once Dunbee decided to abandon operations in America, its Singapore and Hong Kong factories lost over half their existing market. On the other hand, he appeared to concede that DCM had also suffered from bad management. 'Where we went wrong was in interpreting the results of our promotion [Sindy] and in ineffective financial control.' He further acknowledged his own error in not appointing a financial controller to oversee costs on a worldwide basis.[60] As for Marx, it was a company traditionally associated with fast-moving novelties and different market targets and thus required a particular type of managerial flair. This proved to be beyond the capabilities of the new managing director installed by Dunbee. 'Sales and marketing', he confessed, were 'far, far more complex than anything I experienced in the UK.'[61]

In 1982 it was the turn of Berwick Timpo, another company which had expanded rapidly during the 1970s. One subsidiary, Model Toys, was closed late in 1979. An overlong delay in diversifying out of model figure production turned profits of £450,000 in 1973 into losses of £319,000 by 1978. Berwick's own demise came quite suddenly. In 1979 profits were £1,500,000 on sales of £16,800,000. Although a loss of £288,000 was sustained in the first half of 1980, this was not unusual in an industry which made most of its money in the second half of the year. In the event, the anticipated annual profit for the year, of between £500,000 and £900,000, did not materialise, a failure which the chairman put down to the most difficult trading conditions ever encountered.[62] In the first half of 1982 the deficit was £1,287,000: Berwick's new range of child guidance products had not done well while a car racing toy was completely outpaced by a competitor who flooded the market. The trade expected a loss for the year of £1,700,000 but, just before the results were announced, a further deficit of £600,000 was uncovered. Although the Fraud Squad was called in to investigate, Berwick's chief executive moved quickly to allay alarm, stressing that morale was high, that bank facilities were adequate and that no extra support was being sought.[63] His optimism failed to convince the banks, which rejected restructuring proposals from a Berwick board clearly divided about the best way forward. By February 1983 the company was in receivership.

Even more calamitous was the collapse of Lesney, which had made profits of £10,000,000 in 1976. Like DCM, Lesney had invested substantially in America. In 1976 it had acquired the Vogue Doll Company, and then borrowed from local banks to buy the AMT Corporation, America's third largest plastic kit maker, for £4,800,000 in 1978. This proved to be a bad investment. By 1980 the alarm bells were beginning to ring, with the strong pound being blamed for the reduction of Lesney's profit, much of which was generated overseas. In the first half of the year losses of £6,000,000 were sustained; although the annual loss was only £3,600,000, this contrasted with a 1979 profit of £5,100,000. Volume sales were also down by 17 per cent while borrowing had climbed to a peak of £144,000,000. No interim dividend was paid, as Lesney drastically reduced its labour force and its borrowings, closed some of its international operations, strengthened management controls and rationalised lines. Borrowing was cut by half and labour productivity raised by 42 per cent. In the hope of averting further deterioration in a company that was proving to be drastically under-capitalised, talks were opened with potential buyers. Early in the summer of 1981 the board had to ask the banks for further borrowing facilities to avoid the illegality of trading while knowingly insolvent. The banks refused and shares were suspended at 11p. In June 1981 Lesney, whose capitalisation had once exceeded that of Vickers, went into receivership worth a paltry £3,000,000.

The last of the big five to go down was Mettoy which survived to 1983 before succumbing to the combined impact of high interest rates and the increased value of sterling. It should be added, too, that, in seeking to diversify away from its main product lines of die-cast toys and playballs, Mettoy had made a number of bad strategic decisions. Not designing games around micro chips was one such error, as in the course of the 1970s its became ever more obvious that the future lay with electronic control systems. Arthur Katz justified Mettoy's decision in a rather lame fashion, suggesting that, as the Americans and Japanese were leading the way in the development of microchips, it was inevitable that their toy manufacturers would have the best chance of producing electronic toys.[64] Mettoy reported losses of almost £2,800,000 for the year 1980. By the end of 1981 accumulated stocks were worth £7,500,000. The company's overdraft rose 50 per cent to £4,000,000, and interest charges doubled to £1,558,000. In the three years to September 1982 Mettoy lost over £8,000,000. A new chairman was recruited from the Business Policy Unit at Aston University, but it was too late. Rosedale, purchased in 1978 as part of a diversification programme, was sold early in 1983 along with Wembley Playballs and Playcraft, to Tamwade for £1,600,000. in an attempt to raise funds. In the summer, however, another effort at diversification, Dragon Computers, ran into severe problems as competition increased and demand fell away. By the end of the year Mettoy was in the hands of the receivers.

At about the same time a survey revealed that more than half of the manufacturers were cautiously optimistic that the worst was over. Their hopes were borne out when a similar inquiry conducted at the end of the following year revealed that in the course of 1984 60 per cent of the 364 firms questioned had increased their turnovers. This compared with 56 per cent the year before. The proportion whose profits had risen was 45 per cent as against 34 per cent in 1983 and there was also a very slight reduction in the number sustaining trading losses during the year. As chairman of the BTHA, Torquil Norman concluded his report for the year with a relatively upbeat claim that the industry had started to show real signs of recovery after the long, hard recession.[65] If the trade at last appeared to be on the way to recovery, it emerged much changed from the traumas of 1979–1984. For one thing, five of 1979's top eight companies by turnover had been swept away.[66] As a result, the sales of UK manufacturers had slumped disastrously (Table 47).

Table 47
UK Manufacturers' Sales, 1979–83[67]

	Total £m	Die-Cast £m	Dolls £m	Soft Toys £m
1979	326.2	78.7	20.3	8.4
1980	254.5	51.6	n/a	11.4
1981	235.8	47.4	4.9	n/a
1982	212.3	43.4	3.0	11.3
1983	207.5	36.5	2.8	13.9

The demise of DCM played a major part in pulling down doll sales by more than 85 per cent between 1979 and 1982. The collapse of

Meccano, Lesney and Mettoy was reflected in the halving of die-cast output. Die-cast exports also contracted dramatically, dropping by almost two-thirds from £48,200,000 in 1979 to £16,800,000 in 1983.

One half of the top twenty-two toy firms in Britain as listed in a 1984 Mintel report were now foreign-owned. Two years later only three British-founded companies were in the top ten. Pedigree, Adam Leisure and Byron/Britains respectively occupied seventh, eight and ninth positions.[68] Lone Star recovered under the new ownership provided by Wicke of West Germany. The American General Mills Corporation, which had already bought Chad Valley in 1978, took over the Airfix toy division and put its products into the Palitoy range. Universal International (Holdings) of Hong Kong, a company which already had annual worldwide toy sales worth £100,000,000, acquired Lesney's Matchbox Toys business as a means of getting into the Common Market. Sales by May 1984 were 100 per cent up on the previous year and the turnover reached £21,000,000. By 1985 Matchbox was the country's largest toy business with about a thousand employees. Mettoy's Corgi range went ultimately to Mattel via a management buyout backed by the Welsh Tourist Board and Electra Investments, which between them raised turnover by 1985 to £8,500,000 and generated a profit of £300,000.

Not one of 1984's top twenty-two companies had been among the leading eight in 1979. Three were newcomers in the specialist field of computer games, and only five – Pedigree, Britains, J. & L. Randall, Spears and Waddingtons – were long-established indigenous companies. Nor had they all come through the crisis entirely unscathed. Spears had sustained a first-half pretax loss in 1981 of £115,000 as against a £470,000 profit in the first half of 1980. The following year things deteriorated still further. Despite the continued success of Scrabble, Spears made a loss of £285,000. The prompt disposal of unprofitable European subsidiaries brought the company back into profit in 1983 and it proceeded to renew its European interests by investing £889,000 in the Belgian and Dutch subsidiaries of DCM. Waddingtons suffered huge losses of £2,900,000 in 1979 on a single product, Video Master, although other profitable lines reduced the net loss for the year to a relatively modest £418,000. Writing off this experiment restored profitability and by 1983–84 the group made £3,370,000. Britains weathered the storm more comfortably. Unlike some of its peers, the firm had not been tempted to expansion in the 1970s and profits had risen steadily, amounting to £940,000 by 1979. Despite the strong pound, the inherent quality of the firm's products ensured that exports held up at 55 per cent of production and 1980 was Britains' best ever year. With profits hovering just short of £1,000,000, the company appeared an attractive investment. Contemporary experience suggested that involvement in a larger group might confer a greater degree of financial security in the future. Accordingly, at the beginning of 1984 one of the longest-established family-owned firms in the trade passed into the hands of Dobson Park, owners of Byron International, in a deal worth £6,400,000.

When at the end of 1984 retailers were asked to select their top ten manufacturers only two British-owned companies appeared in their list.[69] This reflected not only changes in ownership but also the growing foreign domination of the domestic market. Imports had accelerated sharply from 1976 and by 1980 the balance of the toy trade was heavily in the red with imports of £190,000,000 vastly exceeding exports of £118,000,000 (Table 44). The extent of import penetration was apparent when a 1985 estimate showed that 70 per cent of the toys being sold in Britain were foreign, as opposed to some 30 per cent a few years previously. In a sense, the manufacturing side of the industry had turned full circle and was virtually back to its position of a century earlier.

A further element in the transformation of the British toy business was provided by a second and far more significant invasion of American firms. Knickerbocker opened a manufacturing facility in Reading in 1982. Fisher Price, the nursery toy maker, expanded its Peterlee plant in 1983, bringing the total investment there to £8,300,000 since its opening in 1978. Undeterred by its earlier failures, Mattel finally succeeded in establishing a secure British base. It was so successful that a sales target set at £6,700,000 at manufacturer's prices for 1983 was revised in March to £9,000,000 and then to £11,000,000 in August. By the end of the year it had been raised again, to £13,000,000, four times the sales achieved in 1982. Thanks largely to the success of its Masters of the Universe range of figures, Mattel's turnover in 1984 climbed even more steeply to £30,000,000. Even so, it was completely overshadowed by the General Mills subsidiary, Palitoy, which had about 10 per cent of the British market in 1983 with sales worth £75,000,000.

American influences were developing equally strongly in the retailing and distribution side of the industry, which were also much altered by the difficulties of the 1970s and early 1980s. The crisis had squeezed profits to such an extent that it became clear that toys could no longer sustain multiple margins.[70] Even a major wholesaler like Cowan de Groot had suffered huge reductions in profits, dropping more than

£1,500,000 between 1979 and 1980, for example. Thus some whole-salers were pushed out, becoming in effect nothing more than cash and carry operations. Others survived by diversifying out of toys. On the other hand, some manufacturers reverted to the wholesalers in order to save the cost of maintaining their own sales representatives. By 1982 there were fewer specialist toy wholesalers but they tended to be more substantial: this was a reflection of the way toy distribution had already developed in the United States.

Change was still more far-reaching on the retail side, as was evident from the changing market shares claimed by the various types of outlet (Table 48).

Table 48
Retail Shares of Domestic Toy Market[71]

Outlet	1978 %	1980 %	1982 %
Specialists	35	30	27
Department/Variety Stores	22	22	21
Food Outlets	10	11	14
CTN	8	10	9
Mail Order/Catalogue Showrooms	17	19	22
Others	8	8	7

In the space of four years the specialists had lost about a quarter of their market. One outcome was a reduction in their numbers from 5000 in 1980 to 3800 by 1984. Many of the rest sought security through cooperative buying or participation in retail chains. By 1983 the Zodiac chain, inaugurated in 1969 and backed by Maynards, had seventy-two outlets, including fourteen acquired from the loss-making Youngsters, once owned by Lines. More important still was Toymaster (formerly Unigroup), with 470 outlets in the United Kingdom by 1985.

The influence of American ideas was equally apparent in the devel-opment of toy superstores, which had been appearing across the Atlantic since the mid 1950s. Jolly Giant opened its first shop in Nottingham in 1984 and Toys Я US announced plans to open between eight and ten toy superstores by September 1985. Bulk-buying directly from the manufacturers by such retail organisations further increased the pres-sures on the wholesalers. So, too, did the steady colonisation of toy sales by mail order and catalogue show room organisations. The chair-man of Argos Catalogue Sales was quite open about his intentions as far as existing distributors in the toy business were concerned. He had already declared on television that small retailers would go to the wall because 'they're finished anyway', when he told fellow diners at a trade lunch that he intended to 'murder the toy industry'.[72]

The crisis had also affected the position of the BTHA. The monthly publication, *British Toys*, was one largely unremarked victim. In 1981 it lost £20,000 and the budget for 1984 predicted a loss of £39,261. As its daily operations tied up £100,000 of working capital, it was decided to launch a rather different type of publication, which made its debut in 1984 as *British Toys and Hobbies Briefing*. The toll exacted by the depression was also evident in the association's declining membership. From a peak of 444 in 1978 it fell away to 264 by 1985. At the annual general meeting in 1984 some attempt was made to throw over the existing council, critics suggesting that the association had become too expensive and too labour intensive, and that it had been dominated by the empire-buiding interests of the big companies.[73]

While this last accusation was probably true of earlier years, the record suggests that during the 1970s the BTMA had become more sensitive to the interests and needs of smaller enterprises. To some the pendulum appeared to have swung too far in that direction. In September 1984 the council agreed that it should be take steps to make itself made more aware of the major firms' views.[74] It was partly out of concern for the small companies' interests that the association had resisted union pressure to grant full employee status to outworkers. A similar motivation lay behind its stand against the unions' campaign to get the Wages Council replaced by a joint council. Joint councils had no independent members, and the employers certainly felt that the independents on the Wages Council had done them few favours in the course of the 1970s. On the other hand, the establishment of a joint council would have entailed the BTMA turning itself into an employers' association. It was appreciated that this would be costly and have little appeal to small firms. In similar fashion, the BTMA had opposed a government sick pay scheme because of its unwelcome implications for small companies.[75]

A new flexibility and realism was certainly evident in a strategy paper prepared by David Hawtin, the association's director general in 1983. He pointed out that, as a result of recent events, only a few quality British manufacturers now existed, leaving the market mainly reliant on imports. More and more components were being made overseas, a development that had been recognised in the association's decision to internationalise the annual fair and to open associate membership to overseas manufacturers. He also pointed out that major retailers and buying groups were increasingly importing on their own account. In these circumstances he argued, with some foresight, that an association based solely on local manufacture would inevitably become irrelevant and that it was necessary to move closer towards the other trade associations. He therefore proposed arrangements similar to those existing in America, whereby full membership of the association would be open to British subsidiaries of overseas manufacturers and also to importers. Wholesalers, retailers, designers and toy libraries would qualify for associate membership. Initially too radical for the membership, the plan was deferred for some time before council agreed in June 1984 to recommend that membership be opened more widely to any organisation connected with the toy trade.

In seeking explanations for the series of disasters that overtook the toy industry at the turn of the 1970s two preliminary points need to be made. First, it must be remembered that its problems were by no means unique. British manufacturing in general was under duress and total manufacturing output fell sharply between 1979 and 1981. The proportion of the national workforce engaged in industry had been declining steadily since 1965. In toy making the collapse of the major companies helped to reduce employment from 42,500 in 1979 to 25,400 three years later. The second point is no less important, though often overlooked, and it is that the typical business enterprise is a defunct one. The firm which survives through several generations is the exception. It is self-evident that the concomitant of structural change in any economy must be the disappearance of manufacturing companies. Products, like people, have life-cycles, moving from birth through growth to maturity and eventual decline.[76]

Table 49

Survival Rates of British Toy Businesses, 1930–70

Number of Firms Existing in	1930	Number Still Extant in			
		1940	1950	1960	1970
1920	1,340	560	280	21	16	12
1930	2,460	2,460	1,330	1,110	750	390
1940	2,800		2,800	1,800	1,380	600
1950	3,830			3,830	1,980	1,180
1960	4,850				4,850	1,960

Figures calculated from a 10 per cent sample

As Table 49 indicates, mortality rates in the toy industry were historically high with only a small proportion of enterprises surviving for more than thirty years. Only slightly more than half of those existing in 1950 were still extant ten years later, while under a third lasted for twenty years. Such a high turnover rate was inevitable given that the vast majority of toy firms were small-scale operations. What was unique, however, about the 1979–83 period was the virtually simultaneous collapse of two-thirds of the country's major toy manufacturers in an industry whose six largest firms had accounted for 35 per cent of all home sales in 1979.

Within the trade itself one favoured explanation was couched in terms of changing market structures. Stress was placed upon the effects of a declining birth rate exacerbated by a continued reduction of the age at which children were thought to lose interest in toys. Certainly the number of children under the age of ten had fallen from 9,300,000 in 1970 to 7,700,000 in 1978, but the 1979 Price Commission Report pointed out that there had been no corresponding fall in the per capita expenditure on toys for that age group.[77] Furthermore, the proportion of the population aged between two and four and who attended school was increasing, rising from 11.5 per cent in 1970–71 to 27.2 per cent in 1980–81.[78] Several firms, including Lesney, had sought to capitalise on the ensuing demand for nursery toys in their respective programmes of diversification. Another countervailing tendency was provided by the fact that people were also living longer. This opened up two new possibilities for toy manufacturers. It was widely agreed that grandparents often had more disposable income than parents, allowing them more freedom to indulge their strong natural predisposition to treat grandchildren. As one salesman rather cynically put it, when a granny entered the shop 'they just open the till and wait for the money to fall in'.[79] Greater longevity also provided a further boost to an already expanding leisure market which toy and, more particularly, hobby manufacturers, could exploit. The manufacturers had not been slow to appreciate this fact, changing the title of their organisation to the British Toy and Hobby Manufacturers Association and turning *British Toys* into *British Toys and Hobbies*. At its annual meetings in 1977 the European Toy Institute devoted sessions to considering ways in which the trade could secure a greater share of the adult leisure market.

It is in any case difficult to see how the falling birth-rate by itself could have been a major cause of the collapse. For one thing, British manufacturers producing other types of goods for the juvenile market appear to have been relatively unaffected by it. For another, it was a Europe-wide phenomenon. The main theme of the 1977 European Toy Institute conference concerned the issue of how the industry should react to the falling birth-rate in Europe. The delegates concluded that, while all countries faced similarly falling birth-rates, the fact was that more money was being spent on children than ever before. It was necessary to explore how to get a larger share of the overall market via diversification and also how the appeal of the industry's products could be extended further up the age range.

Even more commonly blamed for the British industry's problems was the general economic situation. Ralph Ehrmann of Airfix attributed his failure to a combination of high interest rates, the high level of sterling and domestic depression. The BTHA's report on the British situation to the ninth annual meeting of the International Committee of Toy Institutes in 1983 commented that the previous four years 'had been amongst the worst in living memory'.[80] Yet while it is true that in Britain the situation was made worse by industrial unrest and rampant inflation, the economic implications of the oil crisis and the ending of the long postwar boom were felt by every major toy producer. At the same meeting the Spanish delegation reported a contraction, the Americans a gloomy year, the Japanese a 6 per cent fall in production and the French an increase of 30 per cent in imports. In Germany, the industry stagnated after 1977 while the rapid export growth that had characterised the Italian industry in the first half of the 1970s slowed down. Only the apparently insatiable Hong Kong toy magnates had done well.

Table 50
UK Toy Expenditure, 1974–79[81]

Year	Current Prices £	Constant 1975 Prices £
1974	52,088,000	64,418,000
1975	63,905,000	63,905,000
1976	73,966,000	64,030,000
1977	84,011,000	63,198,000
1978	96,308,000	66,680,000
1979	112,245,000	69,398,000

If the effects of the depression were thus international in their scope, few appear to have suffered as badly as the British. It cannot plausibly maintained that the state of the domestic demand was a major cause of difficulty. Since the end of the war toy buying had risen consistently, suggesting that it was not especially responsive to changes in the economic environment. Even in a recession, parental desires to ensure that children had a good Christmas meant that toy purchases were not likely to be an early or even a major casualty of adult parsimony. The trend of consumer expenditure on toys was certainly not downwards, even if it was not especially buoyant (Table 50).

Furthermore, as a percentage of all family expenditure, spending on toys and pocket money actually rose from 1.54 per cent to 1.95 per cent between 1974 and 1979.[82] The prevailing economic uncertainty did imply, however, that such expenditure was likely to be more discriminating. Here it is significant that while British manufacturers' volume sales fell by 6 per cent in 1979, foreign imports continued to pour in, accelerating sharply after 1976. This suggests that, whatever difficulty foreign producers were experiencing, they were still able to manufacture more efficiently and produce goods that were seen by the market as representing better value for money.[83] Within the most competitive sector of all, die-cast model vehicles, the Italian firm Burago invested heavily in computerised production control and was able to establish itself in the British market by undercutting the domestic makers.

To some extent imported toys benefited from the effects of the rising value of sterling after 1978. This also pushed up the cost of Britain's exports and had a particularly disastrous effect on American operations of the sort undertaken by DCM and Lesney. Between 1979 and 1980 the dollar-sterling exchange rate moved from $1.90 to $2.32. This was an increase of 22 per cent, catastrophic in an industry which considered a 10 per cent return on sales revenue to be very good. There is no doubt either that the high interest rates which underpinned the rise of sterling created horrendous problems for an industry characterised by extended credit and substantial stock holding. The combination of delayed purchase by customers and demands for extended credit caused manufacturers' stocks to accumulate at a time when their own extensive overdrafts were subject to a 20 per cent interest rate. This, it was said, produced the industry's severe financial problems.[84]

Even so, while the strength of sterling may have worked against the interests of the manufacturers, strong currencies are not necessarily incompatible with continued growth, as the contemporary experience of both Germany and Japan proved. In their cases, however, the strength of the mark and the yen were offset by much greater manufacturing efficiency. This in turn suggests that while monetary factors did play a part in creating difficulties for toy producers, their implications were magnified because the British industry had still not satisfactorily addressed long-standing business weaknesses. For this, management must take most of the blame. Rarely was a business analyst more wrong than the pundit who suggested in 1979 that 'those who criticise British industry for a lack of entrepreneurial flair, poor product design, uncompetitive pricing overseas and poor delivery dates, should look at the best the UK toys and games industry has to offer'.[85]

In particular, financial matters were badly handled in many companies. It was, suggested one expert, unrealistic in an inflationary age to continue to make up price catalogues in January for sales in the following December but 'masochism or self inflicted pain characterises the financing habits of many toy companies'. The industry, he added, generally exercised weak controls over raw material and labour.[86] Certainly this had happened at Meccano, where labour discipline had all but collapsed in the course of the 1970s. Barclay Securities had turned round most of its acquisitions at the beginning of the 1970s simply by improving financial controls. At Sebel a monthly review of overheads had been introduced on the grounds that a company did not deserve to do well if it had to wait to the end of the year before knowing whether a profit had been made. Yet overhead costs at Meccano were subject only to *annual* reviews. As a result, they were largely ignored and subsequently proved remarkably resistant to control.[87] Occasional hints at similar financial mismanagement surfaced also in other firms. One analyst noted that of the 360 toy companies examined in 1978 no fewer than 115 had accounts too old to be of any use.[88] Another pointed out that seven of the major firms could have generated an extra £6,280,000 of cash and raised profits by £1,000,000 by the simple expedient of reducing to sixty-six the number of days credit they allowed to customers. Significantly, the main beneficiaries would have been Airfix (by £1,400,000), Lesney (£2,100,000), and Mettoy (£1,350,000). M. Y. Dart and J. W. Spear, both of whom survived the collapse, would appear to have had better controls on credit as their estimated gains would have been only £49,000 and £46,000 respectively.[89] A financial writer in the *Sunday Times* concluded that Lesney was massively undercapitalised, while Airfix was adjudged to be 'horribly short' on cash controls.[90] Airfix added to its own difficulties by not permitting its subsidiaries to borrow outside the group from independent sources, imposing an internal interest rate that was usually 2.5 per cent higher than the commercial rate. It was also customary to charge 2.5 per cent of profits for the provision of central management services, an unusually high figure.[91]

Stock control was another area of weakness. Meccano lacked effective monitoring mechanisms, as indeed did Airfix. When General Mills took over it was found to possess more than a year's stock of receivables, although in other industries it was usual to hold only between thirty and forty-five days supply. As for outputs, the new chief executive discovered Airfix holding 200 days worth, although he had come from the detergent industry where the norm was about twenty days. Nor did Airfix have any data on stock offtake, pricing or market trends. The usual practice, he noted, had been to offload by generous discounts and extended credit. 'I believe that in the past the toy business has not been seen as a consumer product business but purely as a trading business in which the manufacturer or supplier's only aim was to sell to retailers.' The implication of this was that manufacturers merely transferred goods to the retailer, who naturally expected a high mark up in return.[92]

It meant also that relatively little consumer research was undertaken, a characteristic of the British industry in the 1970s. The establishment by Britains of a panel of children on whom to test new products attracted considerable comment in the industry precisely because it was such a novelty. The usual justification for the neglect of market research was that by the time data was collected it was too late to act upon it, because sales were so heavily concentrated in the few months prior to Christmas. Such considerations had not deterred consumer research and consequential product development by toy makers in other countries. In the United States, for example, the practice of extensive market testing for new toys had become commonplace from the 1960s. Yet as late as 1979 the Price Commission investigation of the British industry drew particular attention to the fact that only about 1 per cent of turnover was being spent by large manufacturers on research and development. 'A number of manufacturers have told us', the report continued, 'that new products often come from abroad where they have already been successful and are 'anglicised' for the British market.'[93] Thus it was that in 1976 both Marx and Mettoy unveiled identical ranges of articulated figures (both originating in Germany) under the respective titles of Playpeople and Busybodies. Certainly a lack of imagination seemed to lie behind the introduction to the British market in the 1970s of no fewer than three new model railway systems. 'One can only wonder', said a trade paper, 'at the large number of similar lines they produce.'[94] Lima trains were brought in by Eisenmann in 1972, Airfix introduced their own system, made in Hong Kong, in 1975. Neither was compatible with the Hornby system. Palitoy's Mainline range was, but it proved so unreliable that Palitoy unloaded £2,000,000 of unsold stock on the market in 1980. It was hardly surprising that one market consultant should have commented caustically on the high level of plagiarism characteristic of the British industry.[95] Such was the general lack of originality that when

Peter Pan brought out its Ladybird toys in 1980 *Toys International* was moved to comment on its novelty, 'there being very few companies indeed, announcing wholly new concepts'.[96] In this respect it is worth noting that in 1972 lecturers at the London College of Furniture Design announced plans to launch the country's first course in toy design. Such courses had existed in Germany for almost a century. In the whole area of design, development and market research, there were symptoms of a deep and long-established reluctance to spend much money.

It may have been as a result of this lack of interest in consumer research and product development that British firms failed to diversify their output sufficiently. This was certainly true of Meccano, Airfix and Lesney. On the other hand, Barclay Securities made money by rationalising product ranges, while Lines Brothers were generally thought to have diversified too widely. Concentration on a narrow set of goods did not prove disastrous to Britains Ltd, and it is relevant in this context to note that in the 1980s the American giant Hasbro generated 65 per cent of its turnover from two products only (Transformers and My Little Pony), while 60 per cent of Mattel's turnover was in Barbie and Masters of the Universe.[97]

This suggests that the main problem with the British manufacturers lay not so much in what they produced but in how they tried to sell it. Marketing remained amateurish, despite the impact of the American example and rising imports. A survey carried out at the 1982 trade fair produced a barrage of familiar criticism from British buyers. Most of it was directed at manufacturers' attitudes and business practices. There was reported to be a good deal of anger and confusion with marketing practices, especially price setting and trade terms.[98] The sales director of Palitoy admitted the validity of many of the complaints directed against his firm, saying that they had created bad feeling by excessive discounting and that deliveries had been unsatisfactory because of the firm's own inefficiency.[99]

The trade fair itself remained the subject of criticism and controversy, too. Throughout the 1970s the image of the British industry was tarnished by it. Compared with the slick professionalism of New York and the polished traditions embodied in the Nuremberg Fair, British Toy Fair press days remained, it was said, 'god-awful . . . with their amateurish free-for-all-may-the-best-man-win approach'.[100] A morning press review was introduced in 1975 but marked no particular improvement. Journalists were crammed into too small a room and only ten of the 400 exhibitors bothered to pay the £20 necessary to show their three products. Displaying toys in draughty hotel bedrooms half a century old, whether at Harrogate or Brighton, was hardly appropriate for a modern international industry. Nor, indeed, was the continued coexistence of the two fairs. Surveys in 1975 and again in 1981 both showed overwhelming support for a single fair but it did not materialise, even when the Brighton Fair moved to Birmingham in 1977 and opened one day after Harrogate closed.

BTMA's decision to move to the midlands was prompted by the knowledge that Brighton was running out of space and that no suitable London venue was immediately available. The intention was that the fair should stay at the National Exhibition Centre for two years before being moved to Earls Court. With venues being scattered about like confetti at a wedding, it was hardly surprising that, as one journalist commented, the rest of the toy world should regard the British as a laughing-stock because they had no proper show to which the manufacturers were committed.[101] It was doubly unfortunate that the first Earls·Court Fair should have turned out so badly. It was undoubtedly hampered by strikes and cold weather, and marred by the cluttering presence of exhibits left over from the recent boat show. Foreign buyers, it was said, were so disillusioned that they were threatening not to return:

> Everything they have ever read about Britain in their own newspapers is true and we, as a nation, have had it. What a terrible indictment but at the same time what a terrible injustice has been served to the British toy trade, by this disastrous start.[102]

Here again was another example of the British toy trade's inability to work together for the common good which seems so to have distinguished it from foreign counterparts. An early 1980s initiative taken by the BTHA to encourage toy buying at Easter had to be abandoned when it received only lukewarm support from manufacturers and retailers alike. With its suggestions for broadening the basis of membership, the director general's position paper got a suspicious reception from manufacturers who usually showed themselves unwilling to cooperate with each other. In the 1970s the industry's mounting problems twice led to proposals for the compilation of corporate trade statistics. Both had died for want of support. When the matter resurfaced at a regional BTMA meeting it developed into a discussion of the wider issue of the extent to which BTMA should adopt dirigiste policies rather than acting in a purely advisory capacity:

> In view of the propensity of British manufacturers to follow their own interest, regardless of the needs of their industry as a whole, it would seem that the former would be best but, in fact, neither Council nor

the members themselves appeared to regard anything other than the second alternative as desirable.[103]

This was in marked contrast to a seminar reported by *Toys International* in 1982 where manufacturers 'came clean' on products, turnover, staffing and future plans.[104] It took place in France, which by that time had moved ahead of Britain and into fourth place in the world league table of toy producers.

It would be wrong, of course, to imply that such inadequacies were unique to toy manufacturing by the end of the 1970s. It would be equally misleading to suggest that they were universal within the industry. After all, the majority of firms survived, even if circumstances were difficult. Granted that after the depression there were few British-owned firms in the top handful of companies but Britains were still there. So, too, were Cassidy Brothers, the Blackpool based, family-owned, employer of some 200 people making plastic toys. The firm had weathered the late 1970s storm by an ingenious combination of short-term working and shrewd property investments. Salters also remained, 'one of the few wholly independent and wholly British toy companies that remain (and, even more rare, one that is still trading profitably)'.[105] A relative newcomer, Action GT, increased its sales during the very depth of the depression, from £2,970,000 in 1980 to £5,600,000 in 1981. Richard Beecham of DCM soon reappeared as the managing director of Tamwade, a new company formed by a consortium of investors to extract the Pedigree Doll business, Combex and Burbank Toys from the wreckage of the old DCM empire. Displaced in a boardroom coup from Berwick Timpo, Torquil Norman emerged to start Bluebird Toys, which turned over £3,400,000 in 1983 and went on to the Unlisted Securities Market at the beginning of 1985. It is also true that it was not long before the various constituent parts of the failed giants recovered under the guidance of new management. Triang was turned round by Sharna Ware. Rovex kept the Hornby trains and Scalextric lines alive, while Peter Pan bounced back so effectively that by 1985 it had bought back Harbutts and Jolycraft. Albeit under foreign control, Airfix and Matchbox recovered while Corgi remained firmly on the road. Nevertheless, the general experience of the toy industry, particularly between 1979 and 1983, seems to bear out the suspicions of those who have argued that British managers did not shine in running large-scale enterprises.[106] The lesson of the failures, it was suggested, would appear to be that 'once you reach a certain size in the UK toy industry you can only go down'.[107]

Chapter 8

The Rest in Pieces

'Justice', remarked H. G. Wells somewhat controversially, 'has never been done to bricks and soldiers by those who write about toys.'[1] It might appear equally contentious to offer an epitaph for a business which by 1993 had a domestic market worth well over £1,000,000,000 and produced goods worth £380,000,000 of which £223,000,000 were exported.[2] Yet it is true that in essence the British industry as it had emerged into its prime years of maturity after 1920 no longer existed. Like all other manufacturing sectors it had been transformed, particularly after the Second World War, by changing patterns of demand, increased competition, technological advance and structural evolution. Multinational corporations produced goods on the other side of the world for toy superstores and catalogue warehouses which were full of heavily advertised toys conforming to international standards of safety, made mainly in plastic rather than wood or metal, powered by electricity instead of clockwork and packaged in a deliberately seductive fashion. The metamorphosis was described by Peggy Nisbet, the soft toy maker, in 1988. She observed that when she entered the trade in the 1950s

> businesses then were smaller, everything moved at a slower pace, and one could plan well in advance. Buyers at the January fairs would place their main spring, summer and even Christmas orders so one could order materials in advance and prepare a manufacturing schedule. Today many buyers can only order one month in advance, their budget being controlled not by their own expertise and experience, but by accountants working from computerised sets of figures in some office hundreds of miles away. Companies change hands with monotonous regularity until one does not know with whom one is dealing. Attitudes, too, have changed. Personal contacts and loyalties have in many cases disappeared resulting in lack of enthusiasm and motivation.[3]

The change was well illustrated, too, in the growing professionalism exhibited by the BTMA, not least in the adoption of a more flexible council structure, and also in two important changes of name. In 1977, the organisation's title was changed to the British and Hobby Manufacturers Association, which was ultimately shortened to the British Toy and Hobby Association. The publication of the *The Toy Industry in the United Kingdom* in 1992 was the most successful outcome of the association's long efforts to generate satisfactory trade statistics and it was intended to be the first in an annual series. Furthermore, the membership seemed now more willing to accept that thinking purely in terms of national industrial boundaries was no longer appropriate. Accordingly, the association took a leading part in establishing a new Federation of European Toy Manufacturers in 1990 and also in efforts to formulate international safety standards, although these were not always very easy to prepare and implement. At home, a 1987 survey of MPs showed that the toy industry was among the least well known and least favourably regarded.[4] In particular, toy makers were criticised, quite unjustly, for being indifferent to safety, and for evading their social obligations by producing toys that encouraged gender stereotyping, sexism and violence. This prompted a more positive approach to the whole matter of public relations. Although that favourite of the Edwardian nursery, the golliwog, almost perished, sacrificed in the interests of maintaining racial harmony, productive seminars were organised on a number of important current topics, including sexism, and the relationship between toys and aggressive behaviour in children.[5] A more considered and systematic defence of war toys was produced, drawing heavily on the work of contemporary social scientists.[6] In similar vein, a new National Toy Council was created in 1989 to link the industry more closely with experts in child welfare, the media and other specialist advisers. The erosion of a long-standing prejudice against outside academic experts was also apparent when the BTHA sponsored research into the relationship between aggression and toys and also funded a University of Leeds project on the impact of televised toy advertising.

The market, too, had changed. While the habit of toy buying had been steadily percolating down through the social scale from the eighteenth century onwards, rising living standards, advertising and changing social norms all combined to create a genuinely mass market in the course of the twentieth century. This was reflected not only in more toy buying by parents but also in greater sums being given to children themselves in the form of gifts and pocket money. The average weekly pocket money was 169p. in 1991. Adding in donations and earnings from jobs raised the average child's weekly income by 1991 to £3.96p.[7] Another important contribution to purchasing power was made by the tendency for families to become smaller, which simultaneously encouraged the greater indulgence of children and released more disposable income for them. The enormous increase in the number of married women entering the labour force after 1945 also served to raise the general level of family income and may have encouraged the buying of gifts as a form of compensation. It has been suggested, too, that the growing divorce rate benefited children in that it led to two sets of parents buying for them at every major present-giving occasion.[8] In so far as divorce created single-parent families, however, the opposite may also have been true, since single-parent families were among the poorest groups in modern Britain. Against this, there is no doubt that historically, especially since the Second World War, even the poorest families felt pressurised by the power of advertising to protect their children from the worst exigencies of deprivation. In the last quarter of 1983, for example, 56 per cent of all adults claimed to have bought toys. The percentage from Class E, which contained the highest proportion of unemployed and pensioners, was not markedly lower at 49 per cent.[9]

Within this mass market the range of children at whom toys were directed changed quite significantly by the 1980s. The upper age limit at which toys were thought appropriate had fallen before the remorseless determination of the twentieth century to invest children with all the burdens of adulthood. Here, perhaps, there occurred something of a reversion to an earlier age when the majority of children entered the adult world quite quickly and at a relatively early age. By the 1990s toy manufacturers acknowledged that their products appealed in the main only to children up to the age of eleven. Even then they still had to compete with the huge range of consumer goods which became available in the course of the postwar years. One survey of children's wants for Christmas in 1991 showed that traditional toys were well down the list, displaced by bikes, sports gear and computer games.[10] Video and computerised games were the fastest growing sectors in the 1980s, drawing a new number of new firms into the industry.

To some extent, however, the loss of older children was offset by greatly increased expenditure on preschool and nursery toys. Emphasis on the pedagogic value of toys was greatly boosted by the extension of educational provision after 1870. In the twentieth century the momentum was maintained by advances made in understanding the learning process, and then by the possibilities afforded by the advent of commercial television. Neither the Abbatts nor the educationalists from whom they drew their inspiration were particularly popular amongst toy manufacturers but they certainly helped to develop interest in this sector of the trade. By the end of the 1980s nursery toys accounted for 45 per cent of the market and some major firms, for instance Bluebird, relied significantly upon them.

Another major market development involved adults. Historically, the bulk of toys had always been purchased by them for children. By the end of the nineteenth century a few, mainly men, were buying toys in the pursuit of their own hobby interests. In the early 1940s George Orwell suggested that one characteristic of the English, 'so much a part of us that we barely notice it . . . is the addiction to hobbies'.[11] After 1945 the general improvement in real incomes, reduced working hours, earlier retirement and better old age pension arrangements, encouraged this development to the extent that, according to one survey in 1983, 12 per cent of the adults who purchased toys were buying for themselves.[12] Manufacturers of construction kits, model railways, soft toys, soldiers and dolls were among the main beneficiaries. Britains catered for this demand, for example, by producing special collectors' sets of its traditional metal toy soldiers, although one senior executive evidently had doubts about the long-term viability of this market. 'Almost all the collectors,' he remarked, 'are men who had metal soldiers in their own nurseries. As they die I'm just not sure whether another generation will have the same interest in all this.'[13] Nevertheless, as in America, such demand prompted the establishment of a number of small, often one-person businesses, specialising in everything from toy soldiers through die-cast vehicles and soft toys to dolls and dolls' houses. To give just one example, by 1989 doll collectors in Britain were served by 125 specialist shops, two specialist magazines, and a Dolls' House Information Service.[14] Two hundred of the firms providing for these types of customers formed their own trade association, the British Toymakers' Guild. Some concentrated on providing spare parts for old toys, the collection of which developed into a major hobby in the postwar period, producing some very handsome returns for auctioneers.[15]

Finally, it is true that the nature of many playthings underwent a fundamental change. For the most part, toys in the past were designed not only to amuse but to prepare children for participation in the adult world to which they might aspire, mortality rates permitting. In the course of the 1960s, and almost unremarked, the inspiration behind toys moved even further into the future. By the 1990s they often reflected an imaginary world which, despite greatly enhanced life expectancy, no child could ever hope to enter, inhabited as it was by creatures of phantasy and magic, masters of the universe, super heroes, transformers, micro machines and the like. Here the impact of television was formative, providing not only fictional contexts for such creations, but also the main media through which they were kept constantly at the forefront of children's minds.

Even so, the play of the late twentieth-century British child was still surrounded by the ghosts and monuments of the past. In the toys themselves, many basic concepts and products survived behind the glitter, old ideas constantly resurfacing in new guises. If it was put more frequently into a future rather than an historical or contemporary context, the struggle between good and evil, implicit in so many children's' toys and games, was still much in evidence; the objectives and settings of board games might have been modernised and repackaged but they were often little more than recycled versions of tried and tested ideas; small articulated figures were the lineal descendants of toy soldiers and dolls, both of which were still widely available, the latter now capable of virtually every bodily function; somersaulting animals still performed, albeit impelled by batteries rather than springs. By the 1990s virtually every artifact associated with human activity was available in miniature, in colour and in plastic.

Increasingly, too, these toys were sold through the toy superstores, mail order companies and catalogue showrooms, which all stood as memorials to the lost legions of wholesalers and independent retailers. Wholesalers were fewer in number and generally larger and more diversified than those of the nineteenth century. They had also become quite capital intensive, more so in fact than many manufacturers themselves. The small independent toy shop, however, was the main victim of change in the pattern of distribution and marketing. Its golden age was very brief. Prior to the First World War demand was not sufficient to allow specialists to develop in any but the very largest centres of population. Growing demand from the 1920s allowed the independents to flourish for about thirty or forty years. Thereafter, the abolition of resale price maintenance and the growing pressure on manufacturers' costs arising from competition made small shops increasingly vulnerable. Chains and buying groups offered some prospect of salvation but it was not guaranteed, as the collapse of the Zodiac chain in 1989 indicated. Even more threatening was the arrival of the toy superstore, yet another American distributive import following the mail order and catalogue showroom. It was reckoned that in the late 1980s eight independents closed whenever a new Toys Я Us store opened.[16] By 1991 Toys Я Us had thirty-three outlets and, along with Argos and

Woolworths, claimed 40 per cent of sales. As a result, the independents, who had had 20 per cent of the market in 1986, were squeezed down to 12 per cent by 1991. Between the early 1980s and 1990 their numbers shrank from 5000 to 2150.[17] Even the leading British toy store, Hamleys, found it difficult to compete. An experiment with provincial branches led to an operating loss of £4,000,000 in 1987–88. Hamleys was sold off to a new owner who promptly put it straight back onto the market.

On the manufacturing side, old firms such as Britains, Galt, Deans, Spears, Hornby and Waddingtons, were still in business. Others, however – Meccano, Airfix, Matchbox, Corgi, Pedigree and Triang – were no more than names, spectres still haunting the nation's toy cupboards long after the original firms had vanished or fallen into foreign hands. Of the twenty-three leading manufacturers listed in an official BTHA publication in 1992 only Bluebird Toys (UK) Ltd, Britains Petite Ltd, Cassidy Brothers plc, Chelful Ltd, Spears, Hornby Hobbies Ltd, Sans Serif Print Promotions Ltd and Waddingtons Games Ltd were wholly British-owned. Most of the rest belonged to multinational corporations, including American toymakers Hasbro, Mattel, and Fisher Price, and the Japanese firms of Bandai and Tomy.

Although it was reckoned that 250 of the BTHA's 285 members manufactured most of their toys in the United Kingdom, the British market was dominated by foreign toys.[18] Between 1974 and 1990 the output of the indigenous toy industry as measured by manufacturers' current selling prices more than doubled to £380,000,000. Over the same period the face value of exports quadrupled. But this growth was completely overshadowed by a thirteen-fold increase in the value of imports, which were worth £980,000,000 by 1993. Import penetration was calculated to be over 70 per cent.[19] In a way, therefore, the industry had gone almost full circle since the beginning of the century. At that time home production was certainly much higher than was indicated by official statistics, and German imports were not rising as fast as interested contemporaries claimed. Yet both the basic structure of the industry and the shape of its activity were very similar to those of 1990 – a home market commanded by foreign toys; the bulk of sales, then about 60 per cent, concentrated in the three months prior to Christmas; a large number of small domestic producers with a few important firms responsible for the majority of production; and a concentration on certain 'British' specialisms. There was a distinct echo of Cremer and Bartley in the observation made in 1994 by a major toy importer, Warren Cornelius, that Britain's manufacturing role was as a provider of traditional craft toys: 'We are very good at wooden rocking horses.'[20]

At the end of Queen Victoria's reign, as in 1990, foreign interests also played a significant role in the industry though in distribution rather than manufacture. Only in one particular was the pattern significantly different. Broadly speaking, in 1900 Britain exported to the empire and imported from Europe. By 1990 western Europe was the main export market with France as the largest individual customer. Conversely, the Far East provided most of the imports. By 1988 Chinese toys (often made for western firms) had 11 per cent of the British market. Taiwan, Hong Kong, and South Korea had 12 per cent between them.[21] By 1993 a fifth of all imports came from China.

As early as the 1960s American manufacturers had started to develop new manufacturing facilities in the cheap labour economies of the east in an effort to reduce costs. This strategy was soon copied by other western toy makers, including some British firms. The relative contraction of Britain's indigenous manufacturing base was not, therefore, unique but it was the most spectacular and the most sudden, tempered only by the continued activity of firms which, like Britains, had secured niche markets for their specialist, high-quality goods; those such as Waddingtons and Spears which made board games; or those like Cassidy and Bluebird, makers of large plastic items whose bulk made imports prohibitively expensive. The decline was also part of a process occurring so widely in the British economy that by the late 1970s economists were discussing it in terms of de-industrialisation.[22] It has recently been argued that this was the inevitable concomitant of the fact that the economy's natural comparative advantage had always been in finance and commerce, rather than in manufacturing.[23] Others have taken a more instrumental view, suggesting that the shrinking of the industrial base was the result of a persistent inclination on the part of governments to sacrifice it in the interests of the financial sector and a strong currency.[24] As far as the toy industry is concerned, there is little doubt that in the late 1970s the strong pound and the high interest rates necessary to sustain it proved the final straw for several major firms. On the other hand, government economic policy was not always detrimental to the industry. In particular, the long period of protection between 1932 and 1960 was something of a halcyon age for the manufacturers, although it subsequently became clear that the opportunity thus provided to improve efficiency and competitiveness had been neglected.

An alternative explanation for industrial decline has been advanced by the American historian Martin Wiener, who claims to have detected an inherently anti-industrial ethic deep in the subconscious of British society.[25] Certainly the domestic toy industry was characterised by what might be termed 'chumminess and gentility'. Graeme Lines attributed this to the fact that the Americans were interested only in product promotion whereas British manufacturers were concerned with 'play value and giving joy'.[26] Little, it seems, had changed since Frank Hornby got the inspiration for Meccano whilst sitting in a railway carriage and turning over in his mind new ways of amusing his own two sons.[27] It was precisely these sorts of attitudes and approaches that John Bentley of Barclay Securities so deplored. Criticised for selling off Triang, he was incredulous that the industry apparently expected him to run his toy companies at low profit levels or even at a loss in order to satisfy the social needs of the country.[28]

On the other hand, Wiener's central hypothesis, that entrepreneurship began to fail in the late nineteenth century, derives no support at all from the experience of the toy business. On the contrary, that period saw not only innovative ideas such as plasticine, rag books, Meccano and hollow-cast soldiers, but also brought to prominence a number of dynamic businessmen like Frank Hornby and Charles Baker. Nor did the flow of ideas and entrepreneurs dry up in subsequent years. The 1920s produced Walter Lines and his brothers who between them developed an organisation which dominated the industry for half a century. In many ways Walter Lines *was* the toy industry, but his achievements should not be allowed to obscure those of more modest empire builders – A. C. Janisch and C. J. Rendle at Merrythought, Alfred Pallett of Cascelloid and the Johnsons at Chad Valley. In the years after 1945 fresh impetus was imparted by new generations of entrepreneurs, the Cassidy brothers, Richard Beecham, Torquil Norman of Berwick Timpo and Bluebird, Hilary Page at Kiddicraft, Leslie Smith and Jack Odell of Lesney and Ralph Ehrmann of Airfix. Graeme Lines' opinion was that Smith and Ehrmann were both 'brilliant businessmen'.[29]

Against all this, however, there stands a substantial body of evidence that British toy manufacturing was characterised by poor service, inadequate presentation and packaging, low quality, inefficient production and indifferent marketing. Some indications of these defects were apparent in the early part of the century, although most can be explained away as the hysterical exaggerations of protectionists or, more commonly, as the result of widespread economic disruption during and after the First World War. It was in the years following 1945, however, that the criticisms of management in the toy industry swelled into a familiar and recurrent litany. Complacency set in, encouraged by the postwar sellers' market, the lack of effective competition overseas and the protected home market.[30] This lends some support to the view that the most plausible causes of Britain's poor industrial performance and low growth record since 1945 were associated with defective human capital and, in particular, poor management. Even in 1992, the chairman of the BTHA admitted that there was 'great scope for management within the toy industry to become more analytical and professional'. Newcomers to the trade, he added, 'frequently comment on the apparently unprofessional 'street trader' management style they perceive'.[31] He went on to justify this in terms of the capricious nature of demand, depending as it did on children's whim. But this had always been universally true and it had not prevented American, German or Japanese toy makers from developing highly effective management styles.

'All that remains of the once flourishing British toy industry', commented a journalist at the beginning of 1994, 'seems to be board games, self-tying shoe laces and hollow imitation vacuum cleaners and lawn mowers.'[32] This may seem an unduly severe verdict but viewed against the backcloth of history it was not wholly unjustified. Certainly a substantial industry may still have existed in Britain but it was overshadowed by the memories and spirits of the past.

> The Olympians are all past and gone. Somehow the sun does not seem to shine so brightly as it used; the trackless meadows of old time have shrunk and dwindled away to a few poor acres. A saddening doubt, a dull suspicion, creeps over me.[33]

Notes

Notes to Chapter 1
Conception

1 C. F. G. Masterman, 'H. G. Wells', *Review of Reviews*, 65 (1922), p. 593.
2 Ibid., p. 594.
3 Winston Churchill and C. P. Trevelyan were also participants, as was the Conservative politician, Leo Amery. See my article, 'Modelling for War? Toy Soldiers in Late Victorian and Edwardian Britain', *Journal of Social History*, 24 (1990), pp. 237–54.
4 L. Sterne, *The Life and Opinions of Tristram Shandy, Gentleman* (1900), 1, p. 186.
5 Details of the performance and structure of the modern industry are provided most conveniently in BTHA, *The Toy Industry in the United Kingdom 1992* (1992).
6 A. Fraser, *A History of Toys* (1966), p. 196.
7 G. C. Bartley, 'Toys', in G. P. Bevan ed., *British Manufacturing Industries* (1876), p. 154.
8 J. H. Plumb, 'The New World of Children in Eighteenth-Century England', *Past and Present*, 67 (1975), p. 64.
9 Good examples of this genre include L. Gordon, *Peepshow into Paradise: History of Children's Toys* (1953); L. H. Daiken, *The World of Toys* (1963); Fraser, *A History*; P. Murray, *Toys* (1968); G. White, *Antique Toys and Their Background* (1971); P. Flick, *Discovering Toys and Toy Museums* (1977).
10 L. Hannas, *The English Jig Saw Puzzle, 1760–1890* (1972), p. 9. The following are among the most useful of the studies of specific firms or products: J. Axe, *The Magic of Merrythought* (1986); M. Fawdry, *British Tin Toys* (1980); R. Fuller, *The Bassett Lowke Story* (1985); C. Gibson, *A History of British Dinky Toys* (1966); P. Johnson, *Toy Armies* (1981); R. Lines and L. Hellstrom, *Frog Model Aircraft, 1932–1976* (1989); B. Love and J. Gamble, *The Meccano System, 1901–1979* (1986); J. Opie, *Britain's Toy Soldiers, 1893–1932* (1985); P. Randall, *The Products of Binns Road: A General Survey* (1977).
11 J. H. Clapham, *An Economic History of Modern Britain: Free Trade and Steel, 1850–1886* (Cambridge, 1967), p. 14. The only other references to toys in serious academic works are confined to studies by anthropologists, sociologists or psychologists concerned with aspects of children's play. For example see,

A. B. Gomme, *The Traditional Games of England, Scotland and Ireland* (1894–99); S. Isaacs, *Intellectual Growth in Young Children* (1930); J. and E. Newson, *Four Years Old in an Urban Community* (1968); J. S. Brunner, A. Jolly and K. Sylva eds, *Play: Its Role in Development and Evolution* (1976); I. and P. Opie, *Children's Games in Street and Playground* (1969): R. Jaulin ed., *Jeux et jouets* (Paris, 1979).

12 M. K. Ashby, *Joseph Ashby of Tysoe, 1859–1919* (Cambridge, 1961), p. 13.

13 R. Roberts, *A Ragged Schooling* (Fontana edn, 1978), p. 30.

14 F. Thompson, *Lark Rise to Candleford* (Penguin edn, 1973), p. 44. My italics.

15 E. Shepard, *Drawn from Memory* (1957), p. 16.

16 For this collapse see my paper, 'The Collapse of the British Toy Industry, 1979–1984', *Economic History Review*, 46 (1993), pp. 592–606.

17 See Chapter 4 below.

18 'British Made Toys', *Industrial World*, 15 (July 1930), p. 33. This assumption informs most work on the industry.

19 See Chapter 3 below.

20 This is the theme of my paper, 'Models in History: A Micro-Study of Late Nineteenth-Century British Entrepreneurship', *Economic History Review*, 42 (1989), pp. 528–37.

21 P. Kropotkin, 'The Small Industries of Britain', *Nineteenth Century*, 48 (1900), p. 270.

22 *Report of the Committee of Inquiry on Small Firms*, Cd. 4811, (1972), p. xix. Britain's 1,250,000 small firms between them employed about a quarter of the country's total labour force.

23 In 1968, for example, Lesney was placed first and Mettoy second in *Management Today*'s list of the most profitable companies in Britain. See *Toys International* (September–October 1968), p. 32.

24 *Daily Telegraph*, 17 November 1988.

25 Engineers, 'the most utilitarian of all academic tribes' are particularly prone to viewing historical work in this light. T. Becher, 'Historians on History', *Studies in Higher Education*, 14 (1989), p. 275.

26 Bartley, 'Toys', p. 200.

27 *The Times*, 4 November 1970.

28 M. Formanek-Brubell, *Made to Play House: Dolls and the Commercialisation of American Girlhood, 1830–1930* (New Haven, Connecticut, 1993), p. 2.

29 See generally G. Speaight, *Juvenile Drama: The History of the English Toy Theatre* (1946).

30 Quoted in V. Greene, *English Dolls' Houses of the Eighteenth and Nineteenth Century* (1955), p. 33.

31 See, for example, L. Stone, *Family, Sex and Marriage in England, 1500–1800* (Pelican edn, 1979), pp. 258ff; P. Ariès, *Centuries of Childhood* (1962), pp. 66–68; L. Pollock, *Forgotten Children: Parent-Child Relationships from 1500–1900* (Cambridge, 1983), pp. 236–38; S. Shahar, *Childhood in the Middle Ages* (1980), pp. 103–4.

32 Brunner and Sylva eds, *Play*, p. 531.

33 D. W. Bell, 'Towards a Sociology of Toys: Inanimate Objects, Socialisation, and the Demography of the Doll World', *Sociological Quarterly*, 8 (1967), p. 447. See also R. Barthes, *Mythologies* (1973); B. Sutton Smith, *Toys as Culture* (New York, 1986).

34 J. Grange, 'Histoire du jouet and d'une industrie' in Jaulin ed., *Jeux*, p. 225.

35 *Report of the Committee of Inquiry on Small Firms*, Cd. 4811 (1972), p. 5.

36 Circular Letter from T. P. Norman to members of the BTHA, July 1984. BTHA, Minute Book, 1984.

37 The Lines material consists mainly of catalogues, whilst only volumes of newspaper cuttings survive from the wreckage of Mettoy. Both archives are housed at the Bethnal Green Museum of Childhood, but neither has yet been catalogued. The Abbatt archive, also at Bethnal Green, is much fuller. For the Meccano archive see my paper, 'Death of a Dinosaur: Meccano of Liverpool, 1908–1979', *Business Archives: Sources and History*, 66 (1993), pp. 22–37.

38 P. Nisbet, *The Peggy Nisbet Story* (Cumberland, Maryland, 1988), p. 5.

39 W. Lines, *Looking Backwards and Looking Forwards* (1958).

40 M. P. Gould, *Frank Hornby: The Boy who Made $1,000,000 with a Toy* (New York, 1915), p. 9.

41 H. Nicholson, *An Autobiographical and Full Historical Account of the Persecution of Hamlet Nicholson* (Manchester, 1892).

42 J. Strathesk ed., *Hawkie: The Autobiography of a Gangrel* (1888).

43 P. Earle, *The Making of the English Middle Class* (1989), p. 236.

44 The phrase was coined by Burke in 1757. See L. Levi, *Wages and Earnings of the Working Classes* (1867), p. vii.

45 For an example of this usage see E. Weeton, *Miss Weeton: Journal of a Governess* (Newton Abbot, Devon, 1969). This journal, first published in the 1930s, refers to the years between 1807 and 1811. For a discussion of the trinket industry see M. Berg, *The Age of Manufactures, 1700–1820* (1985), pp. 286–89.

46 C. Shaw, *When I was a Child* (reprint, Firle, Sussex, 1903), p. 125. My italics. For a similar example see A. Briggs, *Victorian Things* (1988), p. 153.

47 A. Trollope, *Phineas Finn* (Harmondsworth edn, 1985), p. 678.

48 C. K. D. Patmore, 'Toys' in F. T. Palgrave ed., *The Golden Treasury of the Best Songs and Lyrical Poems in the English Language* (Oxford, 1921; first published in 1861), p. 444.

49 *Encyclopaedia Metropolitana*, 25 (1845), p. 702.

50 R. Latham and W. Matthews eds, *The Diary of Samuel Pepys* (1970), i, p. 348.

51 *Journals of the House of Commons*, 28 (1759), p. 496.

52 D. Defoe, *The Complete English Tradesman* (1738), pp. 285–86.

53 *Public Advertiser*, 23 November 1754.

54 In his directory of about a thousand London shops A. Heal, *The Sign Boards of Old London Shops* (1947), identifies twelve toy sellers, five of them in business before 1750.

55 H. Walpole to H. Mann, 8 June 1759. W. S. Lewis, W. H. Smith and G. L. Lam eds, *Horace Walpole's Correspondence*, xxi (1960), p. 296. My italics. Perhaps it was for this reason that when Henry Purefoy went to London in 1749, Deard's was the toyshop he chose to visit. G. Eland ed., *The Purefoy Letters, 1735–1753* (1931), ii, p. 359.

56 'The Princess pleases herself already with the hopes of having at least half Chevenix's shop, *et tant de petites commodités d'Angleterre* but she will have them sent to Lorrain . . . ' H. Mann to H. Walpole, 31 January 1749. *Walpole's Correspondence*, xx, pp. 23–24.

57 N. McKendrick, 'Josiah Wedgwood and the Commercialisation of the

Potteries' in N. McKendrick, J. Brewer and J. H. Plumb eds, *The Birth of a Consumer Society* (1982), p. 142.

58 J. Thirsk, *Economic Policy and Projects: The Development of a Consumer Society in Early Modern England* (Oxford, 1978), p. 182.

59 For example, see J. A. Roper, *Belbroughton, Worcestershire: A Selection of Wills and Probate Inventories, 1543–1649* (Dudley, 1967–68). Most of the forty-four individuals whose goods are listed were scythe smiths or scythe grinders with estates worth, in the majority of cases, less than £40. Some thirty-five possessed pewter, including plate.

60 J. Strutt, *The Sports and Pastimes of the People of England* (1838), p. 397. Strutt's work, originally published in 1801, had sought to 'give some account of the principal sports practised by the children of this country'. Ibid., p. 379.

61 It should be pointed out, however, that this claim is not without its challengers for not all educationalists have been prepared to apply the word 'toy' to everything with which a child plays. See, for instance, the reports of the various conferences organised by Children's Play Activities Ltd, founded by Paul and Marjorie Abbatt.

62 M. Exwood and H. L. Lehmann eds, *The Journal of William Schellinks' Travels in England, 1661–1663* (1993), p. 75.

63 H. Walpole to H. Mann, 20 September 1750. *Walpole's Correspondence*, xx, p. 187.

64 Quoted in G. White, *European and American Dolls* (1966), p. 10.

65 J. Swift, *Gulliver's Travels*, ed. C. McKelvie (Belfast, 1976), p. 98.

66 On this see I. Pinchbeck and M. Hewitt, *Children in English Society* (1969). Also relevant is a study of New England puritans, J. Demos, *Family Life in a Plymouth Colony* (Oxford, 1970).

Notes to Chapter 2

Birth and Childhood, 1700–1850

1 P. Abbatt, 'The Need for Play and the Toy in the Past', typescript lecture, 1 March 1960. Bethnal Green Museum of Childhood (hereafter BGM), Abbatt Archive, uncatalogued.

2 White, *European and American Dolls*, p. 13.

3 Cited in White, *Antique Toys*, p. 14.

4 R. Dodsley, *The Toy-Shop: A Dramatick Satire* (1735), pp. 13–14.

5 M. Hillier, *Pageant of Toys* (1965), p. 38.

6 *Somerset and Dorset Notes and Queries* (June 1938). Quoted in White, *European and American Dolls*, p. 33.

7 N. Whittock *et al.* eds, *The Complete Book of Trades* (1837), p. 447.

8 T. B. James ed., *The Port Book of Southampton, 1509–10* (Southampton, 1989), ii, p. 140.

9 T. South, *Discourse on the Common Weal of this Realm of England* (1549). Quoted in Thirsk, *Policy and Projects*, p. 14.

10   Based on Imports and Exports Ledgers, Christmas 1698 to Christmas 1740, PRO, CUST2/ 6,12,22,30,40.
11   H. Crouch, *A Complete View of the British Customs* (1725), pp. 52, 116, 156, 198.
12   A. Anderson, *An Historical and Chronological Deduction of the Origin of Trade* (1764), p. 167.
13   Certainly this was true of the twenty large items exhibited at Cox's Museum in 1772. See C. Cooke, *Automata Old and New* (1893), p. 81.
14   *A General Description of All the Trades* (1747), p. 210.
15   For the problems of such analysis see P. H. Lindert, 'English Occupations, 1670–1811', *Journal of Economic History*, 40 (1980), pp. 685–712.
16   *New York Journal*, 6 August 1767. Cited in I. and M. McClintock, *Toys in America* (Washington, 1961), p. 65.
17   *Boston Newsletter*, 22 September 1743: *Pennsylvania Gazette*, 2 January 1759. Cited ibid., pp. 30, 69.
18   Crouch, *British Customs*, p. 116.
19   Quoted in McClintock, *Toys*, p. 28.
20   See C. Goodfellow, *The Ultimate Doll Book* (1994), p. 12.
21   J. Hoppit, *Risk and Failure in English Business, 1700–1800* (Cambridge, 1987), p. 186. As suggested above, the fact that these were almost certainly makers of adult toys does not necessarily make them irrelevant to the children's market.
22   *First Report on the Commercial Relations between France and Great Britain*, BPP, 19 (1834), p. 90.
23   J. Locke, *Some Thoughts Concerning Education* (1699), pp. 245–48.
24   G. S. Thompson, *The Russells in Bloomsbury, 1669–1771* (1940), p. 64.
25   Ibid., p. 197.
26   Hoppit, *Risk and Failure*, p. 72.
27   'Children's Playthings', *Chamber's Journal*, 6 (1856), p. 262.
28   Plumb, 'The New World of Children', p. 90.
29   M. and R. L. Edgeworth, *Practical Education* (1812), pp. 1–33.
30   Fraser, *Toys*, p. 116.
31   Ibid.
32   E. Paur to J. Nicholson, 23 June 1827. John Rylands University Library, Manchester, James Nicholson Papers, R 92013, fo. 1473. My italics.
33   *Fourth Report from the Select Committee on Artisans and Machinery*, BPP, 5 (1824), p. 314. One of Mayhew's interviewees subsequently claimed that Osler got this wrong but the evidence of the parliamentary paper seems fairly conclusive.
34   M. Hillier, *Dolls and Doll Makers* (1968), p. 65.
35   Hannas, *English Jig Saw*, p. 13.
36   K. Drotner, *English Children and their Magazines* (1988), pp. 17–18.
37   F. R. B. Whitehouse, *Table Games of Georgian and Victorian Days* (1951), pp. 5ff.
38   Fraser, *Toys*, p. 92.
39   Speaight, *Juvenile Drama*, p. 60. See also A. E. Wilson, *Penny Plain: Twopence Coloured* (1932).
40   *Morning Chronicle*, 25 February 1850.
41   R. L. Stevenson, *Memories and Portraits* (1919), p. 216.

42   G. Sims, *My Life* (1917), p. 12.

43   Strathesk, *Hawkie*, pp. 15–16.

44   C. Hindley ed., *The Life and Adventures of a Cheap Jack* (1881), p. 147. For the persistence of peddling and hawking see M. Phillips, 'The Evolution of Markets and Shops in Britain' in J. Benson and G. Shaw eds, *The Evolution of Retail Systems, c. 1800–1914* (Leicester, 1992), pp. 54ff.

45   'Children's Playthings', *Chamber's Journal*, 6 (1856), p. 261.

46   J. Grant, *Sketches in London* (1838), p. 290.

47   A. Smith, 'A Visit to Greenwich Fair', *Bentley's Miscellany*, 11 (1842), p. 512. That these were children's toys is confirmed by the fact that the author and his companions all purchased penny cornets (without pistons) and noise-makers.

48   *Morning Chronicle*, 25 February 1850.

49   D. Alexander, *Retailing in England during the Industrial Revolution* (1970), pp. .239–55.

50   G. A. Sala, 'Arcadia', *Household Words*, 4 (June 1853), p. 379.

51   *Punch*, 11 (1846), p. 96.

52   E. P. Duggan, 'Industrialisation and the Development of Urban Business Communities: Research, Problems, Sources and Techniques', *Local Historian*, 11 (1975), p. 458.

53   H. and L. Mui, *Shops and Shopkeeping in Eighteenth-Century England* (1989), p. 69.

54   Alexander, *Retailing*, pp. 239–55.

55   *White's Directory of Leeds and the Clothing Districts of Yorkshire* (1853).

56   T. Hood, 'Our Village' in W. Jerrold ed., *The Complete Poetical Works of Thomas Hood* (1906), p. 264.

57   W. Manby Smith, *Curiosities of London Life* (reprint, 1972), p. 398.

58   Figures derived from *Wrightson and Webb's Directory of Birmingham* (1847); *Hunt and Company, Bristol, Newport and Welsh Towns Directory* (1848); *The Dublin Almanac* (1848); *Post Office Directory of Edinburgh and Leith* (1850–51); *White's Directory of Leeds and the Clothing Districts of Yorkshire* (1853); *Gore's Liverpool Directory* (1853); *Post Office Directory of London* (1846); *Slater's Classified Street Register of Manchester and Salford* (1850); *White's General Directory of the Town and County of Newcastle upon Tyne and Gateshead* (1847).

59   In the eighteenth century ironmongers from all over England had travelled to pick up goods from Birmingham. Subsequently, agents performed this task, collecting orders from manufacturers on a commission basis. By the 1830s the factors were executing orders on their own account. See W. Hawkes Smith, *Birmingham and its Vicinity*, 3 vols (1836), ii, p. 18.

60   On this see J. M. Golby and A. W. Purdue, *The Civilisation of the Crowd: Popular Culture in England, 1750–1900* (1984), pp. 150–56.

61   W. Howitt, *The Rural and Domestic Life of Germany* (1842), p. 156, describes the Christmas transformation of everyday German shops into toy bazaars 'filled with every conceivable article of wood that can form presents. It was as if a magical spell had been exerted. '

62   Quoted in J. A. R. Pimlott, *The Englishman's Christmas: A Social History* (reprint, 1978), p. 121.

63   'Christmas in the Metropolis', *Chamber's Journal*, 18 (1852), p. 409.

64   Sala, 'Arcadia', p. 382. Peter Parley was the creation of an American, Samuel

Goodrich, who enjoyed great success with his Peter Parley books before launching a *Peter Parley* magazine in 1833. Some 7,000,000 copies were imported into Britain over the next thirty years, and the name was also pirated by at least two English publishers. Drotner, *English Children*, p. 64.

65 Imports and Exports Ledgers, PRO, CUST3/ 50, 60, 67, 70, 79; ibid., CUST4/ 8, 9, 15.

66 Compiled from the following official reports: *Imports and Exports, BPP*, 22 (1826); *Quantities of Certain Articles Imported and Entered for Home Consumption*, ibid., 18 (1826–27); *Imports from and Exports to France*, ibid., 19 (1828); *Imports for Home Consumption*, ibid. ; *Importation of Manufactured Articles upon Which a Reduction of Duty Took Place*, ibid., 34 (1831–32); *Manufactured Articles and Agricultural Produce, 1850*, ibid., 51 (1852); *Quantities of Declared Value of Foreign Manufactures Imported into and Reexported from the United Kingdom*, ibid., 52 (1850).

67 *Account of Imports into the United Kingdom from France, 1814–44*, ibid., 46 (1845); *Trade with France, 1845–47*, ibid., 58 (1847–48).

68 Reported in *The Times*, 17 June 1932.

69 *Great Exhibition of 1851: Reports of the Juries and Royal Commissioners* (1852), p. 1519.

70 J. R. McCulloch, *A Dictionary, Practical, Theoretical, and Historical of Commerce and Commercial Navigation* (1835), p. 1168.

71 *Great Exhibition Reports*, p. 1522.

72 *Morning Chronicle*, 25 February 1850.

73 Ibid., 21 February 1850.

74 Ibid.

75 Ibid., 28 February 1850.

76 T. C. Barfield, 'German Manufactures and English Corn Laws', *Monthly Chronicle*, 3 (1839), p. 198.

77 Clapham, *Economic History*, p. 14.

78 'British and Foreign Tariffs', *British and Foreign Review*, 4 (1837), pp. 67–68.

79 For the German metal toy trades see C. Neufeld, *The Skilled Metalworkers of Nuremberg* (New Brunswick, 1989). One merchant who issued a trade catalogue was George Bestelmeier of Nuremberg. It contained over 1200 items. See E. R. McKinstry, *Trade Catalogues at Winterthur: A Guide to the Literature of Merchandising, 1750–1980* (1984), pp. 117–18.

80 *Great Exhibition Reports*, p. 1519.

81 Ibid. Of 371 manufacturers in the French capital in 1847, sixty-two had more than ten employees, 142 between two and ten, seventy-seven employed one, while only ninety worked alone.

82 *Select Committee on Import Duties, BPP*, 5 (1840), p. 123.

83 Ibid., p. 124.

84 McCulloch, *Dictionary*, p. 1168.

85 *Morning Chronicle*, 21 February 1850.

86 Ibid., 28 February 1850.

87 C. Dickens, 'A Christmas Tree' in *Christmas Stories from Household Words* (1850), p. 11. For the experts' reassessment, see M. Towner, 'Style on a Small Scale', *Country Life*, 13 May 1993.

88 J. Oddy, *European Commerce* (1805), p. 459.

89 *First Report on the Commercial Relations between France and Great Britain, BPP*, 19 (1834), p. 94.
90 *Imports and Exports (Official Values)*, ibid., 22 (1826), p. 68.
91 Whittock, *The Complete Book*, pp. 449–50.
92 *Morning Chronicle*, 21 February 1850. It is perhaps worth noting that in 1849 the production of the French toy industry, which had a labour force about the same size as Britain's, is said to have been worth the equivalent of £144,467. See H. R. D'Allemagne, *Histoire des jouets* (Paris, 1903), p. 19.
93 Whittock, *The Complete Book*, p. 450.
94 Based on figures for GNP in B. R. Mitchell and P. Deane, *Abstract of British Historical Statistics* (Cambridge, 1971), p. 366.
95 *Morning Chronicle*, 28 February 1850.
96 Based on the *Census of Great Britain, 1841, BPP*, 27 (1844); *Census of Great Britain, 1851*, ibid., 88 (1852–53). The 1841 census also included estimates for 1831.
97 The difficulties of early census interpretation are well set out in J. Bellamy, 'Occupational Statistics in the Nineteenth-Century Censuses', in R. Lawton ed., *The Census and Social Structure* (1978), pp. 165–78.
98 *Morning Chronicle*, 28 February 1850.
99 Ibid., 21 February, 25 February 1850.
100 Ibid., 25 February 1850.
101 C. Dickens, *The Cricket on the Hearth* (1846). In similar fashion R. H. Horne, *Memoirs of a London Doll: Written by Herself* (1846), described how the various stages of doll manufacture were shared between the five members of the Spratt family.
102 *Morning Chronicle*, 21 February 1850.
103 Ibid.
104 Ibid., 25 February 1850.
105 *The Book of English Trades and Library of Useful Arts* (1821), pp. 293, 407.
106 W. Darton, *Little Jack of All Trades* (1814), p. 37.
107 Based on the 1851 census returns. The definitions used in this classification were broader than those used in the listing of toy makers. The figure for males over the age of twenty also covered those involved in games, shows and sports and was thus larger than the occupational figures for toy makers and dealers.
108 *Morning Chronicle*, 28 February 1850.
109 White, *Antique Toys*, p. 220.
110 *Whellan and Company, Alphabetical and Classified Directory of Manchester* (1853).
111 'Report of an Investigation into the State of the Poorer Classes of St Georges in the East', *Journal of the Statistical Society*, 11 (1848), p. 199.
112 *Great Exhibition Reports*, p. 1521.
113 G. A. Sala, 'Down Whitechapel Way', *Household Words*, 4 (November 1851), p. 128.
114 Smith, *Curiosities*, p. 31.
115 G. Dodd, 'Dolls', *Household Words*, 7 (June 1853), pp. 352–53.
116 *Morning Chronicle*, 21 February 1850.
117 Ibid., 28 February 1850.
118 Ibid.

119 Ibid., 21 February 1850.
120 Dickens, *Cricket*, pp. 59–60.
121 Smith, *Curiosities*, p. 272.
122 W. Croft, *Croft's London* (1859), p. 9.
123 *Morning Chronicle*, 28 February 1850.
124 This is the case advanced in Stone, *Family, Sex and Marriage*.
125 Pollock, *Forgotten Children*, pp. 33–95.
126 The debate is usefully surveyed in E. Hopkins, *Childhood Transformed: Working-Class Childhood in Nineteenth-Century England* (Manchester, 1994), pp. 1–3.
127 For a useful introduction to studies of childhood as a concept, see H. Hendrick, 'Children and Childhood', *Refresh*, 15 (1992), pp. 1–5.
128 *Trifles for Children* (1800), n. p.
129 This was in fact the subtitle of J. A. Paris, *Philosophy in Sport*, 3 vols (1827).
130 These are in fact the categories adopted in one of first and most authoritative books on early board games. See Whitehouse, *Table Games*, pp 5ff.
131 'The Bachelor's Christmas', *Blackwood's Magazine*, 23 (January 1828), p. 18.
132 'Children's Christmas Books', *Dublin University Magazine*, 43 (1854), p. 874.
133 S. Sydney, 'Christmas Toys', *Household Words*, 12 (1856), p. 551.
134 A. Bain, 'On Toys', *Westminster Review*, 37 (1842), pp. 112–13.
135 *Punch*, 14 (1848), p. 76. Such responses were not confined to adults either. Children, too, could be serious. Thus Emily Shore was pleased that her thirteenth-birthday gifts in 1832 included a copy of Babbage's *Economy of Manufactures*, 'which I have long wished for', *Journal of Emily Shore* (1891), p. 28.
136 *Guardian of Education*, 2 (1803), p. 424. Dolls were used in a similar way in Anon., *The New Doll* (1826), p. 21.
137 *A Brief History of Trade in England* (1702), p. 169.
138 For the growth of this industry see W. E. Minchinton, *The British Tinplate Industry: A History* (Oxford, 1957).
139 *Morning Chronicle*, 28 February 1850.
140 *First Report on the Commercial Relations Between France and Great Britain*, BPP, 19 (1834), p. 45.
141 F. Eden, *The State of the Poor* (1797), iii, p. 739. For changes in the composition of the Birmingham trades see C. Gill, *History of Birmingham*, 3 vols, (1952), i, pp. 92ff.
142 Whittock, *The Complete Book*, p. 448.
143 W. H. Jones, *The Story of the Japan, Tinplate Working and Iron Braziers' Trades in Wolverhampton and District* (1900), pp. 112–23.
144 Neufeld, *Skilled Metalworkers*, p. 19.
145 W. H. Cremer, *The Toys of the Little Folks* (1873), p. 45.
146 *White's General Directory of the Town and County of Newcastle upon Tyne and Gateshead* (1847).
147 *White' Directory of Leeds* (1853).
148 One at Langham Place was reported on rather critically by H. Morley, 'Playthings', *Household Words*, 6 (January 1853).
149 'Colonies in London', *Chamber's Journal*, 1 (1854), p. 311.
150 E. W. Gilboy, 'Demand as a Factor in the Industrial Revolution', reprinted in R. M. Hartwell ed., *The Causes of the Industrial Revolution in England* (1967), pp. 121–38.

151   N. F. R. Crafts, *British Economic Growth during the Industrial Revolution* (Oxford, 1985), p. 2.
152   The hypothesis of an eighteenth century consumer revolution is advanced in McKendrick, Brewer and Plumb eds, *Birth of a Consumer Society*. It is explored more fully in J. Brewer and R. Porter eds, *Consumption and the World of Goods* (1993).
153   Earle, *English Middle Class*, p. 290.
154   For Haynes and Kentish, see Lloyds Bank Archives, A22d/27.
155   L. Weatherill, 'The English Pottery Trade before 1780' in R. P. T. Davenport-Hines and J. Liebenau eds, *Business in the Age of Reason* (1987), p. 52. For the same writer's regional study see her *Consumer Behaviour and Material Culture in Britain, 1660–1760* (1988). Its conclusions are supported by the findings of A. C. Davies, 'Starting up a Watchmaking Business: James Ritchie of Edinburgh, 1809–1812', *Antiquarian Horology* (Autumn 1992), pp 260–72.
156   T. C. Morgan, 'The Toyman is Abroad', *New Monthly Magazine*, 26 (July 1829), p. 25.
157   P. Gaskell, *The Manufacturing Population of England* (1833).
158   C. Walker, 'Childhood', *New Monthly Magazine*, 28 (January 1830), p. 47.
159   *Morning Chronicle*, 25 February 1850.
160   Ibid., 21 February 1850.
161   This confusion is discussed in G. Himmelfarb, 'Mayhew's Poor: A Problem of Identity', *Victorian Studies*, 14 (1971), pp. 307–20.
162   N. F. R. Crafts, 'English Workers' Real Wages during the Industrial Revolution: Some Remaining Problems', *Journal of Economic History*, 45 (1985), pp. 139–44.
163   S. Nicholas and D. Oxley, 'The Living Standards of Women during the Industrial Revolution, 1795–1820', *Economic History Review*, 46 (1993), pp. 723–49.
164   N. McKendrick, 'Home Demand and Economic Growth: A New View of the Role of Women and Children in the Industrial Revolution' in N. McKendrick ed., *Historical Perspectives: Studies in English Thought and Society in Honour of J. H. Plumb* (1974), pp. 152–210.
165   P. E. Hair, 'Children in Society, 1850–1980', in T. C. Barker and M. Drake eds, *Population and Society in Britain, 1850–1980* (1982), p. 35; E. A. Wrigley and R. S. Schofield, *The Population History of England, 1541–1871: A Reconstruction* (1981), p. 447.
166   C. Nardinelli, *Child Labor and the Industrial Revolution* (Bloomington, Indiana, 1990), p. 155.
167   S. Horrell and J. Humphries, 'Old Questions, New Data, and Alternative Perspectives: Families' Living Standards during the Industrial Revolution', *Journal of Economic History*, 52 (1992), pp. 849–80.
168   H. Cunningham, *The Children of the Poor* (Oxford, 1991), p. 166.

Notes to Chapter 3

Adolescence, 1850–1914

1   J. Hollingshead, *Ragged London in 1861* (1986), p. 23.
2   Ibid., p. 38.
3   Quoted in J. Harris, *Private Lives and Public Spirit: A Social History of Britain, 1870–1914* (Oxford, 1993), p. 85.
4   A. Smith ed., *Gavarni in London* (1859), p. 42.
5   T. Wright, *The Great Unwashed* (1868), p. 205.
6   G. Sturt. *A Small Boy in the Sixties* (1982 reprint), p. 158.
7   Ibid., p. 27.
8   A. Pollock, *Portrait of My Victorian Youth* (1971), p. 53.
9   M. V. Hughes, *A London Child of the 1870s* (1934), p. 4.
10   E. Lyall, *The Burges Letters: A Record of Child Life in the Sixties* (1902), p. 12.
11   Ibid., p. 98.
12   E. E. Nesbitt, *Wings and the Child* (1913), p. 38.
13   Ibid., p. 178.
14   'Christmas', *Chamber's Journal*, 25 December 1875, p. 817.
15   *Routledge's Magazine for Boys* (September 1868), facing p. 576.
16   Taken from *Boys of England*, 28 December 1867; 8 May 1868.
17   Drawn from *Post Office Directory of Birmingham* (1872); *Kelly's Directory of Birmingham* (1900); *Wright and Company's Bristol Directory* (1900); *Western Mail Cardiff Directory* (1900); *Percy, Butcher and Company's Cardiff and Newport Directory* (1873–74); *Thom's Business Directory of Dublin* (1906); *Slater's Royal National Commercial Directory of Ireland* (1870–71); *Post Office Edinburgh and Leith Directory* (1875–76, 1899–1900); *Slater's Royal National Commercial Directory of Glasgow* (1857); *Porter's Topographical and Commercial Directory of Leeds* (1872–73); *Robinson's Leeds Directory* (1901); *Commercial Directory and Shippers' Guide to Liverpool* (1870); *Business Directory of London* (1864); *Slater's Directory of Manchester and Salford* (1876, 1901); *Ward's Directory of Newcastle, Gateshead etc* (1865–66, 1900).
18   *Daily Graphic*, 16 December 1871.
19   Cremer, *Little Folks*, p. 45.
20   Bartley, 'Toys', p. 154.
21   Ibid., p. 200.
22   See R. Church, *The Great Victorian Boom, 1850–1873* (1975).
23   *Morning Chronicle*, 25 February 1850.
24   *Great Exhibition Reports*, p. 1521.
25   *Official Catalogue of the New York Exhibition of the Industry of All Nations* (New York, 1853), pp. 116–37.
26   W. Richards, *A Day in the New York Crystal Palace and How to Make the Most of It* (New York, 1853), p. 135.
27   *The International Exhibition of 1862: The Illustrated Catalogue of the Industrial Department* (1862), vols II and IV.
28   G. A. Sala, *Notes and Sketches of the Paris Exhibition* (1868), p. 151.
29   Taken from Board of Trade, *Annual Statements of the Trade of the United Kingdom*.
30   *Census of Great Britain, BPP*, 88 (1852–53); *Census of England and Wales for the*

Year 1871, ibid., 71 (1873); *Census of England and Wales for 1891*, ibid., 106 (1893–94); *Occupations and Industries*, ibid., 78 (1913).

31 Cremer, *Little Folks*, p. 23.

32 Ibid., pp. 45–49.

33 Ibid., p. 49.

34 Bartley, 'Toys', pp. 157–93.

35 See 'A Day in a Dolls' Hospital', *Strand Magazine*, 10 (1895).

36 *Daily Graphic*, 16 December 1871.

37 Figures from M. French, 'The Growth and Relative Decline of the North British Rubber Company, 1856–1956', *Business History*, 30 (1988), p. 396.

38 *Reports of the Inspectors of Factories for the Half Year Ending 31 October 1869*, BPP, 15 (1879), p. 269.

39 C. L. Mateaux, *The Wonderland of Work* (1881), p. 215.

40 Bartley, 'Toys', p. 155.

41 Taken from Board of Trade, *Annual Statements of the Trade of the United Kingdom*.

42 Bartley, 'Toys', p. 199.

43 A. C. Davies, 'Britain and the American Centennial Exhibition, 1876', *Journal of the Royal Society of Arts* (December 1976), pp. 28–31.

44 *Reports of Her Majesty's Commissioners for the Paris Universal Exhibition of 1878*, BPP, 33 (1880).

45 A. I. Strand, 'Children Yesterday and Today', *Quarterly Review*, 183 (1896), p. 376.

46 See generally A. Forty, *Objects of Desire* (1986).

47 'Children', *Chamber's Journal*, 19 (1863), p. 179.

48 Figures from Hair, 'Children in society', p. 207.

49 On the historical and historiographical evolution of adolescence see J. Springhall, *Coming of Age: Adolescence in Britain, 1860–1960* (Dublin, 1986).

50 A. L. Harris, 'The Toys' Lament', *Girls' Realm Annual* (1900), p. 183.

51 P. Jones, *War Letters of a Public School Boy* (1918), p. 55.

52 R. Finn, *No Tears in Aldgate* (1963), p. 21.

53 H. Mayhew, *London Labour and the London Poor*, 4 vols (1861), i, p. 151.

54 On this see C. Chin, *They Worked All Their Lives: Women of the Urban Poor in England, 1880–1939* (Manchester, 1988), p. 68. See more generally J. Benson, *The Penny Capitalists* (Dublin, 1983).

55 *The Times*, 21 April 1908.

56 Cremer, *Little Folks*, pp. 51–52.

57 Shepard, *Drawn from Memory*, p. 26.

58 'A Word about Toys', *Chamber's Journal*, 11 October 1879.

59 *Fancy Goods and Toy Trades Journal*, 9 March 1891. The identical point was made in *Games, Toys and Amusements* (May 1895), p. 34.

60 *Athletic Sports, Games and Toys* (January 1896), p. 5.

61 *Games and Toys* (August 1914), p. 98.

62 J. Sully, 'Dollatry', *Contemporary Review*, 75 (1899), p. 72. He was attacking the argument advanced in A. E. Ellis and G. S. Hall, 'A Study of Dolls', *Pedagogical Seminary* (1896).

63 'Our Popular Amusements', *Dublin University Magazine*, 84 (1874), p. 233.

64 J. Paget, 'Recreation', *Nineteenth Century*, 14 (December 1883), p. 985.

65 *The Times*, 5 January 1865.
66 W. H. G. Kingston, *Infant Amusements: or How to Make a Nursery Happy* (1867), p. 78.
67 Lyall, *Burges Letters*, p. 44.
68 A. Utley, *The Ambush of Young Days* (1937), p. 142.
69 Sturt, *A Small Boy*, p. 23.
70 Kingston, *Infant Amusements*, p. 138.
71 P. Thompson, *The Edwardians* (1975), p. 197.
72 W. Churchill, *My Early Life* (1930), p. 34.
73 Wilson, *Penny Plain*, p. 19.
74 Nesbit, *Wings*, pp. 19–38.
75 H. G. Wells, *Floor Games* (1911), p. 10.
76 A. J. Holladay, *War Games for Boy Scouts Played With Model Soldiers* (1910), p. 2.
77 R. Ellman, *Oscar Wilde* (1988), p. 268.
78 *Athletic Sports, Games and Toys*, (January 1896), p. 5.
79 *Daily Graphic*, 16 December 1871.
80 Cremer, *Little Folks*, p. 25.
81 C. Feinstein, 'New Estimates of Average Earnings in the UK, 1900–1913', *Economic History Review*, 43 (1990), pp. 595–632; see also the same author's 'What Really Happened to Real Wages?', ibid., 43 (1989), pp. 329–55.
82 H. Maxwell, 'Games', *Blackwood's Magazine*, 152 (1892), p. 406.
83 *Girls' Own Paper*, 18 July 1885.
84 On this generally see R. McKibbin, 'Work and Hobbies in Britain, 1850–1950' in J. Winter ed., *The Working Class in Modern British History: Essays in Honour of Henry Pelling* (Cambridge, 1983), pp. 127–46.
85 G. K. Chesterton, *Autobiography* (1936), pp. 43–44.
86 F. N. Jackson, *Toys of Other Days* (1908). The pageant was reported in *The Times*, 23 April 1909.
87 Quoted in P. Green, *Kenneth Grahame, 1859–1932: A Study of his Life, Work and Times* (1959), pp. 226–27.
88 Museum of London. Ernest King Collection, MS 120109, 'City Street Pen'orths'.
89 *The Right Honourable Hugh Oakley Arnold-Forster: A Memoir by His Wife* (1910), p. 130.
90 C. W. Beaumont. *Flash-Back: Stories of My Youth* (1931), p. 101.
91 British Model Soldier Society, *Bulletin*, 5 (1963).
92 J. Symons, *A. J. A. Symons* (1950), p. 8.
93 H. Cunningham, 'Leisure', in J. Benson ed., *The Working Class in England, 1875–1914* (1985), p. 144.
94 J. Seabrook, *Working-Class Child-Hood* (1982), p. 26. But see also S. Kline, *Out of the Garden: Toys, TV and Children's Culture in the Age of Marketing* (1993), pp. 144–45, where it is asserted that 'until the beginning of the twentieth century toys, like books, had been a specialist product mainly enjoyed by the wealthy'.
95 E. Roberts, 'The Family', in Benson ed., *Working Class*, p. 15.
96 R. Roberts, *A Ragged Schooling* (1978), p. 30.
97 W. Besant, *East London* (1903), p. 120.

 98 R. Bray, 'The Boy and the Family', in E. J. Urwick ed., *Studies of Boy Life in Our Cities* (1904), p. 78.
 99 Ibid., p. 131.
100 M. Pember Reeves, *Round About a Pound a Week* (1913), p. 192.
101 M. Loane, *From Their Point of View* (1908), p. 40.
102 B. S. Rowntree, *Poverty: A Study of Town Life* (1901), p. 171.
103 B. S. Rowntree and M. Kendall, *How the Labourer Lives: A Study of the Rural Labour Problem* (1913), pp. 312–13.
104 It is perhaps worth noting the conclusion reached by J. Burnett, *Destiny Obscure* (1982), p. 241. 'Most children had certain common toys. '
105 For the revival of the custom see *The Times*, 19 January 1872. Ernest Shepard recalled receiving such an egg. It contained the somewhat unseasonable gift of a model soldiers and a miniature pontoon train. Shepard, *Drawn from Memory*, p. 30.
106 Thompson, *Edwardians*, p. 149.
107 T. Thompson, *Edwardian Childhoods* (1981), p. 50.
108 Ibid., p. 53.
109 Ibid., p. 222.
110 Thompson, *Edwardians*, p. 171.
111 C. Dickens, *Our Mutual Friend* (1959), p. 329.
112 Dora Orr, noted in J. Smith, *Edwardian Children* (1983), p. 20.
113 R. Samuel ed., *East End Underworld: Chapters in the Life of Arthur Harding* (1981), p. 36.
114 'Penny Toys', *Strand Magazine*, 10 (1895); 'Outlandish Toys', ibid., 12 (1896); 'How Games are Made', ibid., 11 (1895); 'A Day in a Dolls' Hospital', ibid., 10 (1895).
115 See their advert in *Illustrated London News*, 7 December 1895. They offered a set of twelve costume and historical lithographed paper dolls for three 1d. stamps.
116 *Athletic Sports, Games and Toys* (March 1896), p. 4.
117 See W. Firth, 'Trade Journals', *Cornhill Magazine*, 54 (1886).
118 *Fancy Goods and Toy Trades Journal*, 9 March 1891.
119 *Games, Toys and Amusements* (April 1895), p. 1.
120 This account is from *Toy Trader* (December 1923), pp. 45–46. Tattersall had obviously discovered his niche. Among the more esoteric trade magazines he launched subsequently were *Professional and Greenkeeper* (1911); *Photo Record* (1911); *Glass and China Trader* (1912); *Leather Goods* (1917); *Surgical Appliances* (1919); and *Hatter* (1923).
121 G. Foukes, *Between High Walls* (1972), p. 57.
122 F. E. Power, 'Memories of My Life'. Unpublished manuscript quoted in I. Stickland, *The Voices of Children, 1700–1914* (Oxford, 1973), p. 200.
123 Smith, *Gavarni*, p. 34.
124 'Gossip about Pedlars and Beggars', *Chamber's Journal*, 15 June 1878.
125 F. Willis, *101 Jubilee Road: A Book of London Yesterdays* (1948), p. 137.
126 Mayhew, *London Labour*, i, p. 445.
127 See the recollections of I. Dewhirst, *The Story of a Nobody: A Working-class Life, 1880–1939* (1980), p. 15; Utley, *Ambush*, pp. 194–95; Sturt, *Small Boy*, p 30.
128 *Daily Graphic*, 17 December 1872.

129 *British Toys* (December 1969), p. 31.

130 A. Bennett, *Tales of the Five Towns* (1964), p. 199.

131 A. Adburgham, *Gamage's Christmas Bazaar 1913* (Newton Abbott, 1974), p. 100.

132 R. S. Lambert, *The Universal Provider: A Study of William Whiteley and the Rise of the London Department Store* (1938), p. 215.

133 T. B. and W. Cockayne Ltd, trade accounts, 1898–1914. Sheffield City Archives, 492/B5/50–82.

134 Calculated from figures given in *Fancy Goods and Toy Trades Journal*, 9 March 1891.

135 Calculated from the Board of Trade, *Annual Statements of the Trade of the United Kingdom*.

136 See P. Panayi, *The Enemy in Our Midst* (New York, 1991).

137 *London Directory of Commercial Trades* (1894–95).

138 A. Wilson, 'British Trade', v, 'Austro-Hungary and Germany', *Fraser's Magazine*, 95 (1877), p. 100.

139 R. J. Griffiths, 'New Markets for British Industry', *Quarterly Review*, 163 (1886), p. 152.

140 C. Howard ed., *The Diary of Edward Goschen, 1900–1914* (1980), p. 76.

141 *The Times*, 4 April 1902.

142 Draft chapter of part III, chapter IX of *Life and Labour*, BLPES, Booth Collection, A11, fo. 71.

143 E. E. Williams, *Made in Germany* (1896), pp. 110–11.

144 Ibid., pp. 113–14.

145 E. E. Williams, 'Made in Germany', *New Review*, 14 (June 1896), p. 638.

146 M. D. Griffith, 'The Toy Armies of the World', *Pearson's Magazine* (1898), pp. 641–43.

147 *The Times*, 19 January 1872.

148 Williams, *Made in Germany*, p. 112.

149 'Toys Ancient and Modern', *Chamber's Journal*, 16 (November 1889), p. 727.

150 Derived from Board of Trade, *Annual Statements of the Trade of the United Kingdom*.

151 On this theme see C. Buchheim, 'Aspects of Nineteenth-Century Anglo-German Trade Rivalry Reconsidered', *Journal of European Economic History*, 10 (1981), pp. 273–89.

152 D'Allemagne, *Histoire*, p. 14.

153 A. P. Grubb, 'Toy Territorials: Where the Lead Soldiers are Made', *Boys' Own Paper*, 20 August 1910.

154 *Toys and Novelties* (January 1911), p. 1.

155 *Games, Toys and Amusements* (April 1895), p. 10.

156 *Athletic Sports, Games and Toys* (March 1896), p. 20.

157 Though less so in Britain than elsewhere. P. Bull, *Bear with Me* (1969), pp. 25–39.

158 *Toy and Fancy Goods Trader*, (December 1913), p. 162.

159 H. M. Consul at Nuremberg, Report, 1911. PRO, BT55/ 80, 89.

160 Fuller, *Bassett Lowke*, p. 27.

161 These figures have been extracted from report of the committee appointed by the Board of Trade to consider the application of the Incorporated

Association of British Toy Manufacturers and Wholesalers, 1922. PRO, BT55/80/90.

162 Figures for Beechwood, Parker Bros and Dore, from *Whitaker's Red Book of Commerce* (1913).

163 *Athletic Sports, Games and Toys* (October 1895), p. iv.

164 Quoted in Johnson, *Toy Armies*, p. 72.

165 Quoted in Fuller, *Bassett Lowke*, p. 295.

166 *Toy and Fancy Goods Trader* (February 1919), p. 92.

167 Ibid. (December 1913), p. 162.

168 The whole debate is usefully surveyed in P. L. Payne, *British Entrepreneurship in the Nineteenth Century* (2nd edn, 1988).

169 H. G. Wells, *Mr Britling Sees It Through* (1916), p. 19. See generally M. Wiener, *English Culture and the Decline of the Industrial Spirit, 1850–1950* (New York 1981); B. Collins and K. Robbins eds, *British Culture and Economic Decline* (1990).

170 The revisionist achievement is neatly set out in D. McCloskey, *Econometric History* (1987). Its results are incorporated and discussed in M. Dintenfass, *The Decline of Industrial Britain, 1870–1980* (1992).

171 For the British merger movement at this time see P. L. Payne, 'The Emergence of the Large Scale Company in Great Britain, 1870–1914', *Economic History Review*, 20 (1967), pp. 519–42.

172 P. Kropotkin, 'The Small Industries of Britain', *Nineteenth Century*, 48 (August 1900), p. 270.

173 *Final Report on the First Census of Production of the United Kingdom* (Cd. 6320). *BPP*, 109 (1912–13).

174 D. Elliott, 'In Search of Justice', unpublished manuscript quoted by B. Vernon, *Ellen Wilkinson* (1982), p. 50. Dorothy Elliott was leader of the trade union representatives on the wages board.

175 It is worth noting that in discussing the 1909 American Census of Production, *Games and Toys* (August 1914), p. 108 suggested that while 250 firms had returned their output under toys, a further 500 who also made toys, had returned their output under different headings.

176 *The Times*, 15 July 1915. My italics.

177 Minutes of Proceedings before the Committee Appointed under the Safeguarding of Industries Act 1921 to Consider Complaints with Regard to Toys. 17 February 1922, p. 43. PRO, BT55/80/88.

178 This is a highly tentative estimate. It was arrived at by calculating the retail value of the firm's output. Deductions for wholesalers' and retailers' markups (known), raw material costs (known for antimony and lead but guessed for paint and packing materials), and wages (derived from Booth's figures for the toy trade and adjusted for inflation) for an estimated labour force of about fifty (implied by A. P. Grubb's article in *Boys' Own Paper*, 20 August 1910, although it seems low compared with the 270 known to have been in the factory by 1914) suggest a net profit of £30,000 on an annual sale of 1,000,000 figures. No account has been taken of depreciation, plant expansion, capital equipment, running costs or directors' earnings.

179 Minutes of Proceedings before the Committee Appointed under the Safeguarding of Industries Act 1921 to Consider Complaints with Regards to Toys, 17 February 1922, p. 44. PRO, BT55/80/88.

180 *Factories and Workshops. Summary of Returns of Persons Employed in 1907 in Non-Textile Factories*, Cd. 5398, *BPP*, 88 (1910), p. 795.

181 *Supplement to the Annual Report of the Chief Inspector of Factories and Workshops for 1905*, ibid., 10 (1907), p. 401.

182 *Annual Report of the Chief Inspector of Factories and Workshops for the Year 1902*, Cd. 1610, ibid., 12 (1903), p. 231.

183 Report of the Committee Appointed by the Board of Trade to Consider the Application of the Incorporated Association of British Toy Manufacturers and Wholesalers Ltd, p. 3. PRO, BT55/80/90.

184 *Occupations and Industries*, Cd. 7081, *BPP*, 68 (1913), table 1. Toy makers might well have been missed from this source as well. One wonders, for example, how Sam Standring of Rochdale described himself. This Fabian and secularist lectured at the Working Men's College in the evenings and made toys in his lodgings during the day. I am indebted for this information to Dr Ted Royle of the University of York.

185 O. C. Malvery, *Baby Toilers* (1907), pp. 114, 172–73.

186 C. Black, *Sweated Industry and the Minimum Wage* (1907), p. 12.

187 C. Chaplin, *My Autobiography* (1964), p. 63.

188 The numbers were those claimed by the deputation that waited on the Home Secretary in June 1910 to protest against proposals to ban hawkers from their most popular pitches in the City. *Evening News*, 26 June 1910. The estimates for a day's sale are from *The Reader*, 15 December 1906.

189 Mathematically, this can be set out as £26,500 + 116 × 85(8175–x) + 50 × 15(8175–x), where x equals the unknown number of fishing tackle makers.

190 Minutes of Proceedings before the Committee Appointed under the Safeguarding of Industries Act 1921 to Consider Complaints with Regard to Toys, 17 February 1922, p. 52. PRO, BT55/80/88.

191 *Toys and Novelties* (October 1912), p. 52.

192 *The Times*, 4 December 1913.

Notes to Chapter 4

Coming of Age, 1914–22

1 *The Times*, 7 September 1914.

2 *Toy and Fancy Goods Trader* (August 1914), p. 263.

3 Quoted in R. Macdonald, *1914–1918: Voices and Images of the Great War* (1988), p. 45.

4 For example, *Toy and Fancy Goods Trader* (September 1914), p. 4.

5 Wells, *Britling*, p. 159.

6 Ibid., p. 254.

7 Derived from Board of Trade, *Annual Statements of the Trade of the United Kingdom*.

8 *Toyshop and Fancy Goods Journal*, 20 November 1917.

9 *Athletic Games, Sports and Toys*, 16 December 1895.

10 *Toyshop and Fancy Goods Journal*, 1 December 1916. The journal returned to this theme on several subsequent occasions, remarking for example that ultimately the Japanese would prove to be 'much more dangerous and aggressive competitors than Germany'. Ibid., 20 June 1917.
11 *British Toymaker*, 15 June 1916.
12 *Toy and Fancy Goods Trader* (June 1916), p. 2.
13 When the Board of Trade persisted with a second British Industries Fair in 1916 the editor found it difficult to contain his anger. It would, he wrote, 'surely go down in history as Runciman's Folly . . . one of the most glaring examples of unbelievable thoughtlessness, of lack of business acumen, of an absolute despotic flying in face of all elements of common sense that even this muddling government has given us'. Ibid. (February 1916), p. 16.
14 See pp. 106–07.
15 These workshops were originally set up in 1904 following the South African War. At the peak of their activity during the First World War, fourteen were in operation.
16 *British Toymaker*, 16 October 1916.
17 *Annual Report of the Chief Inspector of Factories and Workshops for 1914*, Cd. 8051, *BPP*, 21 (1914–16), p. 439.
18 *Toyshop and Fancy Goods Journal*, 1 December 1916.
19 One maker was unable to meet a wholesaler's order worth £1500 because the bank would not lend him the capital necessary to finance the operation. Ibid., 20 July 1917.
20 *Toy and Fancy Goods Trader*, 3 May 1915. The same issue, however, also referred to the trade's remarkable progress. Three months later the confusion was unresolved, the paper describing the industry's 'unsatisfactory position'. Ibid. (August 1915), p. 2.
21 *British Toymaker*, 15 September 1915.
22 *Toy and Fancy Goods Trader*, 15 February 1916.
23 Ibid. (December 1916), p. 28.
24 Board of Trade, *Annual Statements of the Trade of the United Kingdom*.
25 Mitchell and Deane, *British Historical Statistics*, pp. 475–76.
26 *Games and Toys* (September 1914), p. 122.
27 Almost certainly this the manufacturer was Britains. *British Toymaker*, 15 January 1915.
28 *Toyshop and Fancy Goods Journal*, 25 April 1918.
29 *Toy and Fancy Goods Trader* (September 1917), p. 104.
30 *British Toymaker*, 15 December 1916.
31 *The Times*, 14 December 1917.
32 *Toy and Fancy Goods Trader* (February 1918), p. 92.
33 M. Clive, *The Day of Reckoning* (1964), p. 31.
34 *British Toymaker*, 15 January 1915.
35 *Toy and Fancy Goods Trader* (November 1915), p. 2.
36 Chad Valley Catalogue 1917.
37 *British Toymaker*, 15 February 1915.
38 It is likely that a small output of toy soldiers was maintained. See D. Featherstone, *Handbook for Model Soldier Collectors* (1969), p. 44.
39 This was the verdict of B. G. Arthur, first secretary of the Incorporated

Association of British Toy Manufacturers and Wholesalers. Minutes of Proceedings before the Committee Appointed under the Safeguarding of Industries Act 1921 to Consider Complaints with Regard to Toys, 6 February 1922, p. 89. PRO, BT55/80/88.

40 W. H. Nicholls, 'Toymaking: Liverpool the Most Important Centre in the Country', in *Liverpool: Its Trade and Commerce* (Liverpool, 1920), p. 99.

41 J. T. Makinson, *Toy Manufacture* (1921), p. 1.

42 *Morning Post*, 14 December 1931.

43 R. S. Attwood and J. Child eds, *The Lancashire Year Book of Industries and Commerce* (1912); Nicholls, 'Toymaking'.

44 The same centres were also identified by *Overseas Buyers' Guide to British Toys and Fancy Goods* (1919), with the addition of the Potteries and also the south west, the latter described as of secondary importance.

45 The Toy Trade: Summary Report, 1919. PRO, LAB2/482.

46 *Harmsworth Encyclopaedia*, 10 (1906), p. 223.

47 Balance Sheets and Profit and Loss Accounts to Year Ending 28 February 1914–19. MMM, Meccano Archive, B/ME/B.

48 *Toyshop and Fancy Goods Journal*, 25 February 1919.

49 See Kenneth D. Brown, *The English Labour Movement, 1500–1951* (Dublin, 1982), p. 223.

50 *Games and Toys* (April 1915), p. 401. There was not much love lost between the two editors at this stage. Tattersall may well have been irked by the way in which *Games and Toys* appeared with the subtitle 'The Leading Trade Journal'. Indeed, he alleged that it was run on behalf of German interests. This charge was based on the fact that a certain Dr Jung had a financial stake in the journal's publishers, the International Trades Press. In fact by the time *Games and Toys* first appeared Jung's connection with the backers had been terminated. For his part, Simmons reported at some length a court case in which Tattersall had been accused of falsifying the circulation figures of his own paper.

51 *The Times*, 23 November 1901.

52 Quoted in *Athletic Sports, Games and Toys* (October 1895), p. 3.

53 Booth, *Life and Labour*, p. 71.

54 *Annual Report of the Chief Inspector of Factories and Workshops for the Year 1902*, Cd. 1610, *BPP*, 12 (1903), p. 231.

55 Black, *Sweated Industry*, p. 13.

56 'Women's Home Industries', *Contemporary Review*, 72 (1897), p. 884.

57 R. H. Sherard, *The White Slaves of England* (1897), p. 41.

58 The worst year was 1913 when four firms making stuffed toys were summonsed for keeping unsavoury premises. *Annual Report of the Chief Inspector of Factories and Workshops for the Year 1913*, Cd. 7491, *BPP*, 29 (1914), p. 716.

59 P. Kropotkin, *Fields, Factories and Workshops* (1909), p. 129. There was no mention of toymaking, for example, in the *Report from the Select Committee on Home Work*, *BPP*, 6 (1907).

60 This information is drawn from two Board of Trade reports commissioned as part of the process of establishing the Trade Board. Toy Trade; Summary Report 1919. PRO, LAB2/482; Summary of Wages Information in the Toy Trade, 31 May 1921. PRO, LAB2/794/11

61 Toy Trade; Summary Report 1919. PRO, LAB2/482.
62 *The Times*, 12 December 1918.
63 *Toy and Fancy Goods Trader* (December 1918), p. 54.
64 Quoted in Love and Gamble, *The Meccano System*, p. 77.
65 The bank manager was not initially enthusiastic, saying that 'that's a lot of money and you are only toymakers'. Lines, *Looking Backwards*, p. 10. Walter Lines' son, Graeme, recalled later that his father replied by saying he had no security to offer save his hands. Author's interview with G. Lines, 10 April 1991.
66 Lines, *Looking Backwards*, p. 10.
67 This was the figure quoted in an interview with Lines and published in *The Times*, 22 December 1966.
68 *Toyshop and Fancy Goods Journal* (January 1923), p. 16.
69 Minutes of Proceedings before the Committee Appointed under the Safeguarding of Industries Act 1921 to Consider Complaints with Regard to Toys, 5 February 1922, p. 46. PRO, BT55/80/88.
70 *Toyshop and Fancy Goods Journal* (October 1920), p. 47.
71 Ibid. (February 1921), p. 27.
72 This information is drawn from Minutes of Proceedings before the Committee Appointed under the Safeguarding of Industries Act 1921 to Consider Complaints with Regard to Toys, passim. PRO, BT55/80/88.
73 Ibid.
74 Application Under Part II of the Safeguarding of Industries Act by the Incorporated Association of British Toy Manufacturers and Wholesalers Ltd. Report of the Departmental Committee of the Board of Trade, p. 6. PRO, BT55/80/87.
75 Minutes of Proceedings before the Committee Appointed under the Safeguarding of Industries Act 1921 to Consider Complaints in Regard to Toys, passim. PRO, BT55/80/88.
76 Toy Trade Board Meetings, 14–15 September 1920; 12–13 October 1920; 20–21 July 1921; 23–24 August 1921. PRO, LAB 35/368.
77 Employers in most of the newly-established trade boards became hostile during the slump. The boards had protected them against excessively high wages during the boom but also made subsequent reductions very difficult. The Association of British Chambers of Commerce gathered local evidence on the rulings of the boards in order to campaign against them. This effort was backed by the Treasury on the grounds that the boards constituted an interference with the free market. See S. Blackburn, 'The Problem of Prices: From Trade Boards to a National Minimum Wage', *Industrial Relations Journal*, 19 (1988).
78 *Toy and Fancy Goods Trader* (June 1921), p. 58.
79 Ibid. (March 1922), p. 38.
80 See, for example, the warning given in ibid. (November 1917), p. 12.
81 *The Times*, 26 August 1919.
82 Ibid., 24 February 1921.
83 Ibid., 2 September 1919.
84 Ibid., 20 September 1920.
85 *Toy and Fancy Goods Trader* (October 1917), p. 32.

86 So, too, had A. W. Gamage. See his comments in H. B. Gray and S. Turner eds, *Eclipse or Empire* (1916), p. 289.
87 *Toy and Fancy Goods Trader* (January 1918), p. 10.
88 Ibid. (July 1918), p. 30.
89 *Toyshop and Fancy Goods Journal* (August 1919), p. 2.
90 Ibid. (September 1919), p. 93.
91 See his comments in *Toy and Fancy Goods Trader* (December 1919), p. 62; (January 1920), p. 56.
92 Ibid. (November 1919), p. 296.
93 *Hansard*, 5th Series, 21, 17 November 1919.
94 Ibid., 135, 24 November 1920.
95 Ibid., 22 November 1920.
96 Application under Part II of the Safeguarding of Industries Act by the Incorporated Association of British Toy Manufacturers and Wholesalers Ltd. Report of Departmental Committee, p. 5. PRO, BT55/80/87.
97 Ibid., p 13.
98 Quoted later in *Toyshop and Fancy Goods Journal* (October 1919), p. 147.
99 *British Trade After the War*, ii, Cd. 8275, *Summaries of the Evidence*, *BPP*, 15 (1916), p. 634.
100 *British Trade After the War: Report*, Cd. 8181, Ibid., p. 608.
101 Memorandum and Short Resumé of the Toy Trade since the Outbreak of War. Submitted 6 Feb 1922. PRO, BT55/80/89.
102 Minutes of Proceedings before the Committee Appointed under the Safeguarding of Industries Act 1921 to Consider Complaints with Regard to Toys, 5 February 1922, p. 33. PRO, BT55/80/88.
103 Ibid., p. 41.
104 Ibid., 6 February 1922, p. 36.
105 Letter from Mr G. W. S. Sherratt, quoted in White, *European and American Dolls*, pp. 159–60.
106 Minutes of Proceedings before the Committee Appointed under the Safeguarding of Industries Act 1921 to Consider Complaints with Regard to Toys, 16 February 1922, p. 127. PRO, BT55/80/88.
107 Ibid., 2 March 1922, p. 19.
108 Ibid., 6 February 1922, p. 71.
109 Ibid., 17 February 1922, p. 83.
110 Ibid., 16 February 1922, pp. 45ff.
111 See the comments in the Bassett Lowke Catalogue, 1922, p. 2.
112 *The Times*, 28 March 1922. The Americans had good cause to be alarmed. As early as 1920 the import of dolls and doll parts from Germany were back to their 1913 levels. See A. Gray, *Postwar Conditions in the German Toy Industry* (Washington, DC, 1924), table 17.
113 *Toy and Fancy Goods Trader* (March 1922), p. 38.
114 Ibid. (January 1923), p. 18.
115 *Toyshop and Fancy Goods Journal* (August 1922), p. 28.
116 Application under Part II of the Safeguarding of Industries Act. Report of the Departmental Committee; Summary. PRO, BT55/80/87.
117 *Toy and Fancy Goods Trader* (July 1916), p. 30.
118 *British Toymaker*, 15 September 1915.

119   *Toy and Fancy Goods Trader*, 31 May 1915.
120   *Toyshop and Fancy Goods Journal*, 15 January 1917.
121   Ibid.
122   Ibid., 20 February 1917.
123   Ibid., 20 October 1917.
124   Ibid. (January 1921), p. 1.
125   *Toy and Fancy Goods Trader* (August 1918), p. 30.
126   *Toyshop and Fancy Goods Journal* (April 1920), p. 196.
127   Ministry of Labour, *Summary Report No. 3, 1921; Fancy Goods, Bazaar, Toys and Games and Sports Goods*. PRO, LAB2/776/ISE 106/14.
128   See for example E. V. Lucas and F. Bedford, *The Book of Shops* (1899), p. 17.
129   *Toy and Fancy Goods Trader* (March 1923), p. 56.

Notes to Chapter 5

Comfortable Maturity, 1923–44

1   Quoted in *Toy Trader* (November 1926), p. 72.
2   Ibid. (January 1930), p. 52.
3   *Final Report on the Third Census of Production* (1924). But note the comment on p. 75 above concerning the reliability of the 1907 figures.
4   *Ministry of Labour Gazette* (July 1923), p. 252.
5   *Toy Trader* (January 1925), p. 58.
6   *The Times*, 22 January 1929.
7   *Final Report on the Fifth Census of Production* (1935), p. 446. It should be noted that the census makers counted only the output of those firms with more than ten workers; its figures are not, therefore, directly comparable with those of earlier censuses which were differently based.
8   Derived from Board of Trade, *Annual Statements of the Trade of the United Kingdom*.
9   Estimated by *Toy Trader* (April 1927), p. 60.
10   *Final Report of the Fourth Census of Production* (1930), p. 329.
11   *The Times*, 24 December 1924.
12   See for example the letter from A. J. Johnson of Chad Valley in *Toy Trader* (December 1923), p. 62.
13   *The Times*, 27 February 1929
14   *Industrial World*, XV (July 1930), p. 33.
15   Derived from Board of Trade, *Annual Statements of the Trade of the United Kingdom*.
16   *Toy Trader* (April 1929), p. 14.
17   Ibid. (September 1926), p. 32.
18   Ibid. (April 1928), p. 70.
19   Ibid. (January 1930), p. 10.
20   See for example, ibid. (April 1923), p. 20; (September 1924), p. 20; (March 1926), p. 30; (March 1928), p. 22; (February 1933), p. 8; (July 1934), p. 30.

21 *Final Report on the Fourth Census of Production* (1930), p. 329.
22 *Toy Trader* (December 1925), p. 20.
23 *Final Report on the Third Census of Production* (1924), p. 369.
24 On this see T. A. B. Corley, 'Consumer Marketing in Britain, 1914–60', *Business History*, 29 (1987), pp. 65–83.
25 *Toy Trader* (December 1927), p. 88.
26 H. Leak and A. Maizels, 'The Structure of British Industry', *Journal of the Royal Statistical Society*, 108 (1945), p. 165, include metal construction toys in their list of commodities in which production was monopolised by one or two firms.
27 *Toy Trader* (November 1923), p. 50.
28 Ibid. (November 1924), p. 56
29 Meccano Ltd, Balance Sheet and Profit and Loss Accounts, 1926–36. MMM. Meccano Archives. B/ME/E.
30 All the employment figures cited in this and the preceding paragraphs are from Reconstitution of the Trade Board, 28 November 1932. PRO, LAB2/2089.
31 This description of G. and J. Lines is from *British Toymaker*, 15 February 1915, by which time there were 300 employees.
32 Toy Trade Board. Perambulator and Invalid Carriage Trade Board. Joint Conference on Scope. Memorandum on the Results of an Investigation into the Overlap between the Two Trades, 25 April 1924. PRO, LAB2/906.
33 Much of this information concerning Lines Brothers is contained in Report of an Investigation into the Overlap between the Toy Trade and the Perambulator Trade, 1924/5. PRO, LAB2/906/TB135/10/24
34 Ibid., p. 18.
35 Ibid., p. 48.
36 Ibid., p. 58.
37 R. O'Brien, *The Story of American Toys* (1990), p. 127.
38 *Toy Trader* (July 1931), pp. 5–8.
39 Ibid. (August 1931), p. 50a.
40 Toy Trade Board Meeting, 11 March 1937, PRO, LAB11/72. He made this claim during wage negotiations at a trade board meeting and may thus have tended to exaggerate.
41 *Games and Toys* (October 1937), p. 40.
42 This claim was made by the managing director of Meccano (France) Ltd, in *British Toys* (July 1973), p. 10. It was subsequently confirmed in the author's interview with Graeme Lines, 10 April 1991.
43 *Games and Toys* (July 1931), p. 24.
44 Calculated from a 10 per cent sample of the lists provided in the *Games and Toy Trade Directory* (1920, 1930, 1940).
45 *Toy Trader*, (February 1932–June 1933), passim.
46 There is some dispute about the longevity of this company. Fawdry, *British Tin Toys*, p. 48, says it lasted until 1980. An earlier date, 1968, is suggested in A. Rose, *The Collector's All-Colour Guide to Toy Soldiers* (1989), p. 15.
47 Cascelloid Directors Minutes, 26 January 1933. Hackney Borough Archives (hereafter HBA). D/B/XYL/11/1.
48 Ibid., 30 September 1935.
49 Cascelloid Directors Annual Reports, 1931–39. HBA, D/B/XYL/11/2.
50 Finn, *No Tears*, p. 22.

51 L. Herren, *Growing Up Poor in London* (1973), p. 43.

52 *Toy Trader* (March 1934), p. 80.

53 G. MacBeth, *A Child of the War* (1987), p. 55.

54 Lines, *Looking Backwards*, p. 25.

55 Figures taken from the annual company statements as reported in *The Times*.

56 For this hypothesis see, for example, D. H. Aldcroft, *The Interwar Economy: Britain, 1919–1939* (1970), pp. 177–201. See also, B. W. Alford, 'British Industry between the Wars', in R. Floud and D. McCloskey eds, *The Economic History of Britain since 1700*, ii, *1860 to the 1970s* (Cambridge, 1981).

57 *Final Report on the Fifth Census of Production* (1935), p. 454.

58 Ibid., p. 574.

59 *The Times*, 22 December 1933.

60 Ibid., 26 October 1937.

61 Ibid., 21 December 1937.

62 *Ministry of Labour Gazette* (May 1937), p. 176.

63 This debate is conveniently summarised in S. Pollard, *The Development of the British Economy, 1914–1980* (3rd edn, 1983), pp. 151–53.

64 N. Gray, *The Worst of Times: An Oral History of the Great Depression in Britain* (1985), p. 12

65 R. Samuel ed., *East End Underworld: Chapters in the Life of Arthur Harding* (1981), p. 226.

66 N. Thompson, *At Their Departing: A Childhood Memoir* (1986), p. 144.

67 The estimates in this table are only approximations. The domestic production figures relate only to the firms making returns to the census while the numbers of children aged under fourteen are derived from the censuses of population of 1921 and 1931.

68 A. H. Halsey ed., *Trends in British Society since 1900* (1972), p. 33.

69 *The Times*, 14 January 1932.

70 Ibid., 27 February 1936.

71 *Toy Trader* (August 1932), p. 6. Cascelloid had to pay 4.5 per cent on a loan raised in March 1932.

72 Derived from Board of Trade, *Annual Statements of the Trade of the United Kingdom*.

73 Memo from H. H. Ryder of the Customs House Secretariat, 23 May 1930, PRO, BT215/1275.

74 Toy and Games Inquiry: Statement of Opposition by Manufacturing Confectioners' Alliance, PRO, BT215/1285.

75 Toy and Games Inquiry: Fifth Day, 19 January 1932. PRO, BT215/1294.

76 Toy and Games Inquiry: George Barnes to the Chairman, 28 January 1932. PRO, BT215/1279.

77 *The Times*, 21 April 1932.

78 *Hansard*, 292, 24 July 1934.

79 Toy and Games Inquiry: Second Day, 12 January 1932. PRO, BT215/1291.

80 Toy and Games Inquiry: Seventh Day, 26 January 1932. PRO, BT215/1296.

81 *Toy Trader* (March 1934), p. 26.

82 J. B. Jefferys, *The Distribution of Consumer Goods. A Factual Study of Methods and Costs in the United Kingdom in 1938* (Cambridge, 1950), p. 131.

83 Ibid., p. 47.

84   G. Orwell, *Down and Out in Paris and London* (1940 edn), p. 143.

85   M. Benedetta, *The Street Markets of London* (1936), p. 124.

86   Ibid., p. 17.

87   *Toy Trader* (October 1930), pp. 36–38.

88   Ibid. (June 1934), p. 8.

89   Ministry of Labour, Information Relating to the Toy Manufacturing Trade, May 1927. PRO, LAB2/1142;TB135/23/1926.

90   *Toy Trader* (January 1930), p. 12.

91   Ibid. (July 1923) p. 24.

92   Ibid. (March 1934), p. 26.

93   Ibid. (July 1934), p. 26.

94   Trade Board Meeting, 11 March 1937. PRO, LAB11/72; ibid., 13 April 1937. LAB11/65; ibid., July 1937. Lab11/82.

95   *Toy Trader* (July 1938), p. 1.

96   *Toy Trader and Exporter* (December 1940), p. 1.

97   *Toy Trader* (February 1933), p. 8.

98   *Daily Herald*, 14 August 1941.

99   Cascelloid Ltd. Directors Annual Report for Year Ended 31 December 1940. HBA, D/B/XYL/11/2.

100 Derived from the Board of Trade, *Annual Statements of the Trade of the United Kingdom*.

101 *Toy Trader and Exporter* (July 1942), p. 4.

102 *Hansard*, 380, 25 June 1942.

103 For example, *The Times*, 6 October 1943, reported the case of a carpenter at an aircraft factory jailed for stealing plywood and paint to make model tanks and other wood toys.

104 See the letter from a retailer in *Toy Trader and Exporter* (September 1943), p. 36

405 On this see V. Bailey ed, *Forged in Fire: The History of the Fire Brigades Union* (1992), pp. 65–66.

106 BTMA, General Meeting Minutes, 5 June 1944.

Notes to Chapter 6

Middle-Age Spread and Hardening Arteries, 1945–70

1   *Toy Trader and Exporter* (September 1947), p. 52.

2   Information reported in ibid. and lifted from the monthly registration of new companies kept at Companies House.

3   Ibid. (May 1946), p. 27.

4   Ibid. (August 1958), pp. 11–12.

5   BTMA, *Annual Report* (1945), n. p.

6   Author's interview with J. G. Thomas, 29 August 1990.

7   *Ministry of Labour Gazette* (February 1953), pp. 42–43; (February 1959), p. 43.

8   *Report on the Census of Production for 1954*, 1 (1957); *Report on the Census of Production for 1963*, 122 (1971).

9   *Toy Trader and Exporter* (January 1952), p. 132.
10 Minutes of 43rd Meeting of the Trade Board, 31 October 1944. PRO, LAB/11/1799.
11 BTMA, Council Meeting Minutes, 5 April 1945.
12 Minutes of Second Meeting of the Toy Manufacturing Wages Council, 3 October 1945. PRO, LAB 11/2134.
13 *The Times*, 19 July 1945.
14 *Toy Trader and Exporter* (December 1947), p. 34.
15 Ibid. (February 1952), p. 62.
16 Details of targets and performance are from ibid., passim.
17 *The Times*, 18 November 1952.
18 A. Briggs, *Friends of the People: A Centenary History of Lewis's* (1956), p. 211.
19 *The Times*, 21 December 1953.
20 *Toy Trader and Exporter Weekly News Sheet*, 8 January 1954.
21 *Toy and Game Manufacture* (November 1954), p. 37.
22 J. F. Wright, *Britain in the Age of Economic Management* (Oxford, 1979), p. 111.
23 *Toy Trader and Exporter* (November–December 1957), p. 53.
24 *Economist*, 28 December 1957. The categories of expenditure were:

Toys	£6 0s. 0d.
Sweets	£6 0s. 0d.
Ice cream	£2 10s. 0d.
Cinema and pantomime tickets	£1 0s. 0d.
Comics and books	£1 4s. 0d.
Fireworks	7s. 0d.
Miscellaneous	£2 10s. 0d.

25 A. H. Halsey, 'Education', in A. H. Halsey ed., *British Social Trends since 1900* (1988), p. 230.
26 D. A. Coleman, 'Population' in ibid., p. 47.
27 G. N. Higgs in *Plastics*, cited in *Toy Trader* (August 1937), p. 35.
28 It was suggested that Page's suicide in 1957 was prompted by his inability to protect his patent against counter claims from the Danish company Lego. Certainly when in 1988 Tyco successfully challenged Lego's own patents and copyrights it was suggested that the Danish company had got the original idea from Page. See *Evening Standard*, 15 February 1988; *The Times*, 17 February 1988.
29 This a stockbroker's survey quoted in *Toy Trader and Hobby and Model Stockist* (June 1960), pp. 20–21.
30 Board of Trade, *Annual Statements of the Trade of the United Kingdom*. Europe is here restricted to Sweden, Norway, Switzerland, Denmark, Portugal, the Netherlands, West Germany, Belgium, France and Italy.
31 Based on ibid. Output figures from the *Reports on the Census of Production*, 1954 and 1968.
32 *The Times*, 24 January 1964.
33 *Toy Trader and Exporter* (May 1952), p. 76.
34 *Toy Trader and Exporter Weekly News Sheet*, 27 June 1952.
35 This of course leaves unaddressed the matter of the efficiency of that investment.
36 *British Toys* (August 1955), p. 1.

37 BTMA, Promotions Committee Meeting Minutes, 15 November 1956.
38 BTMA, Notes for Meeting of the Wages Council, 6 June 1952. Minute Book, 1951–52.
39 Ibid. BTMA to Employers' Side of Toy Manufacturing Wages Council, 22 April 1952.
40 BTMA, Council Meeting Minutes, 21 January 1954.
41 *British Toys* (June 1956), p. 1.
42 See the objections lodged at the council meeting. BTMA, Council Meeting Minutes, 14 November 1950.
43 *The Times*, 21 February 1963.
44 For relevant discussions see generally R. Caves ed., *Britain's Economic Prospects* (Washington, DC, 1968); D. K. Stout, *International Price Competitiveness: Non-Price Factors in International Trade* (1976); Corley, 'Consumer Marketing'.
45 BTMA, Promotions Committee Meeting Minutes, 15 November 1956.
46 *Toy Trader and Exporter* (March 1957), p. 8.
47 Ibid. (March 1949), p. 42.
48 Ibid. (April 1950), pp. 86–87.
49 Ibid. (May 1950), p. 96.
50 Ibid. (February 1952), p. 40
51 Board of Trade Papers on the Leipzig Fair, 4–9 March 1947. PRO, BT211/187.
52 *Toy Trader and Exporter* (October 1947), p. 36.
53 Handwritten note by Paul Abbatt, 17 November 1951. Folder labelled 'C. P. A. Purposes and Objects, 1947–51'. BGM, Abbatt Archive, uncatalogued.
54 Undated typescript in file labelled 'War Years'. Ibid.
55 CPA, *Report on the Design of Toys* (1957).
56 Ibid., n. p.
57 *Design*, 108 (December 1957), p. 31.
58 S. H. Powell to P. Abbatt, 11 November 1958. BGM, Abbatt Archive, uncatalogued.
59 *The Times*, 20 February 1959.
60 Ibid., 7 April 1959.
61 *Toy Trader and Exporter* (August 1952), p. 72.
62 London County Council, *Journal* (January 1958), p. 12.
63 *Toy Trader and Exporter* (September 1956), p. 10.
64 Ibid. (October 1956), p. 43.
65 *Sunday Dispatch*, 16 November 1958.
66 It had only a 27 per cent response. *Toy Trader and Exporter* (May 195), p. 23.
67 Ibid. (August 1954), p. 26.
68 As an Australian child of the 1940s, the broadcaster Clive James has remarked that 'Whatever our convictions, we were children of the Commonwealth, not to say the Empire . . . It was something emotional that went back to Chad Valley tin toys, Brock fireworks, and the every-second Christmas box of W. Britain's lead soldiers.' C. James, *Falling towards England* (1985), p. 22.
69 *Toy Trader and Exporter* (May 1956), p. 21.
70 BTMA, Council Meeting Minutes, 13 September 1948.
71 *Toy Trader and Exporter* (October 1957), p. 15.
72 BTMA, Council Meeting Minutes, 11 February 1958.

73 Confidential Report on the First International Toy Congress to the chairman of the BTMA. BGM, Abbatt Archive, uncatalogued. This particular piece of information was omitted when the report was published in the BTMA, *Newsletter*, 23 July 1958.
74 Reprinted in BTMA, *Newsletter*, 6 November 1959.
75 *Toy Trader and Exporter* (September 1948), p. 86.
76 BTMA, Memorandum on Competition from Japan, 1961.
77 *Toy Trader and Exporter* (June 1959), p. 4.
78 Ibid. (February 1944), p. 20.
79 Ibid. (June 1946), p. 64.
80 Ibid. (June 1950), p. 82.
81 *Toys International* (September–October 1964), p. 25.
82 *British Toys* (August 1956), p. 14.
83 BTMA, Emergency Council Meeting Minutes, 1 July 1954.
84 BTMA, Council Meeting Minutes, 18 October 1956.
85 *Toy Trader and Exporter* (June 1956), p. 31.
86 Ibid. (March 1955), p. 60.
87 BTMA, Council Meeting Minutes, 7 March 1957.
88 BTMA, Memorandum to Council, 13 June 1962.
89 *Toy Trader and Exporter* (June 1956), p. 31.
90 Ibid. (August 1956), p 45; ibid. (October 1956), p. 13.
91 *The Times*, 16 April 1960.
92 Derived from Board of Trade, *Annual Statements of the Trade of the United Kingdom*.
93 *The Times*, 22 December 1961.
94 Ibid., 12 November 1962.
95 Ibid., 2 February 1968.
96 *Toys International* (March–April 1970), p. 8.
97 Ibid. (May–June 1970), p. 19.
98 *British Toys* (February 1967), p. 4.
99 Minutes of the New South Wales Toy Trade Section, 11 May 1964. BTMA, Minute Book, 1964–5.
100 *Toys International* (January–February 1968), p. 62.
101 *The Times*, 20 January 1968.
102 *Toy Trader and Exporter* (July 1948), p. 74.
103 CPA, *Report on the Design of Toys*, n. p.
104 Handwritten notes in preparation for CPA report on toy design. BGM, Abbatt Archive, uncatalogued.
105 *Daily Mirror*, 21 August 1968.
106 *Toys International* (July 1963), p. 7.
107 *Toy Trader and Exporter* (November 1956), p. 44.
108 Lines Brothers, *Annual Statement* (1961), p. 16. He discounted the 1960 figure because it covered an eighteen-month period and two Christmas selling seasons.
109 BTMA, Memorandum to Council Members, 13 June 1962.
110 *British Toys* (September 1963), p. 22.
111 *Which?* (November 1964), pp. 339–42.
112 P. Hammond, *Triang Railways: The Story of Rovex*, i, *1950–1965* (1993), p. 6.

113 *Toys International* (September 1963), p. 13.
114 *Economist*, 22 February 1964.
115 Author's interview with G. Lines, 10 April 1991.
116 W. G. Lines to J. Mullen, 5 August 1969. MMM, Meccano Archive, B/ME.
117 W. M. Lines to fellow directors, 21 May 1969. Ibid.
118 Author's interview with G. Lines, 10 April 1991, and R. Lines, 3 September 1990.
119 *Toys International* (September–October 1980), p. 7.
120 Ibid. (March–April 1970), pp 24–27.
121 Ibid.
122 Ibid. (November–December 1970), p. 26.
123 Ibid. (March–April 1972), p. 19.
124 *British Toys and Hobbies* (July 1981), p. 11.

Notes to Chapter 7

Heart Failure, 1971–85

1 *Toys International* (May–June 1965), p. 1.
2 *The Times*, 10 June 1968.
3 *Report of the Departmental Committee on the Uses of Celluloid.* Cmd. 5790 (1938), p. 11.
4 Portsmouth Junior Chamber of Commerce, *Danger at Play* (Portsmouth, 1959), p. 13.
5 *The Times*, 22 April 1959. It was, said the writer, 'a useful field for public education'.
6 Ibid., 1 August 1966.
7 *Toys International* (May–June 1966), p. 13.
8 W. M. Lines to D. Britain, 25 September 1969. BTMA Minute Book 1969.
9 *Toys International* (January–February 1968), p. 49.
10 BTMA, Council Meeting Minutes, 20 May 1971. This suspicion was still apparent some years later. Reporting the federation's discussion of the rumour that the Italian Government was about to suppress war toys, the BTMA delegates commented that attention was drawn to a relevant study which '*although* it emanated from a university [Hamburg] was nevertheless very sound'. Report on the European Toy Institute Congress, 29–31 May 1983. Filed in BTHA Minute Book, 1983. My italics.
11 *Toys International* (January–February 1968), p. 51.
12 *Toy Trader and Exporter* (August 1951), p. 78.
13 International Council for Children's Play. Verbatim report of the foundation meeting. Ulm, July 1959. BGM, Abbatt Archive, uncatalogued.
14 *Games and Toys* (October 1971), p. 92.
15 *Toys International* (March–April 1971), p. 35.
16 *British Toys* (September 1970), p. 1.
17 Author's interview with G. Lines, 10 April 1991.
18 *British Toys* (December 1971), p. 1.

19 Ibid. (January 1973), p. 1.
20 *Toys International* (January–February 1972), p. 13.
21 McClintock, *Toys in America*, p. 447.
22 Interestingly, it went down because of 'appalling mismanagement'. *British Toys* (April 1968), p. 12.
23 *Toys International* (November–December 1965), p. 25.
24 Ibid. (November–December 1970), pp. 28–29.
25 On this see S. L. Stern and T. Schoenhaus, *Toyland: The High Stakes Game of the Toy Industry* (Chicago, 1990), p. 55.
26 *Toys International and the Retailer* (September 1983), p. 28.
27 It is not possible to quantify this since the figures themselves are of dubious reliability and not always strictly comparable. Some indication of the increase is evident, however, from the fact that in 1980 Mettoy, Waddington and Palitoy planned to spend between them £1,600,000 on televised advertising. In 1969 the same companies had committed about £135,000 to all types of advertising. *Toys International* (July–August 1969), p. 8; ibid. (September 1980), p. 25.
28 See D. Thomas, 'Toy Makers Play the Marketing Game', *Marketing* (December 1969), p. 32.
29 *Toys International* (March–April 1970), pp. 24–27.
30 The normal expectation was that production would absorb about 60 per cent of the sales revenue generated. Mogul took 81.7 per cent, while heavy advertising absorbed another 44.5 per cent. Mogul lost Meccano £102,000. These details are from 'Confidential Profit Plan for Meccano', 26 February 1976. MMM, Meccano Archives, DME/7.
31 Author's interview with J. G. Thomas, 29 August 1990.
32 *Daily Telegraph*, 22 February 1968.
33 *Financial Times*, 29 January 1968. It was indicative of how much costs rose in the 1970s that in 1979 Mettoy put the tooling costs of a standard model at £45,000. *Toys International* (October 1979), p. 19.
34 *Toys International* (July–August, 1969), p. 8.
35 *The Times*, 20 August 1970.
36 Market Studies International, *Western European Toy Industries* (1982), pp 84–85.
37 *The Times*, 2 February 1971.
38 *Toys International* (June 1971), p. 26.
39 *The Times*, 19 January 1972.
40 Ibid., 28 January 1974.
41 R. Price and G. S. Bain, 'The Labour Force', in Halsey ed., *Social Trends*, p. 196.
42 *Toys International* (October 1977), p. 3.
43 Ibid. (January 1978), p. 5.
44 Price Commission, *Prices, Costs, and Margins in the Manufacture and Distribution of Children's Toys and Games*. Cd. 7651 (1979). p. 28; *Toys International* (December 1978), p. 6.
45 *Sunday Telegraph*, 7 March 1965.
46 BTMA, Council Meeting, 28 April 1960.
47 *The Times*, 19 June 1975
48 *Toys International and the Retailer* (June 1981), p. 6.

49 *The Times*, 19 June 1975.

50 J. Stevens, *Toys and Games* (1979), p. 1.

51 A similar conviction appeared to prevail at International Model Aircraft as well. American managers brought in by Dunbee Combex Marx attempted to polish up the company's design processes but were 'successfully fought off by the older hands'. Lines and Hellstrom, *Frog Model Aircraft*, p. 119.

52 I. G. Fletcher to J. Mullen, 18 December 1975. MMM, Meccano Archives, B/ME.

53 Airfix to N. Hope. Accounts for year ended 31 March 1975. Ibid., DME/15.

54 Author's interview with George Perry, 29 August 1990.

55 Author's interview with Bev Stokes, 30 August 1990.

56 *Daily Express*, 1 December 1977.

57 'Confidential Profit Plan for Meccano', 26 February 1976. MMM, Meccano Archive, DME/7.

58 *Toy Trader* (January 1981), p. 80.

59 *The Times*, 20 February 1980.

60 *British Toys and Hobbies* (March 1980), p. 8.

61 *Toys International* (November 1977), p. 17.

62 *Toy Trader* (May 1981), p. 6.

63 *Toys International and the Retailer* (October 1982), n.p.

64 *The Times*, 13 August 1980.

65 BTHA, *Reports and Accounts: Year Ended 31 December 1984*, p. 15.

66 The top eight in 1979 had a combined turnover of £288,700,000. The five major failures accounted for £234,900,00 or 81 per cent of this. The figure rises to 92 per cent if Cowan de Groot is discounted on the grounds that this company had other importing interest beside toys. Stevens, *Toys and Games* (1979), p. vi.

67 Mintel, *Toys* (1984), pp. 11–31.

68 Mintel, *The Toy Market* (1986), p. 26.

69 *Toys International and the Retailer* (January 1985), p. 9.

70 In 1969 the wholesalers' markup was 27 per cent, the retailers' 52.5 per cent, although 20 per cent of the retail price was taken by purchase tax.

71 *Toys International and the Retailer* (August 1982), p. 5.

72 *Toy Trader* (September 1980), p. 17.

73 BTHA, Annual General Meeting Minutes, 24 April 1984. BTHA Minute Book, 1984.

74 BTHA, Council Meeting Minutes, 20 September 1984.

75 G. Goude to Chairman of the Wages Council, May 1977. BTHA Minute Book 1977.

76 For a discussion of this see Northern Ireland Economic Council, *The Duration of Industrial Development Maintained Employment* (Belfast 1985), pp. 12–22.

77 Price Commission, *Prices*, p. 8.

78 Halsey, 'Schools' in Halsey ed., *British Social Trends*, p. 230.

79 *The Times*, 2 February 1976.

80 Minutes of Ninth Annual Meeting of the International Committee of Toy Institutes, 14–15 June 1983.

81 J. Stevens, *Toys and Games Industry Commentary* (1980), p. xiii.

82 Figures from the Family Expenditure Surveys, cited ibid.

83 This seems to confirm the findings of A. P. Thirlwall, *Balance of Payments Theory and the UK Experience* (1982), that generally high levels of import penetration in Britain owed little to comparative price advantages enjoyed by overseas competitors. He stresses rather the importance of non-price factors.

84 *Sunday Times*, 13 June 1982.

85 Stevens, *Toys and Games* (1979), p. i.

86 *British Toys and Hobbies* (January 1980), p. 16.

87 See my article, 'Through a Glass Darkly: Cost Control in British Industry: A Case Study', *Accounting, Business and Financial History*, 3 (1993), pp 291–302.

88 Cited in *Toys International* (December 1978), p. 6

89 Ibid. (February 1979), p. 4.

90 *Sunday Times*, 13 June 1982.

91 Author's interview with Bev Stokes, 30 August 1990. Stokes said that at Bassetts, where he was subsequently employed, the rate was usually about 1.5 per cent, but sometimes as low as 0.8 per cent.

92 *Toys International and the Retailer* (June 1982), p. 37.

93 Price Commission, *Prices*, p. 24.

94 *Toy Retailing News* (April 1976), n. p.

95 Jordan Dataquest Ltd, *Toy, Games and Sports Equipment* (1978), p. vii.

96 *Toys International* (January 1980), p. 35.

97 Mintel, *Toy Market* (1986), p. 27.

98 *Toys International and the Retailer* (April 1982), p. 5.

99 *Toy Trader* (January 1982), p. 62.

100 *Toys International* (September 1974), p. 40.

101 Ibid. (March 1978), p. 2.

102 Ibid. (March 1979), p. 3.

103 BTHA, Members Meeting Minutes, 24 May 1983. Minute Book 1983.

104 *Toys International and the Retailer* (October 1982), p. 1. It is impossible to envisage in a British context the sort of cooperative spirit that enabled fifty-eight small Japanese producers to develop a corporate manufacturing park with government help in 1967. The largest company involved in the arrangement was Tomy.

105 Ibid. (January 1984), p. 135.

106 For example, see the list of managerial deficiencies detected in major British companies and discussed in D. F. Channon, *The Strategy and Structure of British Enterprise* (1973), pp. 221–27. Inadequate management is one of several villains blamed for lagging industrial performance by K. Williams, J. Williams, and D. Thomas, *Why are the British Bad at Manufacturing?* (1983).

107 *Toys International* (March 1980), p. 11.

Notes to Chapter 8

The Rest in Pieces

1 H. G. Wells, *The New Machiavelli* (Harmondsworth, 1970), p. 17.

2 BTHA, *Toy Industry*, p. 3.

3   Nisbet, *Peggy Nisbet*, p. 152.
4   Market and Opinion Research International, *Attitudes of Members of Parliament towards the BTHA* (1987), p. iii.
5   Deans remained as the principal maker of what were quaintly described in 1990 as 'a relic from a less enlightened age'. K. McGimsey and S. Orr eds, *Popular Collectables: Toys* (1990), p. 72.
6   J. H. Goldstein, *Children and Aggressive Toys* (1988). Social scientists whose work was brought to the industry's support included, inter alia, C. Buetnner, 'War Toys or the Organisation of Hostility', *International Journal of Early Childhood*, 13 (1981), pp. 104–12; L. R. Sherrod and J. L. Singer, 'The Development of Make-Believe Play' in J. H. Goldstein ed., *Sports, Games and Play* (Hillsdale, New Jersey, 1989), pp. 1–38; B. Sutton-Smith, 'War Toys and Childhood Aggression', *Play and Culture*, 1 (1988), pp. 57–69; G. Wegener-Spöhring, 'War Toys and Aggressive Games', ibid., 2 (1989), pp. 35–47.
7   BTHA, *Toy Industry*, pp. 57–59.
8   Mintel, *Toy Market* (1986), p. 12.
9   Ibid., p. 124.
10 BTHA, *Toy Industry*, p. 65.
11 G. Orwell, *The Lion and the Unicorn* (Harmondsworth, 1970), p. 39.
12 Mintel, *Toy Market* (1986), p. 124.
13 Tony Crump, marketing and engineering director at Britains, in *Telegraph Magazine*, 19 June 1993.
14 'Little Treasures', *Sunday Express*, 19 February 1989. There were also magazines catering for collectors of teddy bears, toy soldiers, die-cast vehicles and a host of other toys.
15 Most major auction houses hold regular toy sales, with lead soldiers, die-cast vehicles, dolls, tinplate, railways, soft toys and robots being among the most popular purchases. A 1920 Steiff teddy bear sold for £55,000 in 1989, while a sale of 5000 board games realised £25,000 in 1992, See *Independent*, 20 September 1989, and ibid., 11 January 1992.
16 Mintel, *Toy Market* (1989), p. 56.
17 *Independent on Sunday*, 18 March 1990.
18 BTHA, *Toy Industry*, p. 9.
19 Ibid., p. 3. Import penetration is calculated as the percentage of the sum of exports and imports represented by the imports.
20 *Independent on Sunday*, 16 January 1994.
21 Business Ratio Report, *The Toy Industry* (1989), p. 10.
22 F. T. Blackaby ed., *De-Industrialisation* (1979).
23 W. D. Rubinstein, *Capitalism, Culture and Decline in Britain* (1993).
24 Pollard, *Development of the British Economy*, and more especially the same author's *The Wasting of the British Economy* (1982).
25 Wiener, *English Culture*. See also Collins and Robbins eds, *British Culture and Economic Decline*.
26 Author's interview with G. Lines, 10 April 1991.
27 F. Hornby, 'The Life Story of Meccano: Romance of the World's Greatest Toy', *Meccano Magazine* (January 1932), p. 4.
28 *Sunday Times*, 11 June 1972.
29 Author's interview with G. Lines, 10 April 1991.

30 This perhaps lends some limited support to the analysis offered by C. Barnett, *The Audit of War* (1986).
31 BTHA, *Toy Industry*, p. vii.
32 *Independent on Sunday*, 16 January 1994.
33 K. Grahame, *The Golden Age* (n.d.), pp. 10–11.

Select Bibliography

This lists only the items of greatest use to the present work. For the full range of sources utilised see the footnotes. Place of publication is London unless otherwise indicated.

1. Archives

Abbatt Archive, Bethnal Green Museum of Childhood
Booth Papers, BLPES
British Toy and Hobby Association, Minutes of Council Meetings, BTHA, London
Cascelloid Ltd Papers, Hackney Borough Archives
Cockayne Archives, Sheffield City Archives
Ernest King Collection, Museum of London
Lloyds Bank Archives
Makers' Files, Bethnal Green Museum of Childhood
Meccano Archives, Merseyside Maritime Museum
James Nicholson Papers, Rylands Library, Manchester
Tariff Commission Papers, BLPES

2. Author's Interviews

Graeme Lines (10 April 1991)
Richard Lines (3 September 1990)
George Perry (29 August 1990)
Bev Stokes (30 August 1990)
J. G. Thomas (29 August 1990)

3. Official Papers

British Parliamentary Papers
Hansard
Ministry of Labour, *Gazette*
PRO, BT55, BT211, BT215
PRO, CUST2, CUST3, CUST4
PRO, LAB2, LAB11, LAB35

4. Market Reports

Business Ratio Report, *The Toy Industry* (1989)
Euromonitor, *Toys and Games* (1980)
Jordan Dataquest Ltd, *Toys, Games and Sports Equipment* (1978)
Market Studies International, *Western European Toy Industries* (1982)
Mintel, *Toys* (1984)
——, *The Toy Market* (1986)
——, *The Toy Market* (1989)
J. Stevens, *Toys and Games* (1979)
——, *Toys and Games Industry Commentary* (1980)

5. Trade Journals

Athletic Sports, Games and Toys
British Toymaker
British Toys
British Toys and Hobbies
Fancy Goods and Toy Trades Journal
Games and Toys
Games, Toys and Amusements
Toy and Fancy Goods Trader
Toy and Game Manufacture
Toy Retailing News
Toy Trader
Toy Trader and Exporter

Toy Trader and Exporter Weekly Newssheet
Toy Trader and Hobby and Model Stockist
Toys and Novelties
Toys International
Toys International and the Retailer
Toyshop and Fancy Goods Journal

6. Newspapers

Daily Express
Daily Graphic
Daily Herald
Daily Mirror
Daily Telegraph
Evening News

Financial Times
Illustrated London News
Independent
Morning Chronicle
Sunday Dispatch
The Times

7. Periodicals

Bentley's Miscellany
Blackwood's Magazine
Boys of England
Boys' Own Paper
British and Foreign Review
Chamber's Journal
Contemporary Review
Cornhill Magazine
Dublin University Magazine
Economist
Fraser's Magazine
Girls' Own Paper

Household Words
Monthly Chronicle
New Monthly Magazine
New Review
Nineteenth Century
Pearson's Magazine
Punch
Quarterly Review
Review of Reviews
Routledge's Magazine
Strand Magazine
Westminster Review

8. Trade Directories

Jepson's Mercantile Directory and Manufacturers' Guide (1889, 1911)
Lancashire Year Book of Industries and Commerce (1912)

H. R. Simmons ed., *Games and Toy Trades Directory* (1920, 1930, 1940, 1950, 1960, 1970).

W. B. Tattersall, *Directory of Manufacturers and Wholesalers in Toys and Fancy Goods* (1913)

Whitaker's Red Book of Commerce (1913)

9. Books

A: *Firms and Products*

J. Axe, *The Magic of Merrythought* (1986)

P. Bull, *Bear with Me: The Teddy Bear: a Symposium* (1969)

P. Calmettes, *Les Joujous: Leur Histoire, Leur Technique* (Paris, 1924)

J. and M. Cieslik, *Button in the Ear* (1989)

C. Cooke, *Automata Old and New* (1893)

M. Fawdry, *British Tin Toys* (1980)

M. Foster, *Hornby Dublo 1938–1968: The Story of the Perfect Table Railway* (1979)

R. Fuller, *The Bassett Lowke Story* (1985)

C. Gibson, *A History of British Dinky Toys, 1934–1964* (1966)

C. Goodfellow, *The Ultimate Doll Book* (1993)

V. Greene, *English Dolls' Houses of the Eighteenth and Nineteenth Century* (1955)

P. Hammond, *Triang Railways: The Story of Rovex*, i, *1950–1965* (1993).

L. Hannas, *The English Jig Saw Puzzle, 1760–1890* (1972)

M. Hillier, *Dolls and Doll Makers* (1968)

F. G. Jacobs, *A History of Dolls' Houses* (1954)

P. Johnson, *Toy Armies* (1981)

C. Lamming, *JEP: Le jouet de Paris* (Paris, 1989)

R. Lines and L. Hellstrom, *Frog Model Aircraft, 1932–1976* (1989)

B. Love and J. Gamble, *The Meccano System, 1901–1979* (1986)

J. Opie, *Britains' Toy Soldiers, 1893–1932* (1985)

D. Pressland, *The Art of the Tin Toy* (1976)

——, *The Book of Penny Toys* (1991)

P. Randall, *The Products of Binns Road: A General Survey* (1977)

G. Speaight, *Juvenile Drama: The History of the English Toy Theatre* (1946)

A. Ward, *The Model World of Airfix* (1984)

G. White, *European and American Dolls* (1966)

F. R. B. Whitehouse, *Table Games of Georgian and Victorian Days* (1951)

A. E. Wilson, *Penny Plain: Twopence Coloured* (1932)

B: *Autobiography and Biography*

M. P. Gould, *Frank Hornby: The Boy who made $1,000,000 with a Toy* (New York, 1915)

C. Hindley ed., *The Life and Adventures of a Cheap Jack* (1881)

W. Lines, *Looking Backwards and Looking Forwards* (1958)

H. Nicholson, *An Autobiographical and Full Historical Account of the Persecution of Hamlet Nicholson* (Manchester, 1892)

P. Nisbet, *The Peggy Nisbet Story* (Cumberland, Maryland, 1988)

J. Strathesk, *Hawkie: The Autobiography of a Gangrel* (1888)

C: *General*

G. P. Bevan ed., *British Manufacturing Industries* (1876)

BTHA, *The Toy Industry in the United Kingdom* (1992)

W. H. Cremer, *The Toys of the Little Folks* (1873)

L. H. Daiken, *The World of Toys* (1963)

H. R. D'Allemagne, *Histoire des Jouets* (Paris, 1903)

K. Drotner, *English Children and their Magazines* (New Haven, Connecticut, 1988)

A. Fraser, *A History of Toys* (1966)

L. Gordon, *Peepshow into Paradise: History of Children's Toys* (1953)

M. Hillier, *Pageant of Toys* (1965)

F. N. Jackson, *Toys of Other Days* (1908)

R. Jaulin ed., *Jeux et jouets* (Paris, 1979)

J. T. Makinson, *Toy Manufacture* (1921)

C. L. Mateaux, *The Wonderland of Work* (1881)

I. and M. McClintock, *Toys in America* (Washington, DC, 1961)

P. Murray, *Toys* (1968)

C. Neufeld, *The Skilled Metal Workers of Nuremberg* (New Brunswick, 1989)

R. O'Brien, *The History of American Toys* (1990)

G. White, *Antique Toys and their Backgrounds* (New York, 1971)

R. D. Wilson, *The Toy Industry* (1982)

D: *Children*

P. Ariès, *Centuries of Childhood* (1962)

J. S. Brunner, A. Jolly and K. Sylva eds, *Play: Its Role in Development and Evolution* (1976)

H. Cunningham. *The Children of the Poor* (Oxford, 1991)

M. and R. L. Edgeworth, *Practical Education* (1812)

J. Goldstein, *Children and Aggressive Toys* (1988)

—— ed., *Sports, Games and Play* (Hillsdale, New Jersey, 1989)

E. Hopkins, *Childhood Transformed: Working-Class Childhood in Nineteenth-Century England* (Manchester, 1994)

S. Humphries, *Hooligans or Rebels? An Oral History of Working-Class Childhood and Youth, 1899–1939* (1981)

S. Humphries, J. Mack, and R. Perks eds, *A Century of Childhood* (1988).

S. Isaacs, *Intellectual Growth in Young Children* (1930))

W. H. G. Kingston, *Infant Amusements or How to Make a Nursery Happy* (1867)

S. Kline, *Out of the Garden: Toys, TV and Children's Culture in an Age of Marketing* (1993)

J. and E. Newson, *Four Years Old in an Urban Community* (1968)

J. A. Paris, *Philosophy in Sport* (1827)

I. Pinchbeck and M. Hewitt, *Children in English Society*, 2 vols (1969 and 1973)

L. Pollock, *Forgotten Children: Parent-Child Relationships from 1500–1900* (Cambridge, 1983)

J. Seabrook, *Working-Class Childhood* (1982)

S. Shahar, *Childhood in the Middle Ages* (1980)

J. Springhall, *Coming of Age: Adolescence in Britain, 1860–1960* (Dublin, 1986)

E. J. Urwick ed., *Studies of Boy Life in Our Cities* (1904)

J. Walvin, *A Child's World: A Social History of Childhood* (1982)

10. Articles

G. C. Bartley, 'Toys' in G. P. Bevan ed., *British Manufacturing Industries* (1876)

D. W. Bell, 'Towards a Sociology of Toys: Inanimate Objects, Socialisation and the Demography of the Doll World', *Sociological Quarterly*, 8 (1967)

J. Brewer, 'Childhood Revisited: The Genesis of the Modern Toy', *History Today* (December 1980)

Kenneth D. Brown, 'Death of a Dinosaur: Meccano of Liverpool, 1908–1979", *Business Archives: Sources and History* (1993)

——, 'Modelling for War? Toy Soldiers in Late Victorian and Edwardian Britain', *Journal of Social History*, 24 (1990)

——, 'Models in History: A Micro-Study of Late Nineteenth-Century British Entrepreneurship', *Economic History Review*, 42 (1989)

——, 'The Collapse of the British Toy Industry, 1979–1984", *Economic History Review*, 46 (1993)

P. E. Hair, 'Children in Society, 1850–1980", in T. Barker and M. Drake eds, *Population and Society in Britain, 1850–1980* (1982)

J. H. Plumb, 'The New World of Children in Eighteenth-Century England', *Past and Present*, 67 (1975)

M. Walsh, 'Plush Endeavours: An Analysis of the Modern American Soft-Toy Industry', *Business History Review*, 66 (1992)

Index